Hungary and the Soviet Bloc

H U N G A R Y

AND THE SOVIET BLOC

by CHARLES GATI

WITHDRAWN

DUKE UNIVERSITY PRESS   Durham 1986

©1986 Duke University Press
All rights reserved
Printed in the United States of America on
acid-free paper ∞
Library of Congress Cataloging-in-Publication Data.
appear on the last printed page of this book.
second printing

To the memory of my parents

Contents

List of Tables

Introduction

For foreigners, certainly, but even for Hungarians, the intricacies of political life in that country often defy attempts at simple explanation. Take the case of poor Franklin D. Roosevelt, who during the early months of World War II supposedly asked an aide if Hungary was a kingdom or a republic. "A kingdom, Mr. President," the aide replied, whereupon the following dialogue is said to have ensued:

FDR: What's the king's name?
Aide: Hungary doesn't have a king.
FDR: Then who runs the kingdom?
Aide: A regent by the name of Admiral Horthy.
FDR: Admiral? Then Hungary must have a powerful navy.
Aide: Hungary has no navy; it doesn't even have access to the sea.
FDR: Let me see if I understand you right. Hungary is a kingdom run by a regent who's an admiral without a navy.
Aide: That's right, Mr. President.

One can easily imagine similar dialogues about Hungary's postwar Communist leaders as well. It might have happened this way during the presidency of Dwight D. Eisenhower in mid-1956:

Ike: I hear the Russians have replaced Hungary's leader. Who's he?
Aide: Mátyás Rákosi, a Muscovite—one of those clever Communists trained in Moscow.
Ike: Then why did he have to go?
Aide: Many reasons, Mr. President. For one thing, the Kremlin didn't want so many Jewish-born Muscovites to be in charge of this very Christian and anti-Communist country.

Ike: So who's his replacement?
Aide: Ernő Gerő . . .
Ike: . . . who was chosen to pacify the Hungarians because he's neither a Muscovite nor Jewish-born, right?
Aide: Wrong, Mr. President. Gerő is also a Jewish-born Muscovite.

Later in 1956, Ike called in his aide again.

Ike: Tell me about this Hungarian uprising.
Aide: It's the first major anti-Soviet uprising in Eastern Europe.
Ike: Who's leading it?
Aide: Imre Nagy, another Muscovite. He's the last Hungarian "true believer." He really believes in Marxism-Leninism, adores the Soviet Union, and admires Khrushchev.
Ike: Then the Russians must trust him.
Aide: No, they hate him so much that they'll have him shot some day, I think.

Almost three decades after Imre Nagy was indeed shot in 1958, the name of Hungary's new leader, János Kádár, turned up in a memorandum on President Ronald Reagan's desk.

Ron: Is this Kádár I'm supposed to invite to the White House a good guy or a bad guy?
Aide: He was once a bad guy, but he's now a good guy.
Ron: Don't confuse me.
Aide: One day, back in November 1956, Kádár referred to the anti-Soviet uprising as "our glorious revolution," but a few days later he was brought to power in a Soviet tank and then called it a "counterrevolution."
Ron: So he was first a good guy and then a bad guy.
Aide: No, he used to be a very bad guy. As minister of internal affairs in the early 1950s, he put totally innocent people in jail.
Ron: Well, we shouldn't invite him to the White House then.
Aide: But today Hungary is the only Communist country in the world with no political prisoners. And because Kádár is a reformer of sorts who is quite popular with his own people, the Kremlin doesn't trust him very much any more.
Ron: But didn't you just say that he was brought to power in a Soviet tank?

The purpose of this book is to illustrate Moscow's problems of empire by explaining Soviet relations with successive postwar Hungarian regimes.

What I offer here is a series of interpretations and reinterpretations, which place specific Hungarian issues in the broader contexts of Soviet foreign policy, bloc politics, and East-West relations. Hungary, the country I know best, serves as the focus for analyses of issues that have affected and defined Soviet goals and behavior toward Eastern Europe since the mid-1940s. The coverage is neither chronological nor comprehensive. To make my general points, I have frequently if not consistently abandoned pastel shades in favor of poster colors.

The connecting tissue is my attempt to come to grips with the reasons why, even in the best of times, the mighty Soviet Union experienced difficulties in taming its small Communist neighbor. Looking at these reasons, what I find striking is the Kremlin's persistent lack of trust in, and its frequent inability to control, even its most devoted and reliable supporters. As the imaginary little dialogues at the beginning of this introduction are meant to suggest, Moscow has never had confidence in anyone for long. When Rákosi was "in," Stalin—incredibly—was said to have regarded him a British spy, for no better reason, perhaps, than because Rákosi could speak English. Then Rákosi was "out." Khrushchev brought Imre Nagy "in" and then dropped him. Then, again with Khrushchev's approval, Nagy was returned to power during the 1956 revolution, but less than two years later Khrushchev had him shot. And then Kádár, who had spent time in Communist jails, was "in." But today even this ultimate survivor—the man who proved his loyalty to the Kremlin when the empire was on the brink of disaster in 1956—discusses sensitive issues with trusted colleagues during walks in the woods of Buda, apparently convinced that the KGB taps his office.

While Soviet suspicions are no doubt exacerbated by the oft noted Russian inclination to see enemies everywhere, the underlying cause of that suspicion is the very real incompatibility between Soviet and East European national interests. Soviet leaders from Stalin to Gorbachev never admit it publicly, but surely they too must understand the paradox: that however much each East European regime depends on Moscow for survival, its domestic authority and hence its ability to govern is a function of its ability to put distance between itself and the Kremlin. This is so because all Communist regimes in the region, Kádár's Hungary no less than the others, operate in a profoundly anti-Soviet environment. For while the people of Eastern Europe may or may not be attuned to Western-style democratic principles and traditions and they may or may not prefer capitalism to socialism, they all stand together in contemptuous opposition to the Soviet Union. Consequently, the proprietors of power in Eastern Europe attempt to pursue some of their national interests even as they

respond to Soviet expectations and demands, becoming suspected interme-
diaries between their people and their Soviet overlords. That is why the
Kremlin cannot fully trust them, ever. And that is why the Soviet bloc,
though alive, remains unwell.

Part One, which deals with the postwar coalitionary era, calls for a few
special introductory remarks.

For a few years after World War II, diversity and indeed confusion
prevailed among and within several European Communist parties, East
and West. At issue was the appropriate pace of revolutionary transformation under new geopolitical circumstances and hence the timing of the
seizure of power in various European countries. The apparent source of
confusion was Soviet foreign policy, Stalin's postwar policy of "differentiation," which called for the Communist parties of Eastern Europe to seize
power at once and for the Communist parties of Western as well as East
Central Europe to postpone the seizure of power for the time being. Soviet
policy thus sought to mollify the West by expanding—for now—only
along the Soviet periphery.

The unintended and unexpected consequence of the Soviet policy of
differentiation was the rise of diversity in international Communism.
Represented most forcefully by Yugoslav Communists, the "militants" on
the left sought to establish one-party hegemony at once by excluding
non-Communists from the emerging or already existing coalition
governments. At the other end of the Communist political spectrum, the
"gradualists" on the right understood Stalin's signals to mean that they
should seize power without undue violence and without revolution, if
possible, and over a longer period of time. Their more cautious orientation
—upheld especially by the dominant factions of the Italian, French,
Czechoslovak, and Hungarian Communist parties, as well as a large Polish
contingent around Władysław Gomułka—reflected the Soviet Union's
international concerns and circumspection as well as its less than optimis-
tic assessment of immediate opportunities for revolutions everywhere in
Europe. With only some hyperbole, Stalin claimed in a private conversation with Milovan Djilas, then one of the impatient Yugoslav militants,
that, "Today socialism is possible even under the English monarchy. Revolution is no longer necessary."

The Soviet policy of differentiation toward postwar Europe signified
rapid Communist takeovers in Bulgaria, Romania, and Poland, marking
the beginning of the establishment of the Soviet bloc. But elsewhere
—both in Western and in East Central Europe—gradualism, or what
used to be called the Popular Front orientation, prevailed so as to divide

Western governments and publics about Soviet goals and policies. Thus, in response to any Western complaints about the Sovietization of Poland, for example, Stalin was presumably prepared to point to the more or less pluralistic regimes in Austria, Finland, Czechoslovakia and Hungary, claiming that variations in each country's political system should be attributed to local circumstances rather than to Soviet presence or pressures. In adopting and then pursuing his carefully calibrated approach, Stalin was probably also guided by the so-called "percentage deal" he had made with British Prime Minister Winston Churchill in October 1944, a curious agreement that sought to distribute Soviet and Western influence after the war in five of the countries of Eastern and East Central Europe, including Hungary.

The Hungarian Communist party turned out to be a skillful practitioner of Stalin's policy of gradualism. With the help of the Red Army and by relying on force alone, it could have seized power already in the winter of 1944–45—as urged by a few of its leaders at the time. But the Hungarian party, led by Mátyás Rákosi, was directed by Moscow in the fall of 1944 to shelve its ultimate revolutionary objectives for *ten to fifteen years* to come. That is why the Communists competed both in the free elections of 1945 as well as in the still competitive, though no longer untainted, elections of 1947, and that is why they participated in coalition governments led by the centrist Smallholders' party. In the end, as related in chapter 5, the resulting "democratic interlude" only lasted from late 1944 to late 1947.

The Hungarian Communist party's gradualist orientation stemmed from two sources.

First, and foremost, it was a response to external needs: to Stalin's perception of the immediate foreign policy interests of the Soviet Union. The postwar democratic order in Hungary was to last in order to compensate the West for the rapid takeover in Poland; the policy was known among the initiated few as the Polish trade-off. Indeed, one of Rákosi's closest associates at the time, Zoltán Vas, reveals in the unpublished part of his memoirs that the Hungarian Communist leadership was uncertain *even in 1946* whether "Stalin might not let Hungary come under the political influence of the [Western] allies in exchange for Soviet demands on Poland and Germany."

Second, gradualism was a response to particular historical experiences. For the Hungarian party, having committed the cardinal insurrectionist error in 1919 of prematurely establishing an ill-fated dictatorship of the proletariat on the Soviet pattern, had long been haunted by the memory of its missed opportunity. The heavy price of its adventuristic haste and of its narrow-minded eagerness to go alone in 1919 was the subsequent counter-revolution led by Admiral Miklós Horthy, the notorious White Terror, and twenty-five years of right-wing, authoritarian rule. The anti-Communist Horthy regime would so effectively discredit the Communist cause and so thoroughly decimate the party that at the end of 1944 it could claim no more than 2,500 adherents.

Given the party's almost pathological fear of repeating 1919, combined with its long-term goal of political hegemony, gradualism signified neither pure deception nor the permanent acceptance of pluralism. As the party needed a competitive political environment in which to prove itself and gain a modicum of legitimacy, gradualism expressed its extant support for democracy. On the other hand, the party's professed commitment to pluralism was seriously compromised by its efforts to capture many of the key, commanding positions of coercive power in the country. The Communist party was thus engaged in a contradictory and circuitous policy of creating a pluralistic order it would then both uphold and subvert. In doing so, it was guided by the fear, seemingly unwarranted, of once again being excluded from playing an important role in Hungary's political life and by the hope, never forsaken, of eventually seizing power.

The memory of 1919 notwithstanding, the Hungarian Communists abandoned their gradualist strategy after the founding meeting of the Communist Information Bureau (Cominform), held in September 1947. In line with Stalin's uniformly militant approach adopted at that meeting, they presently turned against all of their erstwhile allies in the coalition and began to proceed toward the rapid collectivization of the country's agriculture. Alone in the Politburo, Imre Nagy continued to voice reservations, stressing the dangers of a premature takeover, but the die had been cast at the Cominform meeting, the decision was irrevocable. Feeling that he no longer had anything to gain from his former Western allies, Stalin quite abruptly replaced gradualism in Hungary and, indeed, everywhere else in Europe by the militant, even insurrectionist approach to power. With the United States countering Soviet expansionism by the Truman Doctrine and the policy of containment, the Cold War was under way and hence the consolidation of Soviet control over all of Soviet-occupied Europe and over the international Communist movement became Moscow's overriding concern. Ironically, then, it was the otherwise fully justified if belated American response to the Sovietization of *Eastern* Europe—of Poland, Romania and Bulgaria—that prompted Stalin to speed up the Communist takeovers in *East Central* Europe, including Hungary.

Though Part One thus reinterprets events that by now count as history, it should nonetheless engage those who like to muse over the past, as I do, in search of an answer.

The five chapters of Parts Two and Three require little or no additional amplification. They document and indeed stress the extent to which Soviet policies toward Hungary—and by implication toward all of Eastern Europe —have been conditioned by the circumstances of power in the Kremlin. That was the case in 1953–56, during the 1956 revolution, during the selection process that produced János Kádár as Hungary's postrevolutionary leader, in the mid-1960s when the New Economic Mechanism was adopted, and in the early 1980s, too, when Kádár's Hungary, together with a couple of other Warsaw Pact countries, sought to inch toward the West —without appearing to inch away from the East. Kádár, in particular, has skillfully used periods of Kremlin infighting to enhance his regime's room for maneuver. To use a term Lev Kamenev, his opponent, once applied to Stalin, Kádár has been "a genius of dosage," who has managed not to give sufficient reason for different Kremlin factions to unite and adopt strict countermeasures against his policies. To a lesser extent, other Communist regimes in Eastern Europe have also distanced themselves from Soviet-style cohesion and "internationalism." It remains to be seen whether the West, preoccupied with the *military* balance, can perceive and then exploit the *diplomatic* opportunity offered by a Soviet bloc that is inherently divided.

This book makes use of an assortment of official as well as unofficial —and quite unusual—sources, some of which I had to delve out for myself.

Among the more unusual sources, I managed to obtain minutes of several Central Committee meetings of the Hungarian Communist party. I had access to a few secret documents from the Archives of the [Hungarian] Institute of Party History and from the New Hungarian Central Archive, the latter containing Prime Minister Ferenc Nagy's correspondence in 1946–47. I was fortunate to be able to read the startling five-hundred-thousand-word memoirs of the late Zoltán Vas, Rákosi's intimate friend and occasional Politburo colleague, and of Vilmos Bőhm, éminence grise of the Social Democratic party. I made use of two lengthy doctoral dissertations deposited in the Hungarian Academy of Science, which cite Soviet archival materials. During my frequent visits to Hungary, I conducted extensive interviews with several Communist leaders of the past four decades. In Washington I interviewed the highest-ranking U.S. intelligence agent assigned to Budapest, who represented the Secret Intelligence Branch (SIB) in the Hungarian capital after the war. SIB was so secret that its very name was disclosed publicly—and by mistake—only in the 1980s. I also obtained a comprehensive, inside account of the early structure and personnel of Hungary's Communist-dominated secret police.

The more ordinary sources I have relied on include the contemporary Hungarian, Soviet, U.S., and British press; the official record of heated parliamentary debates in Hungary; the almost complete files of the Department of State and the British Foreign Office; memoirs of non-Communist political exiles; in-depth interviews collected for the Columbia University Research Project on Hungary; and recent contributions by Hungarian historians. I also benefited from Bennett Kovrig's masterful survey, *Communism in Hungary: From Kun to Kádár* (Stanford, Calif.: Hoover Institution Press, 1979).

Many participants in Hungary's postwar political life gave me much help, information, and advice. I am grateful to those who agreed to talk to me, on or off the record, including the late István Bibó, that wise political analyst of postwar Hungary; József Bognár, one-time general secretary of the Smallholders' party; Iván Boldizsár, writer, editor, the man who in another incarnation taught me how to write; Ferenc Donáth, member of the Communist party's Central Committee after the war, then head of Rákosi's personal secretariat, then political prisoner, then Imre Nagy's close collaborator in 1956; the late Ferenc Erdei; Róbert Gábor, a courageous Social Democrat assigned to represent his party in the secret police, who tried to help the democratic cause by cooperating with the United States; George Heltai, the highest-ranking Communist in the ministry of foreign affairs in the 1945–47 period, political prisoner in the early 1950s, member of the revolutionary government in 1956, now professor of history in the United States; Paul Jónás, youth leader in the postwar years and now professor of economics in the United States; the late Imre Kovács, the uncompromising general secretary of the National Peasant party; the late Ferenc Nagy, Smallholder leader and prime minister, a man of simple background and honest intentions; the late Zoltán Pfeiffer, the enfant terrible of the Smallholders' party and of postwar Hungarian politics; the late Zoltán Vas, the Communist mayor of Budapest and frequent Politburo member after the war, who returned to Hungary from Soviet-imposed Romanian exile in 1958 as energetic as, but wiser and more humane than, ever; and—more than anyone else—Miklós Vásárhelyi, once the foreign editor of the Communist daily *Szabad Nép* and then Imre Nagy's earliest supporter, my brave and deeply respected friend of extraordinary knowledge, integrity, and sound judgment. Two high-ranking Hungarian Communist leaders, who requested anonymity, discussed intraparty debates and personal infighting with me. I also received guidance from Milovan Djilas, who helped me understand the significance of the founding meeting of the Cominform and of the politics of international Communism after the war, and from James G. McCargar, a young political officer assigned to the U.S. embassy in Budapest in 1946–47 and concurrently serving as an astute American intelligence agent operating there, who helped me understand what the United States was and was not doing at that time.

Many colleagues and friends were kind enough to respond to my queries or to criticize my preliminary drafts over the years. I shamelessly incorporated into this study their comments, including those of Cyril E. Black, Seweryn Bialer, Randolph Braham, John C. Campbell, Alexander Dallin, István Deák, Péter Gosztonyi, William E. Griffith, Andrew Gyorgy, Johnathan Harris, Joseph Rothschild, George Schopflin, Robert Sharlet, Rudolf L. Tőkés, Robert C. Tucker, Jiri Valenta, Iván Völgyes, and Peter Winn. A number of prominent Hungarian scholars were also helpful, particularly György Ránki, István Vida, and Iván Berend, as well as Ágnes Ságvári. I thank all of them without implying their agreement with my views or conclusions.

Several institutions assisted me in many ways. Union College and Columbia University's Research Institute on International Change provided me with time, secretarial help, and access to duplicating machines, three indispensable commodities. Audrey McInerney typed and retyped most of the manuscript expertly—and more times than either she or I care to remember. Timothy J. Smith was my able assistant in the preparation of the index. I was able to use the libraries of Columbia University, the Library of Congress, the New York Public Library, the National Archives in Washington, and the Public Records Office in London, as well as several libraries and a few archives in Budapest. I received a generous grant from the Joint Committee on Eastern Europe of the American Council of Learned Societies and the Social Science Research Council. Support from the International Exchange and Research Board (IREX) made it possible for me to spend six months in Hungary in 1977 where I greatly benefited from my association with members of the Institute of History of the Academy of Science. Regretfully, what used to be called the Hungarian Institute for Cultural Relations—and particularly the head of its North American department at the time—did much to deny me access to Hungarian archives and indeed to curtail my research.

As I frequently draw here on my previous writings, published and unpublished, I wish to thank those whose permission I had to obtain for allowing me to quote myself.

Excerpts from chapters 1 and 5 appeared in *Survey* (London), vol. 28, no. 2 (Summer 1984). An extended version of chapter 2 was first published in the *East European Quarterly*, vol. 5, no. 3, and of chapter 8 in Stephen F. Cohen, Alexander Rabinowitch, and Robert Sharlet, eds., *The Soviet Union Since Stalin* (Bloomington: Indiana University Press, 1980). Chapter 6 appeared in *Problems of Communism*, vol. 35, no. 3 (May–June 1986) and a shorter version of chapter 9 in *Problems of Communism*, vol. 34, no. 2 (March–April 1985). For chapter 10, I drew on my "Polish Futures, Western Options," *Foreign Affairs*, vol. 61, no. 2 (Winter 1982–83) and on my contribution to Jan F. Triska and Charles Gati, eds., *Blue-Collar Workers in Eastern Europe* (London: Allen & Unwin, 1981).

Finally, my thanks to Toby whose refreshing candor and invariably critical mind I have come to appreciate, if not always enjoy, over the years.

PART ONE

Communists in Coalition, 1944–1948

1

The International Context

The policy and practice of the Russian government has always been to push forward its encroachments as fast and as far as the apathy or want of firmness of other governments would allow it to go, but always to stop and retire when it was met with decided resistance, and then to wait for the next favorable opportunity to make another spring on its intended victim. —Palmerston, May 22, 1853

Although Hungarian political life during the short-lived democratic interlude—from late 1944 to late 1947—was quite complex, its basic features can be easily summarized.

For three years Hungary was governed by a broadly based coalition government composed of representatives from several non-Communist parties and from the interwar regime of Admiral Miklós Horthy, as well as a few members of the small Hungarian Communist party. Legally and concurrently, the country was under the supervision of the Allied Control Commission whose chairman, Kliment E. Voroshilov—marshal of the Red Army and Politburo member—wielded his almost unlimited powers with the disarming charm of a confident overlord. As in Czechoslovakia, Austria, and Finland, but nowhere else in Soviet-occupied Europe, Hungary was also allowed to hold free elections in November 1945, which confirmed the Communists' minority status. They received only 17 percent of the votes in contrast to the 57 percent cast in favor of the immensely popular Smallholders' party alone. Reflecting the outcome of the elections, both the coalition government and the National Assembly were headed by leaders of the Smallholders' party, and when the Hungarian Republic was formally proclaimed in February 1946 yet another leader of the same non-Communist majority party—Zoltán Tildy—became the country's president.

Therefore, until the autumn of 1947, Hungarian political life displayed many of the virtues of political democracy: the composition of the government mirrored the election results, the press was almost free, the National Assembly openly debated controversial issues, the economy was mainly in private hands and based on market forces, and the stock market flourished. Indeed, it was only after the prime minister and the Speaker of the Assembly were forced into exile, the president began to lose his authority, and the Communist Information Bureau (Cominform) was founded in the Polish town of Szklarska Poreba—all of which happened in the summer and autumn of 1947—that Hungary's democratic interlude gave way to Communist hegemony. Czechoslovakia was to follow suit after the Communist coup d'état of February 1948.

This chapter raises a question of interpretation: Why was the Communist takeover of Hungary so gradual? Put in a broader context, why did Moscow prescribe a relatively long democratic interlude in Hungary (and Czechoslovakia) while engineering far more rapid takeovers elsewhere in areas under its control?

The Soviet Vision of Postwar Europe

As World War II was coming to an end, Stalin's foreign policy objectives developed within a framework of conflicting imperatives and inhibitions. On the one hand, the Soviet Union's new European geopolitical position offered a historic opportunity to realize Moscow's long-suppressed desire to expand "socialism in one country" into "socialism in one region," an opportunity pointing toward the adoption of an assertive foreign policy. On the other hand, Stalin's apprehension over potential Western countermeasures—and, to a lesser extent, his view that some of the European countries were not yet ripe for revolution—was an inhibiting factor.

The consequence of such conflicting circumstances and calculations was a highly differentiated Soviet policy toward Europe.[1]

Given the evidence of his negotiating positions in the autumn of 1944, and his subsequent policies, Stalin seems to have regarded it both premature and counterproductive for all Communist parties to adopt a uniformly militant approach even in what would soon be called the "people's

---

1. Cf. Geir Lundestad, *The American Non-Policy toward Eastern Europe, 1943–1947* (New York: Humanities Press, 1975), esp. pp. 435–50. Lundestad speaks of Moscow's "outer sphere" (countries not occupied by the Red Army); the "middle sphere" (Austria, Finland, Czechoslovakia, Hungary, Yugoslavia, Albania, and East Germany); the "inner sphere" (Poland, Romania, and Bulgaria); and the "absolute sphere" (parts of Finland ceded by the Finns in 1940, the three Baltic states of Estonia, Latvia, and Lithuania, Poland to the Curzon Line, and Bessarabia).

democracies" of Eastern and East Central Europe. Although his ultimate objective was surely the establishment of the Soviet Union as the predominant European power, Stalin was prepared to pursue that objective gradually. Accordingly, he appears to have envisioned a Europe made up of three political regions or spheres:

1. a non-Communist, relatively stable region in Western Europe, one that would also include Greece;
2. a Communist region under Soviet control in Eastern Europe—along the vital routes to Germany and the Balkans—that would range from Poland and the eastern part of Germany to the Black Sea states of Romania and Bulgaria; and
3. an intermediate region in East Central Europe of coalitional political systems under only gradually increasing Communist influence, extending from Yugoslavia in the south through Austria, Hungary, and Czechoslovakia to Finland in the north.

For the time being, Western Europe—the first region—was not only beyond Stalin's reach, it was also beyond his ambitions. Seeking a measure of stability in Western Europe to divert attention from the Sovietization of Eastern Europe, Stalin was especially eager to provide no reason for the United States to remain active in Europe after the war and involve itself in the political affairs of the continent. For this reason, Stalin instructed the powerful French and Italian Communist parties to avoid all provocative actions and concentrate instead on such innocuous tasks as the reconstruction of their countries' war-torn economies and administrative structures. Stalin's concerns—that Communist-inspired instability in Western Europe would prompt active American involvement in the affairs of the region and that such an involvement would in turn pose a threat to vital Soviet interests in Eastern Europe—were expressed by Maurice Thorez, leader of the French Communists, who pointedly told his more militant comrades that "Anglo-American troops [would] intervene if the Communists should come to power in France."[2]

Whether any of the Communist parties of Western Europe could have seized power in the autumn of 1944 or early 1945 remains an unanswerable question. It is a fact, however, that the Italian and French Communist

2. As quoted in Fernando Claudin, *The Communist Movement: From Comintern to Cominform* (New York: Monthly Review Press, 1975), part two, p. 336. Arguing against "revolutionary adventurism," Thorez also said: "The most hopeful prospect for our country is the maintenance for a considerable time of a government of national and democratic unity," adding that, "We must fight the Leftist ideas of a few sectarians who think . . . that we may have abandoned the revolutionary line." Ibid.

parties had constituted the largest force within the anti-Nazi resistance during World War II and that they emerged from the war well-organized and quite popular. By professing to fight for national survival and national independence rather than for revolutionary objectives, they had effectively removed the stigma from the Communist name and thus qualified them-selves for participation in a broadly based, democratic coalition government. That they chose to join the postwar governments and postponed all attempts to seize power was not because a Communist-led revolution was definitely destined to fail, but because Stalin settled on a Popular Front or "moderate" strategy for them in order to placate the United States and Great Britain and in order to divert attention from what was happening in Eastern Europe.

In the second region, for which Stalin envisioned Soviet dominance at the earliest possible moment, coalition governments of "national unity" came into being in 1944–45 as they did elsewhere in Europe, but they were coalitions in name only. With a few notable exceptions, such pseudocoalition governments in Poland, Romania, and Bulgaria—as well as in the Soviet-occupied part of Germany—typically included only such non-Communists as the local Communist parties deemed acceptable: fellow-travelers and political chameleons like the Polish Józef Cyrankiewicz, nominally a Socialist, or the Romanian Petru Groza, nominally of the "Ploughmen's Front." Even though a few courageous Agrarian leaders, such as Stanisław Mikołajczyk in Poland, Iuliu Maniu in Romania, and Nikola Petkov in Bulgaria, refused to give up or fade away for some time to come, the Communists in fact obtained controlling influence in the wake of the Red Army almost at once. In contrast to what was happening elsewhere in Europe—and in contrast to the soothing language of democracy and parliamentarism that was deceptively employed in these countries as well—free or almost-free elections were not allowed anywhere in this area; instead, an all-encompassing, Communist-dominated bloc of parties (the Government Front in Poland and Romania, the Fatherland Front in Bulgaria) was to "win" putative elections whose outcomes had been predetermined.[3]

3. As late as mid-1944 the timing of a Communist takeover in Poland was apparently still uncertain. It seemed possible at that time that Poland might end up in Stalin's "intermediate" area and thus enjoy a coalitionary period for ten to fifteen years to come. That was the message Polish Communists then living in Moscow conveyed to their com-rades in a secret letter sent on July 18, 1944, in which they urged the establishment of a "truly national government supported by the majority of the population," a government that would "pursue policies conducive to understanding between the Allied nations." They also recommended acceptance of a "series of concessions and compromises" in order to create "a situation favorable to our long-term plans." As quoted in Antony Polonsky and

In East Central Europe—that intermediate region of states for which Stalin had envisioned coalition governments without Communist hegemony as yet—the trend of events was more ambiguous than elsewhere in Europe, the results rather mixed. Although their political standing varied from country to country, by 1947 all Communist parties in this area, with the notable exception of the Yugoslav party, had witnessed the erosion of their popular appeal, all had suffered setbacks, and all had managed to alienate both Western and domestic opinion. Except for Yugoslavia, which was a source of different problems for Moscow, the Communists could neither consolidate their power nor keep the postwar spirit of national and international cooperation intact, developments that called into question the continued wisdom of Stalin's incremental strategy.

Specifically, three trends emerged within this area:

1. In Yugoslavia, Tito and his colleagues obstructed Stalin's discriminating design by engaging in too much political violence and, indeed, by seizing power too soon.
2. In Finland and Austria, on the other hand, the initially effective Finnish party and the consistently hapless Austrian party simply allowed themselves to be easily outmaneuvered by their non-Communist political opponents, without either gaining a measure of popular support or preparing themselves for the seizure of power later on.
3. In Czechoslovakia and Hungary, the Communists had advanced according to Stalin's early expectations after the war, but by 1947 they appeared to be too complacent, and perhaps even somewhat reluctant, to pick up his increasingly militant signals.

In Yugoslavia, Moscow encountered the unique problem of being unable to hold Tito back. What Stalin had sought was a coalition government composed of representatives of Tito's National Committee and of the London-based Royal Yugoslav Government-in-Exile led by Ivan Šubašić. But Tito, who was eager to establish the first "dictatorship of the proletariat" outside the Soviet Union, failed to abide either by his own November-December 1944 compromise agreement with Šubašić or by the early 1945

Bolesław Drukier, eds., *The Beginning of Communist Rule in Poland—December 1943–June 1945* (London: Routledge & Kegan Paul, 1980), pp. 230–33. In a few short months, however, the party line changed. Before the end of the year the same Moscow-based Polish Communists began to complain, saying that, "Our Party has caught the parliamentary disease. . . . We have been soft with our enemies. Not one had fallen." Ibid., pp. 299–304. The new line emerged after Stalin had concluded in October 1944 that there was "no possibility of a break-up in the alliance over Poland." As quoted in William Taubman, *Stalin's American Policy: From Entente to Detente to Cold War* (New York: W. W. Norton, 1982), p. 76.

Yalta recommendation of the Big Three to put that agreement into effect. Having liberated Yugoslavia without much outside help, and certainly without much Soviet help, Tito also appears to have rejected the 1944 Churchill-Stalin percentage deal that assigned 50 percent influence in Yugoslavia to Moscow and 50 percent to the West; he did not have much patience with Stalin's "capitulationist" policies of gradualism. (In 1947 Tito reportedly confided to a small group of Hungarian Communist leaders that, "Comrade Stalin was too cautious after the war. He should have let the French and Italian comrades seize power the way we did—and he didn't like what we were doing either."[4])

In Finland, where the Soviet-dominated Allied Control Commission frequently intervened on its behalf, the Communist party gained fifty-one of the two hundred seats in the diet of 1945. However, facing a surprisingly determined group of democratic parties,[5] the Communists suffered significant losses in subsequent elections. They opted for a more militant strategy in the winter of 1947−48, as did all other European Communist parties, but the Communists' coup that was planned to take place in the spring of 1948 failed and in its aftermath their political fortunes further declined.

In Austria the Communists emerged in the shadow of the Red Army. As elsewhere in Soviet-occupied Europe, they took control of the ministry of internal affairs in the otherwise respectable and broadly based coalition

---

4. During the course of Tito's visit to Hungary on December 6–8, 1947, he held a small informal meeting with a few Hungarian Communist leaders, including Politburo members Ernő Gerő and József Révai, at the Yugoslav embassy in Budapest. George Heltai, then head of the political department of the foreign ministry and the ministry's highest-ranking Communist, was also present. Stunned by Tito's explicit criticism of Stalin, Heltai asked Révai after the meeting what to make of Tito's remark. "Well, who knows, he may be right, he may be right," said Révai, apparently also puzzled. Story related to me by Heltai. Cf. Alexander Dallin, "The Use of International Movements," in Ivo J. Lederer, ed., *Russian Foreign Policy: Essays in Historical Perspective* (New Haven: Yale University Press, 1962), p. 330, and William O. McCagg, Jr., *Stalin Embattled 1943–1948* (Detroit: Wayne State University Press, 1978), p. 395, n. 32.

5. James H. Billington, "Finland," in Cyril E. Black and Thomas P. Thornton, eds., *Communism and Revolution: The Strategic Uses of Political Violence* (Princeton, N.J.: Princeton University Press, 1964), pp. 117−44. Billington's account of one of the reasons why the Finnish Communist party failed is worth quoting: "First and perhaps most important was the willingness of its opponents to resort to the same tactics of terror and violence that the Communists themselves employed. This is not a conclusion that is pleasing to the liberal mind; but the fact is that . . . calculated threats of terror by otherwise humane Finns were effective, not particularly bloody, and probably indispensable for the preservation of Finnish democracy" (pp. 130−31).

government formed in April 1945 and headed by a Socialist, Karl Renner.[6] Expecting to share power with the Big Two of Austrian politics, the People's party and the Socialists, the Communist party instead gained only four seats in the Nationalrat in the November 1945 elections, while the People's party won eighty-five and the Socialists seventy-six seats. Isolated and disappointed, the Communists lost the ministry of internal affairs, becoming a marginal if occasionally troublesome factor in Austrian politics. For want of a better alternative that Stalin would approve, they continued to participate in the work of the government, holding on to the insignificant ministry of power and electrification, but the party's posture as a partner in the coalition soon gave way to an increasingly confrontationist stance. Apparently with Soviet approval, it made a desperate, all-or-nothing effort to reverse the direction of Austrian politics, but the large-scale riots and strikes of September–October 1950, as the 1948 abortive coup in Finland, were contained and order restored.

In contrast to Finland and Austria, the Czechoslovak Communist party was the most popular political party in Czechoslovakia after World War II, receiving an astonishing 38 percent of the vote in free elections held in 1946—a stunning electoral victory that remains a record for a Communist party in twentieth-century Europe. Concurrently, the Communists infiltrated the several non-Communist, democratic parties of the coalition government, and they also dominated the army and the police from the beginning. The commanding position of the Czechoslovak Communist party was thus unique: it gained an upper hand in the country's parliamentary life by legitimate means and it also controlled and manipulated the coercive levers of power.

Such successes notwithstanding, by 1947 the party began to lose its early momentum. Public-opinion polls showed a substantial decline in Communist support. The party's congenial allies, the Social Democrats, elected a new leader, Bohumil Laušman, to replace Zdenek Fierlinger, a pro-Communist fellow-traveler. Moreover, President Eduard Beneš and Foreign Minister Jan Masaryk, the country's preeminent democratic leaders who had cooperated with the Communists without always submitting to them, were losing interest in making further concessions. Nor was it

6. In 1945, after Stalin learned that Russian soldiers had located the supposedly docile Dr. Renner in a small town near Vienna where he was hiding during the war, he reportedly said: "What, the old traitor is still alive? He is exactly the man we need." Very much alive, Renner turned out to be a formidable and clever opponent that Stalin had no reason to regard as the man he needed. Stalin quoted in William B. Bader, *Austria Between East and West, 1945–1955* (Stanford, Calif.: Stanford University Press, 1966), p. 22.

clear, until Stalin decided to replace the gradualist approach with a militant strategy in the autumn of 1947, that the Czechoslovak Communists actually sought more concessions—more power than they had already accumulated. They had played and seemingly enjoyed the coalitionary game, not infrequently abiding by constitutional rules and presenting themselves as defenders and promoters of Czechoslovak national interests. Indeed, in mid-1947, they supported the Czechoslovak government's acceptance of the American invitation to attend the Marshall Plan preparatory meeting in Paris—a position that was initially unopposed by the Soviet chargé d'affaires in Prague, then abruptly countermanded by Stalin, and then equally abruptly reversed by the Czechoslovak Communist party as well.

The Czechoslovak party adopted a more militant, even insurrectionist strategy only a few months later, after the new Soviet line was put forth at the founding meeting of the Cominform in September. There, the Czechoslovak delegates "were given to understand [by the Soviet representatives] that they had failed to appreciate the consequences of the new situation."[7] By the time they left the meeting, they knew better. Back in Prague, a Communist trade union leader immediately conveyed the message to the party's coalition partners: "If they don't like the slow road, then we can go the quick road,"[8] he exclaimed, suggesting that the democratic parties should surrender rather than invite a civil war. In point of fact, the Communist party had just decided in favor of the "quick road" and preparations were under way to seize power. In November, at a Central Committee meeting, there was talk of an imminent "government crisis," of "the final round in the struggle to win an absolute majority of the

7. Pavel Tigrid, "The Prague Coup of 1948: The Elegant Takeover," in Thomas T. Hammond, ed., *The Anatomy of Communist Takeovers* (New Haven: Yale University Press, 1975), p. 406. Tigrid's essay is based on secret documents and studies that surfaced during the "Prague Spring" of 1968 in Czechoslovakia. In an outstanding study of the period based on careful examination of the same documents and studies, Radomír V. Luža concludes that while the "initial blow" to pluralism in Czechoslovakia came in July (when the government, in the end, was forbidden by Stalin to send its delegates to the Marshall Plan meeting in Paris), it was the "founding of the Cominform . . . [that] put a capstone to this process. It meant the end of the wartime coalition." For example, that was when the party set up a special department in its secretariat "to direct the work within the other parties in the National Front." By November the party "conceived the future national front no longer as a broad platform of national unity but rather as an association of pro-Communist forces headed by the KSČ [Czechoslovak Communist party]." Radomír V. Luža, "February 1948 and the Czechoslovak Road to Socialism," *East Central Europe* 4, no. 1 (1977): 44–55.

8. Joseph Korbel, *The Communist Subversion of Czechoslovakia, 1928–1948: The Failure of Coexistence* (Princeton, N.J.: Princeton University Press, 1959), pp. 205–6.

public for the Party's policy."[9] The code words signified the Communist party's abandonment of the coalitionary strategy and its readiness to rely on force alone. The "final round" came in the form of the successful Communist coup d'état in February 1948.

The Hungarian Approach

Following a strategy similar to the Czechoslovak party's, the Hungarian Communists' quest for power also entailed extensive cooperation with non-Communist elements and participation in a national effort to rebuild the country. As described below, this course had been adopted at a series of secret meetings held in Moscow in the autumn of 1944, after consultation with such leaders of the formally disbanded Communist International (Comintern) as Georgi Dimitrov and Dmitri Manuilsky, and with Stalin himself. The Hungarian Communists were told at that time that since Moscow's primary aim was the rapid Sovietization of Poland (combined with the dismemberment of, and eventual control over, Germany), they had to act in such a way as to placate Western concerns and suspicions.[10] Accordingly, at the first Central Committee meeting held in Soviet-liberated Budapest on January 23, 1945, Ernő Gerő, the party's second-in-command after Mátyás Rákosi, explained the Polish trade-off to a group of puzzled Communist leaders by referring to the complex "international situation" in general and the Churchill-Stalin percentage agreement in particular. "The Soviet Union must win the diplomatic battle in order to obtain decisive influence in Hungary," said Gerő, concluding that Hungarian Communists must "not scare the Anglo-Americans" for the time being. The party was not expected to achieve hegemony in less than ten to fifteen years.[11]

9. Tigrid, "The Prague Coup of 1948," p. 409.

10. Information by Zoltán Vas, Mátyás Rákosi's close associate for over thirty years who spent the war years (1941–44) in Moscow in Rákosi's entourage. Stalin's "Polish trade-off" was also indicated by Gerő (n. 11, below). See also n. 35, below.

11. The Gerő quote is in Mihály Korom, *Magyarország ideiglenes nemzeti kormánya és a fegyverszünet (1944–1945)* [Hungary's Provisional National Government and the Armistice (1944–45)] (Budapest, 1981), pp. 390–91. That the Communist takeover in Hungary should occur in "no less than 10 to 15 years" was a key feature of Communist planning for the postwar years. The phrase itself was repeated in all of my interviews with high-ranking Communist officials, including Vas, Ferenc Donáth, Miklós Vásárhelyi, and others. When asked at a May 1945 party *aktiv*, Rákosi also used the phrase. See Gyula Schöpflin, "A Magyar Kommunista Párt útja, 1945–1950" [The Path of the Hungarian Communist Party, 1945–50], *Látóhatár* (Munich) 7, no. 4–5 (July–October 1955): 239. During a conversation with four leaders of the small Hungarian Radical party on April 18, 1945,

In the meantime, the Communist party was to acquire far more influence than its popular appeal—as expressed in the 17 percent of the vote received in the free 1945 national elections—would have warranted. Ranging from persuasion to intimidation and coercion, the technique it most skillfully applied was known as the "salami tactics," which signified the party's ever-increasing demands to remove step-by-step, or slice-by-slice, elements it deemed undesirable from the coalition. In 1945 it was the leftovers of the interwar regime of Miklós Horthy; in 1946 it was the so-called right wing of the Smallholders' party, led by Dezső Sulyok, and of the Social Democrats, led by Károly Peyer; in 1947 it was Béla Kovács, the Smallholders' popular secretary general, followed by Zoltán Pfeiffer's troublesome faction, followed by the centrist prime minister, Ferenc Nagy, and others. In each case the Communist party reiterated its long-term commitment to political cooperation and harmony within the coalition, adding, however, that first these "reactionary" and "anti-democratic" politicians must be dismissed from positions of influence. The "salami tactics" turned out to be effective, not only because the Communists could claim the support of the Soviet occupation forces, but also because some of the non-Communist leaders readily acquiesced in the removal of a competing faction within their parties from political life.[12]

The Communist party's successes in dividing its adversaries through the "salami tactics" and its advance toward hegemony notwithstanding, the highly competitive national elections of August 31, 1947—in which it received 22 percent of the vote—served as a reminder of its limited appeal. At party headquarters, the atmosphere was gloomy, the leadership embarrassed and bewildered; it seemed as if the whole postwar coalitionary

Rákosi predicted the collapse of the Hungarian bourgeoisie in "10 years." See Imre Csécsy, "A Radikális Párt delegációja Rákosi Mátyásnál" [The Radical Party's Delegation Meets Mátyás Rákosi], *História* 2, no. 2 (1980): 24–25.

12. According to Zoltán Pfeiffer, the term "salami tactics" was coined by him on Fool's Day, April 1, 1946. Frustrated by the accommodationist policies of his own Smallholders' party, this unbending and irreverent opponent of the Communists and of his party's pliable leaders made a practical joke of his predicament. As a Fool's Day gift to Zoltán Tildy, president of the Republic and of the Smallholders, Pfeiffer presented himself in the presidential palace that day. Arriving unannounced and carrying a large salami wrapped in the national colors of red, white, and green, he had President Tildy send out for bread and wine—and the two had a light supper. As Pfeiffer related the story to me in 1980, he used his own pocketknife to slice the salami, all the while demonstrating to Tildy the process by which the Communists were dividing and eliminating the non-Communist parties. "We had a very good time," Pfeiffer concluded, "but Zoltán was not amused and he learned nothing from the experience." In the early 1950s Rákosi publicly boasted about the successful Communist use of the "salami tactics," implying that he had coined the term.

strategy had suddenly collapsed.[13] Publicly, the party claimed victory, but it was hard to explain away 78 percent of the non-Communist vote. Moreover, because of extensive cheating, especially in the countryside, it was widely believed that the Communists had received even fewer votes than the official results showed. On the basis of a confidential secret police calculation it obtained, the U.S. embassy in Budapest estimated that the actual Communist vote was only 7 percent.[14] Although that estimate was almost certainly too low, the election did demonstrate the inadequacy of the gradual, coalitionary strategy in Hungary, as, indeed, that strategy was found to have been inadequate everywhere else in Stalin's third political region by the autumn of 1947.

13. Information by George Heltai. According to Róbert Gábor (who was there), the atmosphere was equally gloomy at the headquarters of ÁVO, the Communist-dominated secret police. Gábor was delegated to the ÁVO by the Social Democratic party. A member of that party's right wing and an anti-Communist, he escaped to the United States a few weeks after the elections.

14. Christopher Felix (pseud.), *A Short Course in the Secret War* (New York: E. P. Dutton, 1963), p. 276. "Felix" was the chief U.S. intelligence agent assigned to Budapest in 1946–47. As James G. McCargar, he was political officer at the U.S. embassy. In an interview Mr. McCargar told me that the estimate was based both on the ÁVO's calculations and on observation by embassy officials. U.S. Ambassador Selden Chapin's August 31, 1947, telegram to the Department of State provides additional details:

> Legation and US Representative ACC [Allied Control Commission] personnel observing elections blanketed country today and collected overwhelming masses evidence conclusively proving scandalous fraud based on great numbers last-minute disfranchisements amounting to 20 percent and over in some places, and multiple voting amounting to 25 percent and above in some localities. This evidence, which includes blue certificates, copies of official protests by all parties participating in elections except Communists, lists of votes cast showing non-resident vote et cetera, indicates fraud possibly reaching over 600,000 votes, and is being assembled by Legation now for telegraphic transmission to Department as soon as possible.

Foreign Relations of the United States, 1947, vol. 4 (Washington, D.C.: GPO, 1972), p. 364. In a vivid account published in Budapest in 1980, Zoltán Vas—who was a member of the party's Central Committee at that time—described the use of the "blue certificates." By making it possible for reliable cadres to engage in multiple voting, he wrote, these absentee ballots were intended to assure the Communist party's victory at the polls. Vas conceded that the party had cheated, but he put the number of blue certificates printed by the party at 100,000 and those actually used at "about 65,000" or approximately half of 1 percent of all votes cast. In other words, Vas argued in retrospect, the party would have won the elections anyway and thus it was a "serious political error" as well as "shameful" to resort to this method. Zoltán Vas, "Az MKP és az 1947–es választások" [The HCP (Hungarian Communist Party) and the 1947 Elections], *História* 2, no. 3 (1980): 17–20.

Dealing with the Old Order

Stalin's projected policy for Hungary was first confronted in a series of three secret meetings that took place in Moscow in October 1944.

One was between the Soviet leadership and an official delegation sent to the Soviet capital by the regent of old Hungary, Admiral Miklós Horthy. At long last, the regent seemed ready to conclude an armistice agreement with the Soviet Union.

The delegation appointed by Horthy left for the Soviet Union on September 28. Headed by Lieutenant-General Gábor Faraghó, who was chosen because he had once served as a Hungarian military attaché in Moscow, the delegation also included Domokos Szent-Iványi, a diplomat, and Géza Teleki, a distinguished scholar whose father, the anglophile prime minister, had committed suicide in 1941 in protest against Hungary's excessively pro-German orientation. The three-man delegation, carrying Horthy's handwritten letter to Stalin that was apparently composed in English by the regent himself, [15] managed to reach Moscow on October 1.

15. The four-page letter first surfaced in 1969 as a footnote to an article written by a prominent émigré historian, Péter Gosztonyi. See his "A magyar-szovjet fegyverszüneti tárgyalások (1944 október)" [The Hungarian-Soviet Armistice Negotiations (October 1944)], *Uj Látóhatár* (Munich) 12, no. 5 (November 1969): 401–18. The regent's letter, which is reprinted below without his numerous grammatical and spelling errors, appeared on pp. 415–16:

Field Marshal:

In the name and for the sake of my people in their extreme danger, I address myself to you. I do so in the name of the Hungarian people, who has no responsibility for this war. For a thousand years and particularly during this last decade, the fate of our people has been influenced by the neighboring German colossus. It was again under this influence that we were carried into this unfortunate war with the Soviet Union.

I must lay particular stress on the fact that my poor country has been practically overrun by the German "Fifth Column." This penetration began on a large scale at the same moment that the German forces marched into Romania and Bulgaria. As a result, every movement and every step in Hungary has been closely watched by German agents and the most important news and reports have never reached me. I have now come to the knowledge that after the air-attack upon Kassa and Munkács, Foreign Minister Molotov during a conversation with the Hungarian Minister emphasized the peaceful aims of the Soviet Union toward Hungary. If this was really so, it was fatal that it did not reach me at the time.

For the sake of justice, I would like to inform you that we have never ever wanted to take even a single inch that was not ours by right from anybody. On the contrary, the Romanians took Bessarabia from their Russian ally after the First World War and wished to take an important part of South Russia during the Second World War, with German help. Furthermore, when in 1940 we intended to put an end to the monstrous treatment of the Hungarian people in Transylvania, it was again the Romanians who asked for support from Germany, begging Hitler to help them retain at least a

The Hungarians expected an armistice similar to the "Finnish pattern": the immediate cessation of hostilities, combined with safe exit for the German forces and participation by British and American troops in the country's occupation. At this late date, the Russians found these terms unacceptable. Moreover, the cumbersome process of negotiations made it difficult to narrow the substantive differences. Despite Horthy's letter, the Russians kept questioning the delegation's credentials. Communications with Budapest were frequently interrupted, not only because the Gestapo closely monitored the regent's activities there but because the delegation had to rely on Soviet radio facilities to reach him. In addition, the Soviet negotiators, Foreign Commissar Vyacheslav Molotov and General F. F. Kuznetsov, did not seem to have full authority either: they kept in constant touch with Stalin (hence negotiations usually took place at night, Stalin's favorite time for work).

One of the important substantive complications—the source of a fundamental misunderstanding—had to do with a previous contact made in mid-September by Horthy's confidant, Count Ladomér Zichy, with Soviet officers then operating in Slovakia.[16] Identified as a certain Colonel Makarov and Captain Volyansky, these officers had conveyed rather favorable Soviet terms to Zichy. Specifically, in exchange for breaking relations with Hitler and allowing the entry of Soviet troops into Hungary, Moscow had supposedly offered to give Horthy free reign in the country's domestic affairs. On the controversial issue of future borders, Moscow was said to have insisted on the return of all land Hungary had recovered since 1938, adding, however, that only a final peace treaty would establish permanent frontiers.

part of this land by the Vienna Award.

When sending my delegates with full authorization to the armistice negotiations I beg you to spare this unfortunate country which has its own historic merits and whose people has so many affinities with the Russian people. Kindly exercise your great influence upon your allies to make conditions compatible with our peoples' interests and honor, as they really deserve a peaceful life and a safe future. I avail myself of this opportunity to express to you, Field Marshal Stalin, my highest consideration.

Yours truly,

Horthy

P.S. As our troops are still on the borders and we are invaded by strong German units, I am asking you to treat my letter with discretion, until we are able to master the situation.

16. The most complete account of Zichy's mission is in Gosztonyi, "A magyar-szovjet fegyverszüneti," pp. 402 ff. Cf. C. A. Macartney, *October Fifteenth: A History of Modern Hungary, 1929–1945*, 2d ed., vol. 2 (Edinburgh: The University Press, 1961), pp. 349–50. For the Soviet view according to which Stalin did not signal to Horthy through Makarov, see Korom, *Magyarország ideiglenes nemzeti kormánya*, pp. 102 ff.

In particular, the Soviet Union appeared to have an open mind about the future of Transylvania.

As the delegation was shocked to learn soon enough, these terms were no longer being offered. On October 8, at one of those midnight meetings, Molotov summarized Moscow's preliminary conditions in this way: Hungary must evacuate all Romanian, Czechoslovak, and Yugoslav territories regained since 1938—including Transylvania, of course—and thus return to "Trianon Hungary" in ten days, and it must break off all relations with, and immediately declare war on, Germany. Although the Soviet government was prepared to "assist" the Hungarians in the implementation of these measures, the Hungarian delegation was simply dumbfounded: these terms were quite different from those transmitted earlier by Makarov. There was no reference now to the continuity of the political order nor to the possibility of settling the issue of Transylvania later on, and the demand to take up arms against the Germans was both unexpected and even abhorrent. But Molotov could not be moved. Only if Hungary had accepted these preliminary conditions would the Allies discuss the final terms of an armistice. The Hungarians' point that they had flown to Moscow via Slovakia with Makarov's help was dismissed as irrelevant. Molotov claimed that he knew nothing about the Makarov contact, that he was not interested in Makarov's professed assertions, and that he had never even heard of Makarov at all.[17]

As three more days of tedious bargaining proved equally futile, a preliminary armistice as presented by Molotov was signed on October 11. Kuznetsov embraced Faraghó. For the first time, Molotov smiled. "We're now allies," he said. But he was wrong. On October 14, claiming he had promised the Germans in March to give Hitler prior notice before he would seek an armistice, Horthy confided to one of his underlings that, "Under the armistice conditions we must withdraw to the Trianon frontiers and join the Russians in attacking the Germans, but I shall find some way out of that somehow"[18]—a rather strange comment from a man so proud of his sense of honor.

The Germans, who had left Finland under comparable circumstances, did not cooperate this time. They kidnapped the regent, forcing him to declare his just-issued proclamation about the armistice null and void and to appoint the lunatic head of the Nazi Arrow Cross party, Ferenc Szálasi, as prime minister. Although the Horthy regime thus formally collapsed, several loyal Hungarian divisions responded to the proclamation by laying

17. Gosztonyi, ibid., p. 409.
18. Macartney, *October Fifteenth*, p. 393.

down their arms and joining the anti-German war effort. The senior General of the Army, Béla Miklós, issued an order on October 21 in which he referred to Szálasi and his "henchmen" as traitors and Gestapo agents and he called on everyone, soldiers and civilians alike, to turn against Germany and "fight together with the Russian Army for Hungary's existence, independence, and honor."

Meanwhile, in Moscow the Russians asked Horthy's delegation —renamed the "Hungarian Committee in Moscow"—to help form a new political order on Hungarian soil and it pledged to do so. The new government would begin its activities in Debrecen as soon as possible; it would be composed of anti-Nazi elements; and it would seek to assure cooperation between the Soviet and the Hungarian armies. As to further specifics, Molotov raised the issue of the composition of a new "provisional" government. He suggested General Miklós to be its chairman, recommended the cooptation of leaders of the Smallholders' party and of the Social Democratic party, and then pointedly asked: 'Are you willing to include in the Provisional Government certain Hungarians residing on Soviet territory?"[19] As the delegation was not told who these Hungarians might be, its response was politely evasive.

Molotov did not press the issue. In line with what they had done in Finland and Romania, the Russians still preferred to create a regime that would suggest a degree of continuity with the past. By relying on the regent's entourage, and perhaps on the regent himself, they sought to do what Hitler had done earlier in 1944: occupy Hungary and thus control the main levers of power, but govern through Horthy's established authority. The difficult months and years ahead would be made easier and the changes to be introduced more palatable if the regent could be persuaded to remain at the helm. Most importantly, Horthy's generals could organize the Hungarian Army against Hitler and indeed inspire their troops in a way certainly no Communist leader—no "Hungarian residing on Soviet territory"—could possibly do.

By the beginning of December, however, the initial Soviet vision of Hungary's postwar development was apparently modified. Instead of leaving open the possibility of keeping the regent in power in order to lend legitimacy to the new postwar order, the Hungarian Communists were told to do without him, after all. Stalin called in three leaders of the

19. As quoted in Péter Gosztonyi, 'Az Ideiglenes Nemzeti Kormány megalakulásának előtörténetéhez" [To the Prehistory of the Founding of the Provisional National Government], *Uj Látóhatár* 15, no. 3 (August 1972): 221. Molotov never used the words "Muscovites" or "Communists." He either referred to "persons in Moscow," or to "Hungarians residing on Soviet territory," or "Moscow-based Hungarians."

Hungarian Communist party—Rákosi, Gerő, and Imre Nagy—to inform them of the new Soviet position: "We would have accepted Horthy. But the Germans took him away. They forced him to sign the document [of de facto abdication]. Once there is a document, it doesn't matter how it's obtained. Now Horthy is morally dead." In a few days Molotov followed up by telling the regent's emissaries, too, that from then on the Soviet Union would have "nothing to do" with Horthy.[20]

For some time to come this was the last change in the increasingly pertinacious Soviet position toward Hungary. At first, as Makarov suggested, Moscow would have accepted an armistice along the Finnish pattern: Horthy stays, the Germans leave, and everything else is subject to negotiations. By the time the Faraghó delegation arrived in October, the terms became less flexible: Horthy could still stay, but he must turn against Hitler and accept "Trianon Hungary." By December, after Horthy had abdicated and after the Red Army had come to control half of Hungary, Stalin made a further adjustment in the Soviet position. His early notion of the "broadest possible anti-German coalition" now gave way to the somewhat narrower "anti-German *and* anti-Horthy coalition," one in which a few leading representatives of the old order could still participate.

Dealing with the West

Coincidentally, though unknown to Hungarian Communists at the time, a second series of secret conferences was taking place in October. Accompanied by British Foreign Secretary Anthony Eden and others, Churchill arrived in Moscow to discuss with Stalin and Molotov the postwar political orientation of five countries in Eastern and in East Central Europe—Greece, Bulgaria, Romania, Yugoslavia, and Hungary. The first meeting between Churchill and Stalin was held on October 9; the substance of their famous "percentage agreement" became known with the publication of Churchill's memoirs in 1953.[21] But their encounter was followed by two days of

20. For the Stalin quotation, see Korom, *Magyarország ideiglenes nemzeti kormánya*, p. 326. For the Molotov quotation, see Gosztonyi, ibid., p. 232.

21. Winston S. Churchill, *Triumph and Tragedy* (Boston: Houghton Mifflin, 1953), pp. 227–29. A copy of the agreement is in Churchill's file at the Public Records Office in London (PREM 3/66/7, PRO). For an excellent summary and perceptive interpretation, see Vojtech Mastny, *Russia's Road to the Cold War* (New York: Columbia University Press, 1979), pp. 207–12. See also Albert Reis, "The Churchill-Stalin Percentages Agreement," *The American Historical Review* 83, no. 2 (April 1978): 368–87; Robert Garson, "Churchill's 'Spheres of Influence': Rumania and Bulgaria," *Survey* 24, no. 3 (Summer 1979): 143–58, and John Lukacs, "The Night Stalin and Churchill Divided Europe," *New York Times Magazine*, October 5, 1969, pp. 36–50.

haggling between Eden and Molotov on October 10 and 11, the details of which came to light only in the mid-1970s.[22]

Churchill was not in a strong position to demand Western influence in Eastern or in East Central Europe. The United States had rejected his recommendation that parts of this region be liberated by Anglo-American forces. Had his plan been accepted by President Roosevelt, the Red Army might not have been the first to reach the Balkans, Austria, and at least the western part of Hungary. Now he could not easily gain at the negotiating table what he had not achieved on the battlefields. Moreover, the United States, and particularly Roosevelt, had never encouraged him to negotiate about "spheres of influence." Washington was always more interested in the broader, more pressing questions of the day; for example, how to end the war as soon as possible and how to implement the principles of the Atlantic Charter.

Under the circumstances, the issue Churchill faced in Moscow was this: will the Soviet sphere include both Eastern and East Central Europe or, alternatively, will Stalin seek a Soviet sphere of exclusive control in Eastern Europe and accept a rather diverse area of states in East Central Europe in which the Soviet Union would exercise extensive, but not exclusive, influence?

Highly skeptical of Soviet objectives, Churchill was still determined to probe Stalin's intentions. Having all but conceded Poland to Stalin in Teheran two years earlier, in 1943, he was now prepared to concede Soviet control over Romania and Bulgaria in exchange for British control over Greece, assuming that in Yugoslavia and Hungary—and perhaps elsewhere in East Central Europe—"some kind of Anglo-Soviet influence-sharing" might be possible.[23] Expressing his ideas in percentages (see table 1.1), Churchill, writing "on a half-sheet paper," presented Stalin with the now-famous or notorious formula for the distribution of great-power influence after the war.

At the follow-up meetings on October 10–11, Molotov's apparent purpose was to increase Soviet influence in Hungary, while Eden, guided by British interests in the Mediterranean, would have preferred to focus on

22. The British record of these two meetings is at the Public Records Office: "Record of Meeting at the Kremlin, Moscow, on 10th October, 1944, at 7 P.M." (PREM 3/343/2) and "Record of Meeting at the Kremlin on 11th October, 1944, at 3 P.M." (PREM 3/434/2). Brief reference to these meetings is made in Anthony Eden, *The Reckoning* (Boston: Houghton Mifflin, 1965), pp. 559–60. For an excellent summary, see Mastny, *Russia's Road to Cold War*, pp. 208–12.

23. Elisabeth Barker, *British Policy in South-East Europe in the Second World War* (London: Macmillan, 1976), pp. 267–68.

Bulgaria and the Balkans in general. (Neither side brought up Greece and Romania anymore.) Molotov quickly turned to the 50:50 Hungarian deal Stalin and Churchill had made the day before, offering the rather disingenuous argument that, "Marshal Stalin thought that, after learning of the considerable losses sustained by the Red Army in Hungary, the army would not understand it if a principle of 50:50 were alloted." As if Stalin had spent the night consulting "the army"! The British minutes of this meeting then continue: "M. Molotov had been instructed by the Marshal to raise this question and to give his opinion."

A long, rather petty, and somewhat disjointed haggle followed. Much of the time was spent on Bulgaria, with Molotov promising that if the British could only accept a 90:10 distribution of influence in that country, instead of 75:25, "agreement could easily be reached on all the rest." Eden was prepared to go along with the Soviet proposal for the duration of the war, but for the period after Germany's surrender he sought to change what he called the West's "observer status" to "active participation." Not knowing how this idea could be translated into percentages, though, Eden offered no specific counterproposal, saying that "all he wanted was a greater share [in Bulgaria] than we already had in Romania . . . which was almost nothing."

During the assiduous, if surrealistic, babble about percentages that ensued (see table 1.1), Molotov, claiming that "the idea of percentages . . . was worthy of consideration," proposed the first package deal of the day. He wanted to change Bulgaria and Yugoslavia, as well as Hungary, to 75:25 each. When Eden quickly brushed aside this proposal—it "would be worse than on the previous day"—Molotov countered with a second package deal: 90:10 for Bulgaria, 50:50 for Yugoslavia, and Hungary "subject to an amendment." Eden said "he was ready to meet Molotov's wishes with regard to Hungary," but he still sought a larger role for the West in Bulgaria "after the Germans had been beaten."

Sensing an opening, Molotov proposed a third package deal: Hungary and Bulgaria 75:25, Yugoslavia 60:40. In response Eden first claimed that his prime minister "was greatly interested in Yugoslavia" and then put forth the first, and only, British offer of the day: Hungary 75:25, Bulgaria 80:20, Yugoslavia 50:50. This way the Churchill-Stalin agreement on Yugoslavia would have remained intact, while Moscow would have ended up with 25 percent more influence in Hungary and 5 percent more in Bulgaria. Still, Molotov was not satisfied. Leaving Hungary aside, he said, he could "now agree to 50:50 for Yugoslavia if Bulgaria were 90:10." As Eden would not accept this, Molotov immediately retorted with still another modified offer: 75:25 for Bulgaria, 60:40 for Yugoslavia. The

Table 1.1   The Soviet-British Bargain of 1944 (in percentages)

	Churchill-Stalin agreement (October 9)	Molotov's initial revision proposed (October 10)	Molotov's 1st "package deal"	Molotov's 2nd "package deal"	Molotov's 3rd "package deal"	Eden's only counterproposal	Molotov's counteroffer	Molotov's modified counteroffer	Molotov's October 11 final proposal (apparently accepted)
Soviet influence in Hungary	50	—	75	50 +	75	75	—	—	80
Soviet influence in Yugoslavia	50	—	75	50	60	50	50	60	50
Soviet influence in Bulgaria	75	90	75	90	75	80	90	75	80
Soviet influence in Romania	90	—	—	—	—	—	—	—	—
Soviet influence in Greece	10	—	—	—	—	—	—	—	—

session ended with no agreement on Bulgaria and Yugoslavia, but the Soviet Union was conceded to have 75 percent influence in postwar Hungary.

Until the next day, that is. For when the meeting continued in the Kremlin on October 11, Molotov made what appears to have been the last Soviet proposal: *Hungary* 80:20, *Bulgaria* 80:20, and *Yugoslavia* 50:50. The British record shows no opposition to the Soviet offer. Compared to the Churchill-Stalin deal, then, there was no change in the "status" of Yugoslavia because Great Britain, given its Mediterranean interests, resisted Molotov's pressure for adjustment. The change for Bulgaria was only cosmetic: Moscow was allowed 80 rather than 75 percent influence in that country. Whatever its meaning, the change for Hungary was more substantial (from 50:50 to 80:20).

Oddly, Eden was to recall in his memoirs that while Molotov "showed a disposition to haggle over the percentages," he [Eden] "was not interested in figures. All I wanted was to be sure that we had more voice in Bulgaria and Hungary than we had accepted in Romania." Eden believed that ". . . we obtained what we wanted on almost all points. I should say 90 percent overall."[24] Aside from the irony of judging the results of this

24. Eden, *Reckoning*, p. 560.

encounter in percentages, Eden was surely mistaken. Compared to the Churchill-Stalin deal, he gained nothing. And if Molotov's main purpose was to obtain British consent to Soviet primacy in Hungary, then that purpose was achieved. Vojtech Mastny put it well: "The British could hardly congratulate themselves on their accomplishment. For the sake of an ephemeral role in a country [Bulgaria] for which Churchill felt little but disgust, they resigned themselves to the status of bystanders in Hungary, perhaps the most Anglophile nation of all of East Central Europe."[25]

Still, what each side actually expected to gain by the agreement remains unclear. Perhaps the best explanation is that the British, concerned about Soviet presence near the Mediterranean, saw in the deal a chance to preserve Western influence in the two countries that mattered to them, Greece and Yugoslavia. As for Stalin, who both respected and feared Great Britain, he sought the British stamp of approval for a gradual extension of Soviet influence.

The extent of American knowledge about or responsibility for the percentage deal is also unclear.

Among high-ranking American officials only George F. Kennan supported the spirit of the Churchill-Stalin agreement explicitly. Writing from Moscow as minister-counselor of the U.S. embassy, he told Charles E. Bohlen, then chief of the State Department's Division of Eastern European Affairs, that the United States should "divide Europe frankly into spheres of influence" and thus "keep ourselves out of the Russian sphere and keep the Russians out of ours." More importantly, however, President Roosevelt's attitude was ambivalent. Guided by his long-time opposition to spheres-of-influence arrangements, he had informed Stalin early in October that the United States would not be bound by a deal he might make with Churchill. On the other hand, when he was informed by Ambassador W. Averell Harriman of the "division of responsibility" that was reached in Moscow, he seems to have accepted it. Replying to Harriman the same day, on October 11, the president noted that his "active interest at the present time in the Balkan area [was] that such steps as [were] practicable *should be taken* to insure against the Balkans getting us into a future international war."[26]

The president's ambivalence, based on principle as well as political considerations, prompted State Department officials to ignore the

25. Mastny, *Russia's Road to Cold War*, pp. 210–11.

26. President Roosevelt to Ambassador Harriman, October 11, 1944, U.S. Department of State, *Foreign Relations of the United States, Diplomatic Papers, 1944, Europe*, vol. 4 (Washington, D.C.: GPO, 1966), p. 1009. Emphasis added.

"percentage deal." Yet when they prepared Roosevelt for the February 1945 summit of the Big Three in Yalta, their "Briefing Book Paper" not only referred to the deal, but included the specific percentages as well. Therefore, the United States was certainly aware of what had taken place. More than that, Lynn E. Davis may be right by suggesting that "the United States government, by its actions and inactions, in effect granted the Soviet Union . . . a sphere of influence in Eastern Europe."[27]

Dealing with the Muscovites

The third set of secret meetings held in Moscow in the autumn of 1944 was the gathering of Hungarian Communists. The cream of Hungarian Communist émigrés got together on September 13, 20, and 28, and on October 7, 1944 to hammer out their program for and define their role in postwar Hungary. At least twenty-four leading cadres participated in the debates, some proposing specific measures, some debating seemingly obscure theoretical propositions, some raising rather silly questions. These were the veterans of the Hungarian Communist movement in exile, the "Muscovites," who had survived the short-lived Soviet Republic or Commune of 1919, Hungary's prisons during the interwar years, and Stalin's purges in the 1930s. They were exhilarated by the prospect of returning to their homeland, not as conspirators and agitators facing certain arrest and imprisonment but as free citizens of a new Hungary. Yet, as their speeches and comments showed, they bore the scars of more than two decades of intense factional disputes and personal antagonisms.[28]

27. Lynn Etheridge Davis, *The Cold War Begins: Soviet-American Conflict Over Eastern Europe* (Princeton, N.J.: Princeton University Press, 1974), p. 170.

28. The most detailed report on these meetings is in Korom, *Magyarország ideiglenes nemzeti kormánya*, pp. 243–60. See also Bálint Szabó, *Népi demokrácia és forradalomelmélet* [People's Democracy and Revolutionary Theory] (Budapest, 1974), pp. 75–105. For a fine summary in English based on Szabó, see Bennett Kovrig, *Communism in Hungary: From Kun to Kádár* (Stanford, Calif.: Hoover Institution Press, 1979), pp. 154–56. Zoltán Vas, one of the participants, gave me a vivid account of the meetings. Another participant, Gyula Háy, described the atmosphere among the Moscow émigrés—residents of the Lux Hotel—as follows:

One had the impression that the one-time great men of the political emigration hated one another's guts. They clung to the Soviet Union with quaking hearts as constituting henceforth their sole source of contact with life, with humanity. Yet they felt at the same time that the Soviet Union had shamefully betrayed them and robbed them of their former greatness. So they hated their new homeland no less bitterly than they had hated their old.

They had nothing of any consequence to do but they behaved as if they had. They practised assiduously something they referred to as politics, plotted one another's

The timing of this gathering could not have been more propitious. The first Soviet military units crossed the Romanian-Hungarian border on September 23, the southeastern town of Makó was liberated on September 26, and the Red Army reached the Tisza River on October 8. In less than two weeks, Szeged and Debrecen—not counting Budapest, Hungary's largest cities—would be in Soviet hands, and by the end of October the vast military offensive to free Budapest itself would get underway. It was practically certain that all of Hungary would soon be liberated by Soviet forces alone; indeed, in Stalin's eyes Hungary was now "in the center of our interests."[29]

Neither of the two main speakers at these gatherings even intimated that the Communist party might seek to rule postwar Hungary. One of them, the ideologist József Révai, a particularly articulate spokesman for the Popular Front approach, argued that his party should seek the slow, long-term transformation of Hungarian society. He put considerable emphasis on the necessity of inspiring a national effort in the months and years ahead, stressing that even "a democratic revolution will not happen at once, only a transformation whose point of departure will be national [in scope and character]." He added, however, that since "the bourgeoisie will [not] play the leading role in the national movement," the coming transformation could be and indeed "will have to be developed into a democratic revolution."[30] The primary task was the distribution of land, Révai stressed, and hence the Communist party must not allow such popular issues as Hungary's proper borders with its neighbors—the much-desired revision of "Trianon Hungary"—to distract the country's attention from the implementation of land reform and from the pursuit of other social and economic reforms.

Gerő was both the second main speaker and a frequent participant at all of the sessions. In his lecture of October 7, he noted that although Horthy's ultimate fate was uncertain, the old regime was expected to survive. He also argued that the party had to stand for a democratic transformation and not for the dictatorship of the proletariat because the

downfall, and generally pranced and cantered and whinnied like superannuated parade horses at the knacker's gates.

Julius Hay, *Born 1900: Memoirs* (La Salle, Ill.: Library Press, 1975), pp. 218–19.

29. As quoted in Mastny, *Russia's Road to Cold War*, p. 205.

30. Korom, *Magyarország ideiglenes nemzeti kormánya*, pp. 249, 257. For further details on Révai's speech, see Korom's three-volume doctoral dissertation (1974), which is deposited in the Archives of the Hungarian Academy of Science: *Az ideiglenes nemzeti kormány létrejötte és Magyarország átállása az antifasiszta koalíció oldalára* [The Formation of the Provisional National Government and Hungary's Switch to the Side of the Anti-Fascist Coalition], vol. 2, ch. 6, pp. 424, 427. See also Szabó, *Népi demokrácia*, p. 79.

Communist cause in Hungary was now weaker than even in 1918–19 (prior to the establishment of the Commune), because anti-Bolshevism was widespread, and because a large part of the industrial working class was corrupted by Horthy's counterrevolutionary propaganda. Looking at more positive developments, Gerő observed that some of the "undemocratic but anti-German" elements in Hungary had begun to seek contact with the left. He concluded by saying that all European Communists, the Hungarians included, should "enter those governments in which [at least] the minimal possibility exists for movement toward a people's democracy."

The term "people's democracy" had a special meaning during the meetings. Only after the war was it to signify a transitional form of economic, social, and political order in which capitalist and socialist forces, features, and characteristics would coexist side by side, in which socialist elements would only gradually gain the upper hand. Now the term meant something more specific and immediate: a "reduction," as Gerő put it, in the number of "our enemies, the destruction of feudalism and pro-German capitalism." The party's program for a people's democracy must be so flexible, Gerő emphasized, that no important stratum of Hungarian society would find it necessary to oppose it. Put another way, the Communist party should be prepared to form an alliance with all classes and not only with the industrial proletariat and the peasantry.

During the rather extensive debate that followed Révai's and Gerő's presentations, all participants agreed that the new postwar government would have to be broadly based. Most of them seemed to assume that such a government should include those leaders of the Horthy regime who, toward the end of the war, had finally turned against Hitler—notably Count István Bethlen, one-time prime minister and the regent's most influential adviser throughout the interwar period. Therefore, the discussion focused on the role that the Communist party would play in such a political order. Sándor Gergely expressed concern about the possibility that, given the expected "continuity," the Communist party would be outlawed even after the war and thus operate as an illegal entity. Zoltán Lippai wondered which party would have the largest say in the country's political life, listing the Smallholders' party, the Social Democratic party, and the anti-Nazi Horthyites as possibilities—not even mentioning the Communist party.

Such naive and atypical views aside, a number of participants, apparently surprised if not irritated, openly questioned the leadership's conciliatory guidelines. Gerő, acknowledging the existence of "mistaken views," found it necessary to repeat the reasons for the party's gradualist approach.

Still, some kept returning to the issue of how the Communist party would make headway: how it would proceed to hasten the process toward a people's democracy. Responding to that question, the leaders referred to a system of local national committees that the party would establish concurrently with the formation of a central government. Expecting these national committees to be more responsive to Communist influence and pressure, György Lukács, the noted Marxist philosopher, argued that a national committee in Budapest could play an especially vital role in the country's political life and indeed "push the government forward."[31]

Given this explanation, some participants assumed that a "duality of power," as in Russia in 1917, would thus be inevitable. "Whether we want it or not, there will be dual power," said László Rudas, for example. But this was not the leadership's position. "Dual power: we mustn't have," Rákosi retorted in one of his few recorded interjections.[32] Yet the leadership could not define the exact relationship between the local soviets and the central government. "It depends on the circumstances, on where our power will be," said Lukács. "It's a function of the class struggle," explained Révai. "What's better for us: that the government control them [the local soviets] or they control the government? [It depends on] where the party will have greater influence! We cannot give an answer in advance."[33]

On the basis of these somewhat vague if not disjointed discussions, Révai and Gerő composed the party's "action program" during the second half of October. A copy of the draft was given to Dimitrov, who forwarded it to Stalin and Molotov for approval. The program emphasized the need for national collaboration and unity against Nazi Germany, speedy reconstruction, and the urgency of land reform. Dimitrov laughingly told Gerő that the Hungarian Communists were ever so lucky to have the unresolved problems of vast landholdings in Hungary, for this way they could easily champion a popular and quite noncontroversial cause.[34] So

31. Szabó, *Népi demokrácia*, pp. 84–85.
32. Ibid., p. 85.
33. Ibid.
34. Mihály Korom, *Magyarország ideiglenes nemzeti kormánya*, p. 268. Rákosi called Vas "around November 20" to tell him that the action program had just been "approved in Moscow" (ibid., pp. 295, 314). In a barely modified form it was then published in the November 30 issue of *Néplap* (Szeged), pp. 1–2. Entitled "Magyarország demokratikus ujjáépítésének és felemelkedésének programja" [Program for Hungary's Democratic Reconstruction and Advancement], it is reprinted in Sándor Rákosi and Bálint Szabó, eds., *A Magyar Kommunista Párt és a Szociáldemokrata Párt határozatai, 1944–1948* [Decisions of the Hungarian Communist Party and the Social Democratic Party, 1944–1948] (Budapest, 1967), pp. 37–41.

approved, the Muscovites' program virtually amounted to temporary self-abnegation. Even the party's name would soon be changed to "Magyar Kommunista Párt" (Hungarian Communist party) from the previous "Kommunisták Magyarországi Pártja" (the Communists' party in Hungary), a slight semantic distinction to emphasize its Hungarian character and de-emphasize its ties to international Communism. Rákosi was instructed to stay in Moscow for a while because his return to Hungary might frighten too many of his countrymen. The party was to display both its red flag and the Hungarian national colors of red, white, and green. Although all participants of the Moscow meetings were not informed about it explicitly, Stalin had told the leadership that in order to distract the attention of the Western Allies from the rapid Sovietization of Poland, the pluralistic phase in Hungary—the democratic interlude—would have to last at least ten to fifteen years.[35]

35. William O. McCagg, Jr., was the first to notice overwhelming *public evidence*, by the end of December 1944, that Stalin's gradualism in Hungary was "designed to compensate Western discontent over Poland." McCagg points out that whenever *Pravda* reported on the new, broadly based coalition government in Hungary—on December 24, 25, 29, and 30—in each instance "contingent comments [appeared] praising the activities of pro-Soviet elements in Poland." McCagg, "Communism and Hungary, 1944–1946" (Ph.D. diss., Columbia University, 1965), p. 158. It should be noted, too, that Stalin, who paid close attention to Hungarian affairs during the autumn and winter of 1944–45, repeatedly reminded the Hungarian Muscovites not to hurry and especially not to antagonize anyone. On December 5, for example, he made extensive comments on the Hungarian Communist party's draft of a new policy declaration, saying (according to Gerő's private notes taken that day) that while the draft was "generally good," it would benefit from greater emphasis on the "protection of the average person's private property" and on the possibility of "private initiatives" [po gushche o chastnoy initsiative]. Additional comments made on the draft included the following: "More flexible formulations." "State with particular clarity that private property will remain untouched." "More flexibility on the land question. Do not address [issue of] numbers." "Underline private property more heavily." "Speak more flexibly about the clean-up of the [old] administrative apparatus." (Marked by Stalin's initials "I. V." and underlined in Gerő's notebook.) Concerning the nature of the coalition government, the Soviet—almost certainly Stalin's—advice was also based on tactical considerations: "Don't be grudging with words, don't scare anyone. But once you gain strength, then move ahead. . . . Conclusion of an armistice is the government's [main] task. . . . Must utilize as many people as possible, [those] who could be of service to us [Mozgatni kell minél több embert, akik basznot hozhatnak]." Korom, *Magyarország ideiglenes nemzeti kormánya*, pp. 333–34. On another occasion, Stalin told the Hungarian Communists that although they could count on Soviet fraternal assistance, "Soviet power cannot do everything for you. You must do the fighting, you must do the work." Ibid., p. 330.

The Provisional Government: Made in Moscow, Ratified in Debrecen

Until the first week of December, discussions in Moscow about the distribution of portfolios in a new provisional government had moved along two separate tracks. First, as previously noted, the subject had come up between Horthy's delegation and the Soviet government. The three sessions known to have been held took place on November 13, 16, 22, all during the night so that Stalin could be consulted. Second, there had been extensive consultations between the Soviet government and the "Moscow-based" Hungarian Communists, too. Stalin was present on at least one such occasion, on December 1, when the Hungarian Communist side was represented by Rákosi, as well as by Gerő and Nagy, who had just returned from Szeged for new instructions.[36]

The three sides finally got together for what turned out to be a decisive session on December 5. Rákosi stayed away. General Kuznetsov introduced Gerő and Nagy (these two "gentlemen" as he put it) to the "gentlemen" of Horthy's Hungarian Committee.[37] They had not met before—these professional revolutionaries and these well-bred officers and politicians of the old order—but they all knew by now what kind of government they were expected to form. As Molotov had told the Hungarian Committee on November 13: "The institution to be created should be democratic, with the participation of every party. It may be that the Moscow-based Hungarians could be useful, too, but especially those should be regarded as suitable who are respected in Hungary. Jews must be counted out."[38]

Gerő presented the list. He said that the Provisional Government should be headed by General Miklós and the remaining four members of the Hungarian Committee should each be given either a cabinet position or — in one case — stay in the Soviet capital as the government's representative. The list read as follows: defense—General János Vörös;

---

36. In preparation for this and other meetings with either the Soviet government or the Hungarian Committee, the three Muscovites—Rákosi, Gerő, and Nagy—frequently consulted with Eugene (Jenő) Varga, the Hungarian-born Soviet economist. From 1927 until he fell out of favor with Stalin in 1947, Varga had directed the prestigious Institute for World Economy and World Politics in Moscow. Respected by both Lenin and Stalin, Academician Varga was considered a Soviet economist rather than a Hungarian exile. Nonetheless, he participated in some of the discussions leading to the formation of the fiirst postwar Hungarian government and advised Rákosi, Gerő, and Vas about the stabilization of the Hungarian currency and other economic matters after war. Because he was such a significant figure in the Soviet hierarchy, his role in matters relating to Hungary was seldom publicized.

37. Gosztonyi, "Az Ideiglenes," pp. 228–29.

38. Ibid.

culture/education—Professor Géza Teleki; ministry of food—Lieutenant-General Gábor Faraghó; and liaison with Moscow—Domokos Szent-Iványi. Gerő further recommended that the other seven portfolios should be distributed among four political parties as follows: two "Moscow-based" Communists in charge of agriculture (Imre Nagy) and commerce (József Gábor); two Social Democrats in charge of industry (Ferenc Takács) and welfare (Erik Molnár); two Smallholders in charge of foreign affairs (János Gyöngyösi) and finance (István Vásáry); and one representative of the National Peasant party in charge of internal affairs (Ferenc Erdei).[39]

Gerő's list was accepted without debate. At a follow-up session with Molotov at 2:30 A.M. that night, there was some talk about the absence of any mention of the regent and hence about the legitimacy of the Provisional Government, but the Hungarian Committee was clearly pleased with the list. What with the Horthyites and five non-Communists assuming all but two of the cabinet seats, there was reason to believe that the Soviet Union was indeed committed to continuity, albeit without Horthy, and to the ideal of forging a genuine coalition government.

In reality, Gerő seems to have set at least two political traps for the unwary Hungarian Committee.

First, the Communists were about to take control of not two but four, and perhaps five, ministries in the government. For in addition to Nagy and Gábor, the man to head the important ministry of internal affairs, Ferenc Erdei, was a Communist even though he remained formally associated with the National Peasant party at Zoltán Vas's request. Then there was Erik Molnár, listed by Gerő as a Social Democrat. In fact, Molnár had been a home Communist, a party member since 1928, whose assignment in the 1930s was to penetrate the Social Democratic party and influence its policies from within. Lastly, there was the dubious case of János Gyöngyösi,

39. Ibid. Cf. Jób Paál and Antal Radó, eds., *A debreceni feltámadás* [Resurrection in Debrecen] (Debrecen, 1947), p. 148. Relying mainly on Gerő's recollections, Korom maintains that the cabinet was not established in Moscow, only "partial agreement" was reached there at the time. According to his account (Korom, *Magyarország ideiglenes nemzeti kormánya*, pp. 337–50), six of the eleven cabinet members were chosen by the Provisional Assembly in Debrecen. The records kept by two participants (Teleki and Szent-Iványi) of the December 5 Moscow meeting as well as the very reliable 1947 Paál-Radó book contradict Korom's argument. It may be that Korom wants to make it appear that the Soviet Union played a smaller role in the creation of the Hungarian government than it did—and was widely believed to have done. Another Hungarian historian has also confirmed that "The list of the new cabinet . . . was put together in Moscow, its final version . . . was clarified at home." István Vida, *A Független Kisgazdapárt politikája, 1944–1947* [The Politics of the Independent Smallholders' Party, 1944–1947] (Budapest, 1976), p. 31.

the designated foreign minister and a Smallholder, who was already working for and on behalf of the Soviet High Command in Western Hungary.[40]

Second, Gerő offered a cabinet seat to all members of the Horthyite Hungarian Committee probably because he expected that the Communist party would be able to use their past against them — some day. After all, Béla Miklós, the new prime minister, could be accused of collaboration with the Third Reich: he had served as the senior General of the Army until mid-October 1944 and in that capacity he had directed Hungary's war effort against the Soviet Union. The same could be said about the other officers, Vörös and Faraghó. As for the civilians, even Professor Teleki and Szent-Iványi had been identified with some of the policies of the Horthy regime. In short, Gerő's coalition appeared to be far more genuine and inclusive than it actually was.

Pleased with the agreement and anxious to have it ratified, the Soviet government was to fly members of the new Hungarian Provisional Government, together with a few Soviet officials, to Debrecen the next day. But the weather was bad and so the group left by train on December 7. When they arrived five days later, they found Debrecen — a county seat in eastern Hungary — already bustling with political activity. The so-called Preparatory Committee for a Provisional Assembly was wrestling with the legalities and politics of creating a new legislature, which would have proper authority to elect the members of the Provisional Government. From the liberated areas, delegates to the Provisional Assembly began to arrive, some having been elected at town meetings, others selected by the newly created local committees. In the end forty-five cities and towns sent 230 delegates, of whom 89 (38.7 percent) turned out to be Communists; 57 (25 percent) Smallholders; 43 (18.7 percent) Social Democrats; 16 (7 percent) National Peasant party members; 13 (5.6 percent) Citizen's Democratic party representatives; and 12 (5 percent) were identified as unaffiliated.[41] The Communist leadership was not pleased with the results. As Gerő put it in a letter sent to Rákosi in Moscow: "As far as the

40. According to Vas, near the end of 1944 both Erdei and Gyöngyösi applied to him for membership in the Communist party and that they became secret members. All other sources deny Gyöngyösi's membership.

41. Because of rather chaotic conditions, the actual party affiliation of some of the delegates could not be easily determined at that time. Thus, the first official count referred to only seventy-one Communists (rather than eighty-nine), together with fifty-five Smallholders, thirty-eight Social Democrats, sixteen National Peasants, twelve members of the Citizen's Democratic party, nineteen trade unionists, and nineteen unaffiliated delegates. Most of those originally listed as "trade unionists" turned out to be Communists — hence the discrepancy. For the official list, see *Ideiglenes Nemzetgyűlési Napló* [Diary of the Provisional Assembly] (Budapest, 1946), p. 160.

proportion of Communist representatives is concerned, we have certainly gone too far. It happened partly because we were in a hurry, partly because the local comrades were overzealous."[42]

But everything else was under control. The delegates argued about who should serve as deputy head of one ministry or another, and the election of the chairman of the Provisional Assembly caused something of an uproar. However, there was no argument about the two key issues of the day: the distribution of cabinet portfolios as decided in Moscow on December 5—the list to which a Social Democrat, Ágoston Valentiny, was added as minister of justice—and the new government's professed objectives. Thus, at the year's end, as Budapest was still to be liberated, the country's postwar political order was already in place. The radical transformation of Hungary's social and economic life was underway. Not incidentally, the Soviet-ordained gradualist approach of the Communist party was not only an eminently workable strategy in Hungary, but it also turned out to be an effective Soviet signal to the West as well. The *Economist* of London assured its readers on December 30 that the composition of the new Hungarian government had proved the accuracy of "Mr. Molotov's promise" that Russia would not attempt to influence the "domestic structure" of countries under its temporary supervision.

Two Tactics of Soviet Conduct

In a more general sense, Stalin's early postwar policy toward Europe was as effective as it was because it combined expansion along the Soviet periphery with considerable deference to Western sensitivities elsewhere. Exploiting the opportunity created by the Red Army's momentous victories, Stalin undertook the early Sovietization of Bulgaria, Romania, and Poland, convinced that Western acquiescence in Communist control over Eastern Europe in exchange for Communist restraint in Western Europe was not only fair, but that it would be acceptable to the United States and Great Britain. He also proceeded on the assumption that the strong postwar momentum of the left throughout Europe, together with growing Soviet power and influence, would bring under Communist control most if not all of the five states in the intermediate area of East Central Europe in ten to fifteen years.

To realize his intricate scheme, Stalin simultaneously employed two traditional approaches in Soviet conduct.

First, he relied on the "inclusionary," quite flexible, Popular Front

42. Dated December 28, 1944, Gerő's letter to Rákosi is deposited in the Archives of the [Hungarian] Institute of Party History (274—7/13).

orientation of the 1934–44 period, encouraging most Communist parties to join forces with non-Communists in coalition governments and to promote such anodyne causes as postwar reconstruction, land reform, anti-Fascism, and the like. He accepted the costs associated with this orientation—that is, the danger of ideological erosion by Socialists, Social Democrats, and others—because he believed that only a broad left coalition in Western Europe and in East Central Europe could ensure the security of the Soviet Union. In the realm of international relations, his inclusionary approach entailed a measure of continued cooperation with Moscow's Anglo-Saxon allies. By making the necessary compromises and concessions, and by proceeding gradually, Stalin sought to gain time and indeed to await a favorable turn in the international balance of forces.

Second, Stalin concurrently relied on the "exclusionary," more rigid, pre-Popular Front orientation as well, one that called for little or no common effort with non-Communists. Along the Soviet periphery and as time went on elsewhere as well, he increasingly sought to transform genuine coalitions into pseudocoalitions, attempting to exclude from these formations those liberal, agrarian, Christian, and social democratic elements who were willing to cooperate, but unwilling to collaborate, with Communists. In international relations, the exclusionary approach entailed an ever more hostile stance toward the West, particularly the new target —"American imperialism." By avoiding compromises and concessions and by proceeding rapidly, Stalin sought to consolidate Moscow's geopolitical gains, protect the Communist movement from evolutionary tendencies and influences, and thus prepare his own country and Communists everywhere for the hard times ahead.

By alternating between the two orientations, Stalin intended to offer non-Communist publics and politicians a difficult choice. They had to decide whether long-term partnership with Moscow and with the several European Communist parties was or was not a likely possibility. If it was—if the inclusionary approach would last—then they should reciprocate by adopting a correspondingly tolerant course and engage in the give-and-take of the political process. If it was not—if the exclusionary orientation was the genuine article—then, by refusing to be fooled by the language and tactics of Popular Frontism, they should adopt such tough countermeasures that would curtail Communist power and influence.

For a few years between 1944 and 1947, both in Europe and in the United States, public opinion was split between those for whom more conclusive evidence was needed to prove Stalin's intransigence and those for whom the evidence was sufficiently conclusive already. In the United States, for example, Democrats around Henry A. Wallace preferred to wait, Democrats around Harry S. Truman did not. In Italy the left wing of the Socialist party seemed patient, its right wing was not. In Hungary the apparent tolerance of the leaderships of the two centrist parties, the Smallholders' party and the Social Democratic party, ran counter to non-conformists in the same parties who opposed the Communists early and directly.

These differences were as natural as they were understandable. So soon after World War II few in the West were ready for yet another confrontation; the memory of wartime partnership was fresh and vivid. Despite a flash of skepticism here and there, the spirit of Soviet-American camaraderie was alive and well. Respectable people in the West could still divine that Stalin's "occasional stubbornness" must be due to the intransigence of his colleagues in the Politburo. Even in East Central Europe, where the presence or proximity of the Red Army alerted quite a few politicians, many others could not yet find the evidence of Moscow's unyielding behavior conclusive. After all, for every Poland under early Soviet control there were several pluralistic regimes in such countries as Czechoslovakia, Austria, or Hungary, where the Communists could have gained hegemony but supported coalition governments instead. In short, Stalin's two-track policy made it possible, even reasonable, for the optimists to be hopeful and the pessimists to be incredulous.

As new evidence helped the pessimists gain political momentum by 1947, the Truman Doctrine, the Marshall Plan, and the expulsion of Communists from the Italian and French coalitions marked both the end of the postwar phase of limited partnership and the beginning of the cold war. The emerging Western consensus held the Soviet Union responsible not only for the Sovietization of Eastern Europe, but for the Greek civil war and for other violations of international agreements and understandings as well. With the new doctrine of containment intended to stop further Soviet advances and with the United States assuming a key role in the affairs of the old continent, Stalin's differentiated scheme for postwar Europe presently lost its relevance.

Therefore, at the founding meeting of the Cominform in Szklarska Poreba (see chapter 5), Stalin repaired to the one-track policy of almost unmitigated militancy inherent in his exclusionary approach. His gradual, inclusionary approach—international Popular Front with the West and coalitions with Communist cooperation in most European countries—had outlived its usefulness. With that change in the autumn of 1947, Stalin drew the curtain, the iron curtain, on the democratic interlude he had composed for Hungary, too, only three short years earlier in Moscow.

2

The Domestic Context

Given the evidence presented in the previous chapter and in numerous studies describing and analyzing the Communist seizure of power in Eastern and in East Central Europe, it is tempting to explain the Communists' ultimate success exclusively in terms of external circumstances and influences.[1] After all, persistent Soviet political and economic pressure combined with Western inaction was the necessary condition of the Communist takeovers. The very presence of Soviet troops, by itself, made other political outcomes all but impossible, even though only in Czechoslovakia did a Communist party enter the postwar era enjoying considerable indigenous support.

Without denying the primacy of external influences, this chapter treats the domestic sources of Communist hegemony in Hungary. The main point is that while the Hungarian Communist party's postwar success was a function of Soviet power, fundamental changes in the fabric of the Hungarian economy and society, particularly on the eve of and during World War II, had set the stage for the approaching revolutionary change. Indeed, the question after the war was no longer whether the country could choose between evolutionary or revolutionary change; this question had been settled—primarily by previous economic, social, and even political developments—in favor of revolutionary change. The question actually facing Hungary was the nature and direction of revolutionary transformation, with the choice limited to two competing radical models of development—the populist-agrarian model and the Communist-

1. Outstanding studies of this kind include Hugh Seton-Watson, *The East European Revolution* (New York: Praeger, 1956); Zbigniew K. Brzezinski, *The Soviet Bloc: Unity and Conflict* (Cambridge: Harvard University Press, 1967); Stephen D. Kertesz, *Diplomacy in a Whirlpool: Hungary between Nazi Germany and Soviet Russia* (Notre Dame, Ind.: University of Notre Dame Press, 1953).

industrial model. In this context the Soviet Union can be viewed as the catalyzer rather than the sole creator of revolutionary change.

The validity and implications of this interpretation are developed in the four sections of this chapter. The first section presents the salient features of the modernizing process in Hungary, with emphasis on the efforts and characteristics of Horthy's syncratic political system in the interwar period. The second section analyzes the two competing revolutionary formulas (populist and Communist) for Hungary's economic, social, and political development. The third section deals with the results of the 1945 elections and with the respective positions of the prominent political parties at the time, to ascertain the extent of popular support for the various paths of development. Finally, a brief section at the end offers a few concluding remarks on modernization and Communist power in Hungary.

Stages of Modernization

The process of modernization in Hungary might be divided into three stages of development.[2] The first or initial stage lasted from the second half of the nineteenth century, particularly from 1867, to the onset of World War I; the second or transitional stage occurred during the interwar period; the third or revolutionary stage began in 1944.[3]

The initial stage. If "modernization," in its most general meaning, denotes increasingly rapid political, social, and intellectual change under the impact of industrialization, Hungary had been barely touched by the wind of modernization until the second part of the nineteenth century. As late as the 1830s, less than 5 percent of the population had lived in communities officially designated as towns or were employed in industry or trade. As of 1848, political rights, or rather certain political rights, had been enjoyed by only 44,000 of the 136,000 "noble" families. Most functions of the courts were exercised by the landed aristocracy.

After the revolution of 1848−49 and particularly after the establishment of the Dual Monarchy in 1867, however, the challenge of moderniza-

2. This is a modified version of the periodization offered by C. E. Black in his *The Dynamics of Modernization: A Study in Comparative History* (New York: Harper & Row, 1966), pp. 67−94. Black's study also includes an excellent bibliographic essay on the literature of modernization.

3. Further breakdowns of each stage of development can only be indicated here. The initial stage may thus be subdivided into the 1848−67 and 1867−1918 periods, the transitional stage into the 1920−33 and 1933−44 periods, the revolutionary stage into the 1944−48 and 1948−53 periods, with the postrevolutionary—consolidating—period commencing in 1953. Systematic elaboration on these subdivisions is beyond the scope of this chapter.

tion could no longer be denied. Economic retardation was increasingly becoming a source of embarrassment even for the landed aristocracy, and for this reason industrialization was stimulated by necessity as well as national pride. In the wake of Count István Széchenyi, a small group of intellectuals, merchants, and artisans spearheaded the movement aimed at the adaptation of Western ideas and institutions. Progress was indicated by the decrease of uncultivated land from 22 percent in 1870 to 15 percent in 1890 to 5 percent in 1910. With the introduction, on a small scale, of fertilization and mechanization, the wheat crop per hectare[4] increased by nearly 60 percent between 1870 and 1890. The number of banks and savings and loan institutions grew from 41 in 1867 to over 600 by the early 1890s. The length of railways—an important prerequisite to, and indicator of, industrialization—was drastically extended from 1,350 miles in 1866 to 8,226 miles in 1896 to 13,625 miles in 1913. Trains that carried fewer than 3.5 million persons and less than 3 million shipping tons of goods in 1866 increased their capacity so that by 1894 the corresponding figures were 50 million persons and 27 million shipping tons of goods.

This intrusion of modernity, particularly during the last decade of the century, slowly began to leave its imprint on the country's social structure. The industrial population grew by 127 percent between 1870 and 1910 in contrast to a 36 percent increase of the whole population. By 1900, 16.7 percent of the population was employed in transportation and industry (mainly the former) as opposed to 13.8 percent in 1890; in the same period, the agricultural population decreased from 72.5 percent to 68.4 percent. Concurrently, the number of "large" factories, those employing more than twenty workers, grew from 1,129 in 1890 to 1,756 in 1900 to 2,180 in 1910. Labor unions came into existence in 1899, and in the capital city of Budapest almost one out of three workers joined the labor movement. The scope of governmental activities was indicated by the growth of the state bureaucracy: the number of public servants increased from 25,000 in 1870 to 230,000 by the end of World War I.

The government's growing interest in education was revealed by the budget of the ministry of religion and education, which increased from 0.82 percent of the total governmental budget in 1868 to 3.54 percent in 1900, to 5.54 percent in 1913. As a result, while about two out of three Hungarians were illiterate in 1869, by 1890 it was less than one out of two, by 1900 about two out of five, and by 1910 only one out of three. The output of graduates at the nation's universities also increased, although

4. One hectare = about 2.5 acres.

they still produced more lawyers than doctors, engineers, and scientists together. Finally, the impact of modern culture was illustrated by the publication of such periodicals as *Huszadik Század* (Twentieth Century) and of *Nyugat* (West) whose orientation clearly reflected the intelligentsia's growing interest in Western culture.[5]

Such economic, social, and cultural developments obviously required, or should have required, political readjustments. On balance, however, the landed aristocracy and the slowly emerging gentry, which dominated the top echelons of the government after 1867, could not govern effectively, let alone guide or direct the processes of modernization.[6] Specifically, the various governments of the 1867–1914 period faced four crucial problems,[7] none of which did they seem able to resolve or substantially mitigate.

First, the non-Magyar nationalities became increasingly dissatisfied with their economic and political status during this period, and their opposition to what they conceived to be Hungarian domination remained complete. Their assimilation into and hence the integration of Hungarian society—a major component of modernization—was left unresolved. Second, the poverty and hopelessness of the agrarian population, if anything, continued to increase. As C. A. Macartney noted, "It was calculated that by the end of the century [agricultural] laborers got enough to feed themselves and their families adequately only when the harvest had been 'exceptionally good'; another authority said that the conditions of the laborers had gone down by at least 50 percent since 1848. Starvation diseases were common. Hours of work had been lengthened to the extreme limit. The agrarian legislation of the period consisted almost exclusively of enactments designed to prevent the laborers from defending their interests against those of the landlords."[8] The third problem was that, particularly after 1867, industrial growth was accomplished overwhelmingly at the expense of the industrial working class. The government in fact encouraged low wages, especially for unskilled labor, so as to develop native industrial strength in the

5. Most of the preceding data has been derived from Zoltán Horváth's informative *Magyar századforduló: A második reformnemzedék története 1896–1914* [Hungary at the Turn of the Century: History of the Second Reform Generation 1896–1914] (Budapest, 1961). For a thorough and important study of the social composition and growth of the industrial proletariat, see Miklós Lackó, *Ipari munkásságunk összetételének alakulása 1867–1949* [Development of the Composition of Our Industrial Proletariat, 1867–1949] (Budapest, 1961).

6. For the social background of high government officials, see Ernő Lakatos, *A politikai magyar vezetőréteg* [The Hungarian Political Elite] (Budapest, 1942).

7. C. A. Macartney, *October Fifteenth: A History of Modern Hungary, 1929–1945*, 2d ed., vol. 1 (Edinburgh: The University Press, 1961), pp. 8–13.

8. Ibid., p. 10.

face of competition from the great manufacturing centers of Austria and Bohemia. The fourth problem, persistent nationalist agitation against the Dual Monarchy, provided for an acute crisis of the political elites throughout the period as the country's two political parties collided on the issue of Hungary's proper relationship with Austria: the Independence party considered the Dual Monarchy a disadvantageous and dangerous arrangement, while the Liberal party regarded it as a guarantee of Hungary's undisturbed future.

Within the political elite, the growing influence of the Hungarian gentry at the expense of the landed aristocracy was a development of major significance. The gentry, to be sure, was divided: its lower stratum —economically less privileged, culturally deprived, and fearful of losing untenable prerogatives—allied with the aristocracy against modernization and argued for closer ties with Vienna. However, the higher stratum of the gentry, educated, quite well-to-do, distinctly cosmopolitan and urbane—offered itself as a substitute, as it were, for the urban middle class and welcomed Western influences. Thus the Hungarian political elite was becoming rather evenly divided between the conservative aristocracy and the poorer segment of the gentry, on the one hand, and the progressive well-to-do segment of the gentry, on the other. Accordingly, the elite as a whole showed but a casual attitude toward industrialization: it neither impeded nor guided it.[9]

As a result, the tempo of industrialization was moderately slow by European standards, with the rate of economic growth reaching 3.0 percent in agriculture and 4.4 percent in mining and manufacturing by 1910.[10] A genuine opportunity for more rapid industrialization was missed in view of the "uniquely favorable institutional and economic setting for the development of both agriculture and industry" provided by the economic setup of the Dual Monarchy, that is, a guaranteed market for Hungary's agricultural exports coupled with administrative measures protecting the emerging Hungarian industry.[11] The opportunity was missed largely because the transfer of power from traditional to modernizing leaders had only begun and no decisive break with a predominantly agrarian life as yet occurred. In the countryside, practically all of the country's cultivable land remained in a few hands and land ownership remained a determining factor in both politics and social advancement. Indeed, social mobility lagged behind Hungary's economic development. Such early

9. See table 2.2.
10. Alexander Eckstein, "National Income and Capital Formation in Hungary, 1900–1950," in Simon Kuznets, ed., *Income and Wealth*, 5th ser. (London, 1955), p. 176.
11. Ibid.

Table 2.1   Occupational Distribution in Hungary, 1900–1941
(Percentages per year)

Economic Branch	1900	1910	1920	1930	1941
Agriculture, forestry, and fishing	59.4	55.8	58.2	54.2	50.0*
Mining, metallurgy, manufacturing, commerce, transport, and communications	23.0	26.9	26.3	30.4	32.6
Government, community, business, and recreational services	4.6	5.7	6.1	7.7	8.0
National defense	1.7	1.6	2.4	1.0	3.2
Domestic service	6.2	5.7	4.3	4.5	3.7
Other	5.0	4.3	3.6	3.2	2.8

*Without forestry and fishing, 48.7 percent.
Source: Alexander Eckstein, "National Income and Capital Formation in Hungary, 1900–1950," in Simon Kuznets, ed., Income and Wealth, ser. 5 (London, 1955), p. 182.

channels of social mobility as the social service and the military were still closed to members of the lower classes.

Nonetheless, in a casual, almost haphazard fashion, the feudal features of Hungarian society were being left behind. The influence of a progressive gentry increased and that of the landed aristocracy declined. Railroads were built. Illiteracy was significantly reduced and the country's school system was expanded. Western ideas impregnated Hungary's intellectual life. In short, the socioeconomic foundations of traditional society were being undermined even if the intrusion of modernity did not yet cause social upheaval or political transformation.

The transitional stage.   The casual but steady process of modernization, which had characterized the first stage of development, led to a serious and largely successful attempt by the landed aristocracy to slow down the pace and ease the consequences of change during the premiership of Count István Bethlen (1921–31). However, a dramatic reversal occurred in the 1930s; so much so, in fact, that by the eve of World War II Hungary became "industrialized" as illustrated by the fact that less than 50 percent of the country's population engaged in agricultural pursuits (see table 2.1).

This was the setting: Hungarian political life in the interwar period centered around two major questions. First, the regime of Regent Miklós

Horthy (1920–44), which came into being after the collapse of the revolutions of 1918–19, was so repulsed by the revolutions that it allowed if not encouraged the White Terror of 1920–21 to run its course, during which hundreds of Communists, Socialists, and Jews were murdered without trial. Worse, the Horthy regime failed to come to terms with the revolutions' modernizing alternatives. Clearly, the first revolution in 1918 offered a bourgeois-democratic model of industrialization and political development whose substance, meaning, and appeal the Horthy regime could have utilized; in its abhorrence, it spent its time and energy denouncing them.

Second, the Horthy regime's other major preoccupation was the Treaty of Trianon, which, it claimed, represented a national defeat for Hungary. Indeed, when the new boundaries were drawn, only 28.6 percent of the old kingdom remained as Hungary proper, with the rest being assigned to the neighboring countries. As a consequence of the new boundaries, Hungary's population decreased by over 60 percent. Supported by all shades of political opinion, the Horthy regime argued that the punishment meted out to Hungary was too severe: more than half of the 3.5 million Hungarians now separated from Hungary lived in areas contiguous to their homeland, and thus a more equitable and just arrangement would have been possible. Indeed, the new states of Czechoslovakia and Yugoslavia were not homogeneous either; both were composed of several different nationalities. At any rate, the Horthy regime kept the question of revision alive at least partly in order to divert attention from economic stagnation, social injustice, and political repression.

To be sure, economic and fiscal reconstruction after the war ran into real and serious obstacles. The currency was rapidly depreciating and the budget was unbalanced. It was clear from the beginning that reconstruction depended overwhelmingly on the government's ability to secure financial assistance abroad; mainly for political reasons, however, foreign loans were unavailable until 1924.[12] With the protection of the Dual Monarchy removed, however, the economy was now dependent on foreign markets and foreign supplies, and the country faced a serious balance of payments problem as well. Since Hungary's major product for export was wheat, whose world price tended to fluctuate, each time the price of wheat fell the whole economy was affected. In short, disruption and destruction inflicted by the war and readjustment necessitated by the boundary changes made rapid reconstruction exceedingly difficult.

Yet World War I and the boundary changes effected by the Treaty of

12. Cf. Macartney, *October Fifteenth*, pp. 61–66.

Trianon were not without potential benefits to economic and social change in Hungary. First, Trianon provided the basic conditions for the creation of national unity—a primary prerequisite for further modernization—since it led to the disappearance of the divisive separatist movements of the ethnic minorities. Because of *ethnic homogeneity*, the Horthy regime could have attained firm political authority more easily and used it for the encouragement of the process of modernization. Second, the war had accelerated the development of industrial production in general and of the metal processing and engineering industries in particular; Hungary emerged from the war with an enlarged industrial capacity. The horsepower capacity of large-scale manufacturing, for example, had increased by 50 percent between 1913 and 1921, from about 400,000 to 600,000.[13] Moreover, the largest Hungarian manufacturing centers—Budapest, with its industrial suburbs, in particular—were not detached from the country. The largest financial and cultural centers also remained within Hungary and so did most of the trained personnel needed for industrialization. Third, while the proportion of "very large" holdings in the countryside, those over 1,000 hold (1,420 acres), did increase somewhat, the proportion of "very small" and thus uneconomical holdings, those from 0 to 10 hold (0 to 14.2 acres), declined to 30 percent of what it had been prior to World War I.[14]

In short, while difficult and costly economic readjustments undoubtedly had to be made after the war, what added up to a temporary halt in the modernization process was caused primarily by the political leadership's determination to circumvent the consequences of modernization. Let us emphasize: Trianon offered a combination of opportunities as well as impediments for modernization; under Count István Bethlen's premiership in the 1920s the opportunities were deliberately ignored. As a representative of his class, Bethlen sought order and stability at the same time that he longed for a return to the undisputed rule of the landed aristocracy.

The political system to serve such objectives can be identified as a *syncretic political system*, using A. F. K. Organski's conceptual framework.[15] The system was characterized by the common or shared rule of the landed aristocracy and the lower segment of the gentry, on the one hand, and the upcoming industrial elite and the upper segment of the gentry, on the other. As elsewhere, too, syncretic politics occurred in Hungary during

13. Eckstein, "National Income," p. 177.
14. Macartney, *October Fifteenth*, p. 26.
15. A. F. K. Organski, *The Stages of Political Development* (New York: Alfred A. Knopf, 1965), pp. 122–56. The word "syncretic," Organski explains, is derived from the Greek *syn*, which means "together," and from *cratic*, which, of course, means "rule."

Table 2.2   Rates of Economic Growth, 1899–1901 to 1940–1941
and 1942–1943 (Percentages per year)

Period	Mining and manufacturing	Agriculture
1899–1901 to 1911–13	4.4	3.0
1911–13 to 1928–29 and 1930–31	1.7	−0.7
1928–29 and 1930–31 to 1940–41 and 1942–43	5.7	−1.5
1934–35 to 1939–40	10.8(!)	2.0

Source: Eckstein, "National Income," p. 176.

the transitional stage of modernization, at a time when the goal of industrialization had not yet been attained and when the industrial elite was still weaker than the old agricultural elite. Syncretic government, then, expressed the desire of the landed aristocracy "to slow the pace of industrialization and to control its consequences. . . . Faced with certain defeat, they nevertheless managed to maximize their power and postpone its final shift into other hands."[16]

As table 2.2 illustrates, the Bethlen regime did not seek to stop the trend of industrialization altogether; it sought to *control* the process of industrialization and to *slow* its pace without completely disrupting its cordial relationship with the partly Jewish financial and industrial elite. Unable and unwilling to stop industrial expansion, the government aimed at the conservation of the balance of power between the old agricultural and new industrial elites. If the latter, however slowly, still continued to gain ground, it was because the government feared economic isolation and because the possibility of another war, this time with Hungary's neighbors, required larger industrial capacity and advanced know-how.

What were the consequences of such "syncretic balancing"? Organski's apt generalization applied to the Hungarian case: "The main effect of syncretic government is typically to exempt the agricultural elite from paying the economic and social cost of industrialization and to lessen the cost paid by the peasantry. . . . To a very large extent, the savings in the industrial sector are created by increases in productivity in the modern portion of the economy and by decreases in the living standard of the industrial proletariat."[17] A second consequence of such "balancing" was growing social unrest as expressed in the intensification of the three major

16. Ibid., p. 155.
17. Ibid., p. 155 and p. 139.

conflicts of the Hungarian, as of all, syncratic political systems: (*a*) the conflict, already mentioned, between the old agricultural and new industrial elites; (*b*) the conflict—or class struggle—between each of the elites and their respective employees; and (*c*) the underlying urban-rural dichotomy.[18]

The latter, urban-rural tension, was particularly acute in Hungary where urban civilization became identified with foreign civilization; a sizable portion, perhaps two-thirds, of the ambitious urban middle class was of Jewish and German extraction. This growing middle class of the cities, estimated to make up from 8 to 10 percent of the population, was not the enterprising middle class of the Anglo-Saxon world; it consisted of relatively few entrepreneurs but many professionals. Its special character was indicated by the fact that, in order to qualify for membership, it was normally sufficient to possess a university degree. Not surprisingly, the city's conception of rural life was at best condescending, at worst hostile; life in the countryside became a source of mockery. The prevailing image of the peasant was that of an uneducated, uncultivated, unsophisticated, and simple soul, respectful though often sly. The city appreciated folk music, witness the acceptance of Béla Bartók and Zoltán Kodály, but this attitude was marred by the enormous popularity of folksy, Viennese-type operettas that caricatured the peasant way of life.

Conversely, the city seemed strange, alien, non-Magyar, and on the whole unacceptable for traditionally rural Hungary. In a sense, the city was attractive *and* dangerous: it offered both somewhat higher wages and the ills of urban civilization, that is, slums, concentrated unemployment, loneliness. At best, it was a place to visit. Also the average peasant or small farmer who had always marketed his own produce considered it rather odd, if not outright immoral, for a city merchant to make a living by simply buying and selling that which he himself did not produce. Preferring conditions prevalent prior to the advent of industrialization, then, rural Hungary did not conceive of some of the advantages of industrialization and modernization: better schools and hospitals, advanced methods of agricultural production, and the like. Also rural resistance to modernity was exacerbated by bitter anti-Semitism, diligently promoted by the lower stratum of the gentry whose members found it uncomfortable, even degrading, to deal with Jewish financiers in the 1920s; even worse, their declining estates tended to drift into Jewish hands after the economic crisis of 1929—31. Rightly or wrongly, rural Hungary identified industrialization with Jewish influence and blamed the Jew for the real or imagined

18. Ibid., pp. 125 ff.

humiliation it was suffering. In short, as rural Hungary was being bypassed, a stubborn and provincial opposition set in against the outward-looking urban society of the cities.

As to the political conflict between the industrial and agricultural elites and their respective employees, Bethlen's syncratic regime sought to secure its hegemony by placating, indeed paralyzing, the two political parties expressing and representing the interests of the agricultural and industrial proletariats: the Smallholders' party and the Social Democratic party.

The Smallholders' party had attained some recognition during World War I, and at the first national elections in 1920 it sent a surprisingly large group of ninety-one representatives to the legislature in contrast to the fifty-nine of the establishment's Christian National party (as it was called at the time). Led by István Nagyatádi Szabó, a farmer, the Smallholders' party won the election on a platform of land reform, secret ballot, and progressive taxation. Count Bethlen, a nonparty deputy at the time with close ties to the Christian Nationals, recognized that Szabó would probably prefer to share his power (he was somewhat "frightened by the responsibility of creating a new state"[19]) and approached him with the idea of working together in a united party. He suggested that the Smallholders' platform could be carried out more effectively by a new party that would undoubtedly obtain more than sufficient majority in the legislature.[20] The apparently naive and definitely inexperienced Szabó agreed and became minister of agriculture in a cabinet dominated by the Christians; indeed, the Smallholders' party was soon swallowed up in the new United party. Its program, too, was disregarded: the secret ballot, already in force, was withdrawn; the pseudo land reform—with only about 1.5 million acres or about 5 percent of the arable land distributed —did not meet the needs of Hungary's landless population; and progressive taxation was simply forgotten. By the time of Szabó's death in 1924, the Smallholders' party no longer retained its former political strength and appeal and it was only in the 1930s that the new Independent Smallholders' party made a renewed attempt to represent the political and economic interests of the peasantry.

Bethlen also succeeded in curtailing the activities of the Social Democratic party and of the trade unions. Although the Social Democrats had greatly suffered during the White Terror and many of their best leaders

19. Ferenc Nagy, *The Struggle Behind the Iron Curtain* (New York: Macmillan Co., 1948), p. 14.

20. Several documents related to the establishment of the United party are reproduced in Dezső Nemes, ed., *A fasiszta rendszer kiépitése és népnyomor Magyarországon, 1921–1924* [Development of the Fascist System and Destitution in Hungary, 1921–1924] (Budapest, 1956).

Table 2.3   Workers in Industry and Craft, 1929–43

Year	Number	Index (1929 = 100)
1929	613,300	100.0
1930	559,800	91.3
1931	508,500	82.9
1932	447,600	73.0
1933	451,300	73.6
1934	489,900	79.6
1935	526,900	85.9
1936	581,100	94.7
1937	638,000	104.0
1938	688,800	112.3
1939	759,700	123.9
1940	794,100	129.5
1941	853,600	139.2
1942	872,700	142.3
1943	919,000	150.0

Source: Béla Kovrig, *Magyar szociálpolitika (1920–1945)* [Hungarian Social Policy (1920–1945)] (New York: Hungarian National Council, 1954), p. 39.

were forced to escape to Western Europe, their moderately socialist program retained some popularity among the industrial proletariat. The aim of the Social Democratic leadership was to gain more freedom of action from the government in order to expand socialist activity at least in the industrial centers. Bethlen's primary goal was to prevent the trade unions and the Social Democrats from organizing the peasantry. The compromise between the government and the Socialists became known as the Bethlen-Peyer pact.[21] The parties, inter alia, agreed that the Social Democratic party would not attempt to organize among the peasants, trade unions would deal only with economic, not political, issues, and the Socialists would cooperate with the government in presenting Hungary's case in the West. The government, in turn, agreed to permit the publication of socialist propaganda, the party was allowed to organize industrial workers, and it could once again be represented in the legislature.

The cleverly manipulated and balanced syncretic political order thus established was nevertheless unable to withstand the enormous impact of the economic crisis of 1929–31. Factories became idle and the number of employed workers dropped (see table 2.3), while the price of most agricul-

21. Károly Peyer was the head of the Social Democratic party throughout the interwar period—its Norman Thomas. A detailed, though exceedingly biased, study of the agreement is László Réti, *A Bethlen-Peyer paktum* [The Bethlen-Peyer Pact] (Budapest, 1956).

tural produce diminished. What amounted to a social and economic upheaval, then, forced Bethlen to resign in 1931. He was first replaced by another member of the landed aristocracy, but in 1932 Gyula Gömbös, a former officer in the army, took over the premiership (1932–36). Gömbös's program contained something for all, and in this respect at least he emulated Fascism from the beginning. His program was carefully phrased so that the first part of a particular statement usually neutralized the second part. He announced, for example, that the "safeguarding of the liberty of the press is a national asset," but he added: "so long as the press faithfully serves the nation." In another passage, Gömbös called for the reintroduction of the secret ballot, adding, however, that "at the same time the great national ideals of the Hungarian people must be safeguarded."[22]

Of course, Gömbös was a demagogue, at best a sincere demagogue, and so it is tempting to dismiss or underestimate him. Nevertheless, two major developments occurred during his premiership, each of which pointed to far-reaching consequences. First, he succeeded in curtailing the influence of the old agricultural aristocracy. Second, his definitely pro-German foreign policy resulted, inter alia, in German economic and political penetration, with German economic influence becoming a decisive stimulus for Hungarian industrialization and modernization.

As to the first development, Gömbös was acutely aware of the lack of a Western-type middle class in Hungary. He was also aware of the apparent inability of Bethlen's syncretic coalition to govern effectively, let alone guide the seemingly inevitable economic and social transformation of Hungary. "Mind you," he repeated time and again, "there isn't a single count in my government." Antagonistic to the vested interests of the 1920s, Gömbös altered the syncretic balance created and cherished by Bethlen. His new coalition relied heavily on the gentry, the army, the bureaucracy, the industrial elite, and only after that on the landed aristocracy. In short, he changed the orientation of the governing elite, which became less cautious and more radical, pro-Italian *and* pro-German, less nostalgic and more outward-looking, anti-Semitic, somewhat vulgar, but more receptive to change. To be sure, some of this "change" was to lead Hungary to political catastrophe in World War II, but it also led to rapid industrialization under German tutelage. At any rate, *Gömbös finally concluded the transfer of power from a traditional to a modernizing leadership.* Indeed, the political system Gömbös built, to use Edward Shils's category,[23]

22. Macartney, *October Fifteenth*, p. 148.

23. Edward Shils, "Political Development in the New States," *Comparative Studies in Society and History* 2, no. 3 (April 1960): 265–92, and no. 4 (July 1960): 379–411.

Table 2.4   Germany's Share in Hungarian Foreign Trade, 1920–1939

Year	Import (% total)	Export (% total)
1920	8.4	11.1
1921	12.9	9.3
1922	16.6	9.1
1923	14.3	6.2
1924	12.5	7.9
1925	15.0	9.9
1926	16.6	12.9
1927	18.2	13.3
1928	19.5	11.7
1929	20.0	11.7
1930	21.2	10.3
1931	24.1	12.7
1932	22.5	15.2
1933	19.7	11.2
1934	18.3	22.2(!)
1935	22.7	23.9
1936	26.0	22.8
1937	26.2	34.1
1938	NA	NA
1939	52.5(!)	52.2(!)

Source: Iván T. Berend and György Ránki, *Magyarország a fasiszta Németország "életterében" 1933–1939* [Hungary in the "Living Space" of Fascist Germany 1933–1939] (Budapest, 1960), p. 175.

was a modernizing oligarchy strongly motivated toward economic development. Its impulse for modernization stemmed from the system's concern for efficiency, its dislike for traditionalism, and its correct appraisal of the depth and extent of social and political disaffection and economic deprivation. The system was further characterized by its verbal commitment to democratization, something, however, that it opposed in practice.

The second major development associated with Gömbös's premiership was the aggressive German economic penetration of Hungary. As table 2.4 shows, Germany's share in Hungarian foreign trade rapidly increased in the 1930s. Of Hungary's total export in 1930, for example, only 10.3 percent went to Germany; the corresponding figure in 1939 was 52.2 percent. Of Hungary's total import in 1930, 21.2 percent came from Germany; the corresponding figure in 1939 was 52.5 percent. Guided by political considerations, Nazi Germany was increasingly willing to purchase Hungarian agricultural products in larger quantities, a development of definite interest to the struggling and capital-lacking Hungarian economy.

Economic growth thus stimulated by Germany was only barely short of being phenomenal. The rate of industrial growth between 1934–35 and 1939–40 reached an impressive 10.8 percent per year (as table 2.2 shows). The up-to-then declining agriculture also began to grow, at the more modest rate of 2.0 percent. The number of workers employed in industry more than doubled during the decade between 1933 and 1943 (see table 2.3), while the number of people employed in agriculture further declined to 48.7 percent of the total population (see table 2.1). For the first time, then, the majority of the working population was engaged in nonagricultural pursuits, one of the great watersheds in Hungarian history, which by most standards qualified Hungary as an industrial country.[24]

Unfortunately, reliable social indicators pointing to the full impact of industrialization are difficult to come by. The available data clearly illustrate, however, the profound social impact of industrialization. For example, the number of secondary schools increased by nearly 60 percent in four years, from 167 in the 1934–35 academic year to 262 in 1938–39. The general improvement and extensive utilization of communications were indicated by the fact that about 4.5 million long-distance telephone calls were made in 1932 and nearly 8 million in 1939. Illiteracy declined to about 7 percent by 1941.

Some of the most profound modernizing measures were initiated during the premiership of Pál Teleki (1939–41). First, Teleki sought to reform the country's antiquated bureaucracy. Concerned about widespread corruption, he wanted to eliminate the traditional practice of *protekció*, a system of special advantages or "pull," whereby political connections and family patronage served as the necessary prerequisite for holding a position and for advancement in the bureaucracy. He was hoping to introduce objective entrance examinations to bring competent and qualified personnel into state administration. Under his premiership, bureaucrats were reminded of their primary function, which was to serve the general public, rich and poor alike. As Béla Kovrig pointed out, Teleki did not pursue these objectives because of any deep commitment to democratic principles, a commitment he was lacking, but because of his conviction that without

24. It should be pointed out that the indicator frequently used for industrialization is the percentage of economically active *males* engaged in nonagricultural pursuits. In the Hungarian case, the difference between economically active males and economically active males *and* females engaged in nonagricultural pursuits was negligible.

a thorough reform of the bureaucracy the integration of Hungarian society was not possible.[25]

Second, Teleki sought to improve the esprit de corps of the Hungarian people by initiating a number of cultural and educational programs. He encouraged the establishment of about twenty so-called popular colleges whose purpose was the education of poor, mainly peasant-born youth. He commenced the publication of Hungarian classics in inexpensive paperback editions and organized a speakers' bureau, which provided large and small communities around the country, free of charge, with qualified scholars lecturing on cultural and historical subjects. To bring knowledge and current information into the often remote villages of Hungary, Teleki initiated a program of wall-newspapers that carried apolitical and topical news, and an executive order from the ministry of internal affairs required county and village officials, who disliked the idea, to prominently display such wall-newspapers. Teleki's objective was to fight traditional provincialism and narrow perspectives and to overcome the knowledge-gap between city and countryside.[26]

Teleki's suicide in 1941 in protest against Hungary's forced participation in the German attack on Yugoslavia marked the conclusion of the transitional stage of modernization. Hungary had come a long way toward being "industrialized." The state bureaucracy had established nearly uniform practices and procedures throughout the country. The knowledge-gap between urban Hungary and rural Hungary had narrowed. Ethnic division no longer inflicted major damage to the fabric of society. The steady modernization of social relations was clearly in evidence, particularly just prior to and during World War II. Extensive kinship units began to lose their pervasiveness. As illiteracy significantly diminished, the number of qualified men with productive skills increased. The movement of people from the countryside into urban centers assumed considerable proportions. In the political realm, this phase of development witnessed the conclusion of the rule of the landed aristocracy as the syncretic balance gave way to the modernizing leadership.

The revolutionary stage. The passing of traditional society, combined with the most unsettling impact of World War II, created a revolutionary situation: against the background of very high expectations, too many old problems had remained unsolved and too many new problems had come to the surface. Specifically, no genuine land reform had taken place until 1945; less than one-tenth of one percent of the landowners still owned

25. Béla Kovrig, pp. 174–79.
26. Ibid., pp. 179–83.

24.5 percent of the land in the 1930s, while 45.9 percent of the "landowners," that is, small farmers, owned only 19.3 percent of the land. In terms of improvements in the general standard of living, the benefits of industrialization were not very discernible. The otherwise improved state bureaucracy could not rid itself of traditional habits and customs, and it was still used to protecting old privileges. In addition, national unity had suffered as the country lined up behind Germany's war effort, a development opposed by Count Bethlen's conservative group of politicians, by most intellectuals, and others. Above all, destruction and dislocation caused by World War II inflicted heavy damage on the whole country and the whole population.

Thus, when the Horthy regime collapsed in the spring of 1944, well before the arrival of Soviet troops, it was not simply because Hitler no longer trusted and supported Horthy. Hitler invaded and occupied Hungary, and kept Horthy as a figurehead for the time being, only after it became clear that the Horthy regime was disintegrating—and hence already lost whatever usefulness it had once had as Germany's rather reluctant ally. In any case, the Horthy regime's disintegration was the result, first, of internal pressures generated by the disequilibrated social system as the population, exhausted by the war, vainly sought further change on the road to modernity. Second, the political system could not initiate a process of resynchronization or rejuvenation,[27] for the political elite was neither able nor willing to mobilize the political system's coercive forces against either external, that is, German, or internal pressures. By 1944, then, both Hungarian society and the political order had thus reached the point of no return. Given its ineffective and discredited political authority,[28] the country was ripe for revolutionary change.

Two Revolutionary Models of Development

What direction could the revolutionary transformation take?

Not considering the various radical groupings of the right,[29] two revolutionary movements of the left, the populist and the Communist movements,

27. Chalmers Johnson, *Revolutionary Change* (Boston and Toronto: Little, Brown, 1966), pp. 90–91.

28. Ibid., pp. 98–99.

29. A judicious treatment of the radical right is István Deák, "Hungary," in Hans Rogger and Eugen Weber, eds., *The European Right: A Historical Profile* (Berkeley and Los Angeles: University of California Press, 1965), pp. 364–407. Cf. Macartney, *October Fifteenth.* See also, Miklós Lackó, *Nyilasok, nemzetiszocialisták 1935–1944* [Arrow Crossists, National Socialists 1935–1944] (Budapest, 1966); Kálmán Szakács, *Kaszáskeresztesek* [Scythe Crossists] (Budapest, 1963).

had come to possess qualities for the leadership of the revolutionary transformation to come. As Horthy's political and social order was falling apart during the war, both presented alternative platforms for Hungary's future development. Their appraisal of the immediate past was similar in that they saw no merit in the modernizing trends of the 1930s and early 1940s. Their appraisal of the country's immediate objectives also coincided as they agreed that the restoration of old privileges was undesirable, land reform was imperative, the social immobility of the past should be erased, and the overhaul of the bureaucracy was overdue. On the other hand, their appraisal of future economic development differed in that the populists preferred a predominantly agrarian, small-scale, village-based, and decentralized economy, while the Communists believed in rapid, centralized, and thorough industrialization, including the development of heavy industry.

Main features of populist thought. As the war was coming to a close, the populists' ideas were widely known and probably widely shared. A prominent sociologist, János Kósa, observed in 1942 that virtually the entire Hungarian youth identified itself with populism.[30] The British historian C. A. Macartney noted that populism was "genuinely native" and it was "destined to have a not unimportant future" in Hungary.[31] The chief Hungarian Communist ideologist, József Révai, in one of the first fullscale studies on the populist movement in 1938, called it "the most important intellectual current of the last two decades in Hungary."[32]

In its basic platform and attitudes, Hungarian populism[33] differed little from Russian populism of the nineteenth century and from populism in the developing countries. It was more an attitude and a state of mind than a coherent and ordered set of specific ideas. It is nevertheless possible to

30. János Kósa, "Magyar társadalomkutatás" [Hungarian Social Research], *Magyar Szemle* (1942), p. 260.

31. Macartney, *October Fifteenth*, p. 156.

32. József Révai, "Marxizmus és népiesség" [Marxism and Populism], reprinted in his *Marxizmus, népiesség, magyarság* [Marxism, Populism, Hungarianism], 4th ed. (Budapest, 1955), p. 298.

33. On Hungarian populism, see Charles Gati, "The Populist Current in Hungarian Politics 1935–1944" (Ph.D. diss., Indiana University, 1965). Cf. Rudolf L. Tőkés, "The Hungarian Populist 'Third Road' Ideology—Three Case Studies: 1932–1943" (M.A. thesis, Columbia University, 1961). For a contemporary account, see Géza Juhász, *Népi írók* [Populist Writers] (Budapest, 1943). The most important contemporary (1938) Communist appraisal of populism is Révai, *Marxizmus, népiesség, magyarság*, pp. 297–466. The renowned Hungarian Marxist György Lukács also published several studies of Hungarian populism on the eve of and during the war in *Uj Hang* [New Voice], the Moscow-based Hungarian periodical; his studies were reprinted later in *Irástudók felelőssége* [The Responsibility of Intellectuals] (Moscow, 1944), pp. 79–94.

extricate certain commonly held propositions from the voluminous populist literature.

In the economic realm, populism was an "ideology of delayed
industrialization."[34] As a movement, it emerged in the 1930s in response
to the impact of the economic crisis and renewed industrialization. In
their economic (as in their political) program, the populists subscribed to
a "third road" position—neither capitalism nor Communism, neither
West nor East. Capitalism and large-scale industrialization were considered beneficial for others, that is, the West, but largely harmful for Hungary.
This was so, first, because industrialization required foreign assistance and
investment that would place the country at the mercy of foreigners. Second,
industrialization would definitely be uneven because the controlling foreign interests would neither understand nor appreciate tradition; they
would be guided exclusively by profit considerations. Third, the populists
feared the social and cultural consequences of industrialization; they were
concerned, in particular, about the uprooting of peasant youth whose life
in the "sinful" and alien city would turn him against native values and
culture.

Thus, the Hungarian populists opted for an agrarian-oriented economy.
László Németh, a leading populist writer and ideologist, for example,
advocated the creation of cottage industries or what he called a "garden-
Hungary." In his conception of the good economic system, emphasis was
not on mass production but on creativity, handicraft, and light industry.
Perhaps a small furniture factory here and there, utilizing local talent for
wood-carving, food processing plants catering to regional tastes and eat-
ing habits, or factories producing farm machinery that would ease the
heavy workload of the peasant. The populists opted for small-scale production because it would bring industry to the countryside and thus the
movement to the already overgrown cities would stop. In addition, they
sensed that the development of heavy industry was extremely costly and
the peasantry would likely carry the main burden of it. In short, they
would have fully agreed with Stuart Chase who once advised Mexican
peasants, ". . . If I were you, when and if the new highway comes looping
over the mountains into your village street, I would buy all the boxes of
extra-sized carpet tacks I can afford."[35]

As to agriculture, the populists focused on the plight of the peasantry
and advocated a radical land reform. Much of the best populist literature

34. Mary Matossian, "Ideologies of Delayed Industrialization: Some Tensions and
Ambiguities," *Economic Development and Cultural Change* 6, no. 3 (April 1958): 217–28.

35. As quoted in John Kenneth Galbraith, *Economic Development in Perspective* (Cambridge:
Harvard University Press, 1962), p. 9.

was devoted to the description and analysis of the misery and exploitation of the peasantry. The publication of *Puszták népe* (People of the Puszta), by Gyula Illyés, became both a literary bestseller and a political event in 1936, as did Imre Kovács's *Néma foradalom* (Silent Revolution), Zoltán Szabó's *Tardi helzet* (The Situation at Tard), and Géza Féja's *Viharsarok* (The Stormy Corner), all of which have since been reissued in numerous editions and translated into several languages. In these partly sociological, partly impressionistic studies, the populists sought to reveal the intolerable conditions of the peasantry and to express their uncompromising demand for a radical land reform, even though they could not always agree on the step beyond land reform. Most of the populist writers, like Féja, Illyés, and Péter Veres, envisaged a social system of peasant communities with voluntary cooperatives, that is, agrarian socialism. Others, like Ferenc Erdei, Kovács, and Szabó, opted for the utilization of modern technology in farming: large-scale agricultural production on the advanced Western pattern, they thought, would eliminate the misery and retardation of the peasantry.

In the political realm, the populist platform was blurred by the basic eclecticism of Hungarian populism. Rudolph L. Tőkés identifies the main Western ingredients or sources of Hungarian populism as the German school of sociological positivism, Marxism, West European reformist socialism, West European leftist radicalism, peasant romanticism, Rosenberg's race myth, the Fascist corporate system, and Scandinavian socialism;[36] and the list may be even extended to include Eastern influences. At any rate, eclectic though the Hungarian populist political platform was, it definitely included, first, the notion of nonalignment, a kind of "third road" foreign policy to be steered between Germany and the Soviet Union. As Németh explained the meaning of "third road" in an oft-quoted analogy, "Let us suppose that there is a political party in New Guinea which maintains that New Guinea should belong to the British. According to another party, New Guinea could be happy only under the Dutch. Then someone stands up and asks, 'couldn't New Guinea belong to the [native] Papuans?' This is the third road."[37]

Second, Western-style political democracy and freedom were not part of the populist platform. To be sure, the populists often demanded the "democratic reorganization of the country," "freedom of thought, speech,

36. Tőkés, "Hungarian Populist," pp. 33–38.
37. *Szárszó* [an incomplete but exceedingly informative record of a major populist gathering at the resort town of Balatonszárszó in 1943] (Budapest, 1943), p. 54. This volume was reissued in Budapest in 1983, reflecting continuing public interest in populist thought.

press, assembly, and organization," "universal, equal, and secret suffrage,"[38] and the like; yet they were also apprehensive about the misuse of freedom in a democratic political system. Illyés, for example, once remarked that his commitment to freedom of the press was limited because, as he put it, "when the press was genuinely free, it freely prostituted itself."[39] Indeed, the populist notion of freedom and democracy meant, above all, freedom for the peasantry to possess land and it meant the "democratic," perhaps equal, distribution of wealth in society. On the whole, the populists were prepared to accept almost any form of government so long as it served the interests of the peasantry, their assumption being that the interests of the peasantry were strictly identical with those of the nation. Put differently, the populists concluded that the socioeconomic transformation of Hungary, and of the peasantry in particular, had priority over the development of a democratic political order. Very much like some present-day leaders in the Third World, the populists believed that political democracy might well be used against the interests of the people by foreigners or by semi-native, that is, Jewish, industrialists.

Finally, the cultural platform of Hungarian populism can best be characterized by emphasizing its nationalist and historical perspective. The populists were proud of indigenous talent, of folk music and folk art, of those Hungarians of the past who had shown courage, of the ostensibly uncorrupted simplicity of primitive culture. They looked *up* to "the people" and *down* on "the masses."[40] Depending on the need of the moment, they glorified one or another period of Hungarian history — once it was a war of independence to demonstrate bravery and sacrifice, then it was clever and wise political maneuvering between wicked foreign powers to demonstrate the overriding value of survival for the nation. The uses of the past were many. History served for national self-assurance to prove that the West was not superior; after all, didn't Hungary defend the West time and again against Eastern hordes? In a psychological sense, history served for escape from the undesirable present into an ostensibly "golden age" in the past.

To sum up, the Hungarian populists offered both an attitude and a platform. Their orientation was eclectic in its foundations; romantic in tone; nationalist in cultural outlook; archaic in its attempts to resurrect the "golden age" of the past; utopian in its hope for moral regeneration to combat the perversions of modern life; negativistic in its anticapitalist, antiurban, anti-German, anti-Semitic, and anti-Communist sentiments;

38. See the twelve points of the populist March Front of 1937, for example: "A Márciusi Front kiáltványa" [The Manifesto of the March Front], *Válasz* (1937), p. 697.
39. As quoted in Lukács, *Irástudók felelőssége*, pp. 90–91.
40. Matossian, "Ideologies," p. 227.

emotional in its search for foreign conspiracies and scapegoats; sentimental in its absolute commitment to the cause of the peasantry; calculating in its foreign policy orientation; anarchic in its distaste for organization; conservative in its hatred of advanced social differentiation and division of labor; progressive in its belief in the value of education and in its deep commitment to social equality; and irrational in its contradictions. Above all, the populist orientation was both revolutionary and profoundly Hungarian. The populists were prepared to turn society upside down — redistribute the land, provide educational opportunities for all, exclude the old elites from positions of influence and replace them with "the people," and defy the great powers. In a sense, populism was also a microcosm of Hungary:[41] it mirrored the confusion and contradictions of the country's struggle with, and for, modernization. Significantly, the populists lacked the attributes required for further modernization once the war was over: an organizational base, the acceptance of the necessity of industrialization, and a wider, less provincial, indeed international perspective.

Communist preparations for a postwar role.   The other revolutionary movement of the left, the Communist movement, possessed qualities the populists lacked and lacked what the populists possessed. With no more than 2,500 members, the outlawed and illegal Communist party enjoyed little or no popular support. It was not considered an indigenous movement with an indigenous ideology. Its best leaders were in exile, in Moscow and in Western Europe, and some of them had not been in direct touch with Hungarian reality since 1919. Those who were in Hungary engaged in underground activities that seldom went beyond journalistic and polemic endeavors, even though during World War II there were a few demonstrations with Communist participation as well as isolated instances of sabotage. Unlike the populists, however, the Communists paid attention to organizational matters, possessed an ideology that embraced industrialization and urbanization, and showed great familiarity with international politics.[42]

The Communist International's 1935 resolution, which called on all Communists to work together with Socialists and others against the rise of Fascism in Europe, represented an impossible assignment for the Communist party in Hungary, because, after the arrest of its leadership in January 1936, it consisted of a small group of largely inexperienced men. Their objective was the creation of a Popular Front; however, the Social Demo-

41. Cf. Paul E. Zinner, *Revolution in Hungary* (New York: Columbia University Press, 1962), p. 16.

42. For a thorough history of the Hungarian Communist movement, see Bennett Kovrig, *Communism in Hungary: From Kun to Kádár* (Stanford, Calif.: Hoover Institution Press, 1979).

cratic party rejected any cooperation with the Communists initially and the Communists did not even approach the Smallholders' party at this time. By necessity, therefore, it was the populist movement that represented the greatest attraction for the Communists. First of all, the populists also pursued revolutionary objectives. Second, the Communists could reasonably expect that, given the populists' political dilettantism, leadership within the movement would easily slip into their hands. Third, as most populists were known non-Communists, this was an ideal "front," a convenient hiding place. Finally, the Communists were naturally attracted by the populists' popularity and national appeal.

At any rate, the Communists' flirtation with the populist movement marked the beginning of their alliance policy between 1936 and 1947. The early objective was clear: the penetration of non-Communist groups and organizations. On assignment from the party's leadership in Prague and later in Moscow, they cooperated with almost any movement or group opposed to Hitler or Horthy or the war. Yet, on balance, their immediate accomplishments were minimal. A few Communist journalists were able to join the staff of Népszava, the daily of the Social Democratic party. They later participated in a number of antiwar demonstrations and issued, together with the Socialists and the Smallholders' party, antiwar manifestos. The Communist party's membership, however, did not increase during the war, nor could it organize a single effective strike against the government or against Hungary's participation in the war.

Such young home Communists as László Rajk, Ferenc Donáth, János Kádár, Gyula Kállai, and others nonetheless succeeded in making the Communist party a palatable, if not quite a desirable, political ally. By 1941 but especially by 1943–44, the Social Democrats, the populist National Peasant party, the Smallholders' party, and nonparty intellectuals found it possible to make a few common appeals with the Communists against the war. After all, they agreed with the Communist program, which at this time was limited to the goals of independence from Germany, peace, and social and political equality. Indeed, the party did not offer anything specific or detailed to counter the populist platform; it emphasized "broad" agreement on "fundamental" issues. As a result, the indigenous Communist leadership became part of the small antiwar effort and made useful contacts with the democratic left, but its professed program was vague, superficial, and elusive.

In the meantime, the party's politically more sophisticated leaders in Moscow (Rákosi, Gerő, Révai, Imre Nagy, Mihály Farkas, and Vas) were preparing for their imminent return to Hungary. Looking at the war from Moscow, they knew of the strains and tensions between the Soviet Union and its Western allies and understood their meaning and possible consequences for East Central Europe. Their experience and training had taught them about the relevance of political organization and about what they considered the inevitability of industrialization in Hungary after the war.

Therefore, when the new Provisional Government came into being in Debrecen in the winter of 1944, the Communist party—Muscovites and home Communists—possessed much more than the support of the Soviet Union, however decisive that support was. First, it possessed a leadership with an international outlook, trained in the worst kind of political infighting in the Soviet Union, lacking in any great concern about the brutal impact of social and economic dislocation that was to come, and unhesitatingly committed, as was to be seen later, to the long-term goals of forced industrialization and political hegemony. Second, the Muscovite leadership was reinforced and complemented by the party's indigenous leaders who, through an elusive program that emulated populism, had partly destigmatized the Communist name within the new postwar democratic elite. Third, the Communist party faced a divided opposition, made up of the Smallholders' party, the Social Democrats, and the National Peasant party. While each of these parties possessed a few gifted leaders (Zoltán Tildy and Béla Kovács; Antal Bán and Anna Kéthly; Imre Kovács and István Bibó, respectively), their political perspective was provincial in comparison with that of the Communist leaders now returning from Moscow. The latter understood the revolutionary momentum caused by the war and by the process of modernization in the 1930s. They were skilled politicians and professional revolutionaries. The Communist party also had an economic program of development that went beyond reconstruction and land reform: it was, of course, the program of industrial socialism. In short, the Communist party was prepared to carry the process of modernization to its ultimate conclusion, irrespective of cost and consequences, through revolution if necessary.

Who Wanted Radical Change?

After the war, the country's immediate objectives were self-evident. Aside from creating order and fiscal stability, the most pressing task of the Provisional Government was to realize the age-old dream of land reform,[43]

43. Many important documents related to the planning and execution of the 1945 land reform are included in *Földreform 1945* [Landreform 1945] (Budapest, 1965), which contains an informative introduction by Magda M. Somlyai. Cf. Job Paál and Antal Radó, eds., *A debreceni feltámadás* [Resurrection in Debrecen] (Debrecen, 1947). See also Imre Kovács, *Im Schatten der Sowiets* (Zurich, 1948) and Ferenc Nagy, *Struggle Behind the Iron Curtain*.

which was largely completed in 1945. In addition, the new regime sought to reduce the size and change the social composition of the bureaucracy. The government's first measures also included the improvement of the country's communication network, the expansion of educational opportunities (by giving preferential treatment to the so-called popular colleges), the betterment of the social security system, the enlargement of health services in the countryside, and the like.

With reconstruction proceeding quite rapidly and national elections scheduled for November 1945, which path of development would the electorate want the country to adopt?

The 1945 elections were decided on a large number of issues, of course, including the country's proper relationship with the Soviet Union, the desirable extent of land distribution, the nature of the Horthy regime, the role of religion in the country, the future of modernization and economic development, and many other issues. However, if one had been able to isolate the issue of modernization and economic development alone, support for the Smallholders' party *on this issue only* would have been less convincing.

Consider the following. Broadly speaking, Hungary could pursue one of three alternative paths of development after the war:

    (*a*) the bourgeois-democratic path, characterized by its objective of measured modernization through evolution and the democratic political process, continued industrialization without the significant disruption of the country's social and economic structure, and an agriculture based on the independent small farmer; or

    (*b*) the populist-agrarian path, characterized by its emphasis on light or cottage industries, an agricultural policy leading to a vaguely defined agrarian socialism, the radical eradication of social immobility still infecting the fabric of Hungarian society, and a willingness to accomplish these objectives through almost any form of government; or

    (*c*) the Communist-industrial path, characterized by a long-term commitment to one-party rule, the rapid development of heavy industry, the establishment of cooperatives and state farms in the countryside, and the breakup of the social structure to make room for members of the industrial and agricultural proletariat.

Needless to say, the electorate's precise choice among the three alternative models of development cannot be ascertained. However, it is possible to extrapolate from the results of the 1945 elections the voting public's probable orientation. Considering, inter alia, the substance of some 250 interviews in the Columbia University Research Project on Hungary,[44] it seems that the bourgeois-democratic path was supported by approximately two-thirds of the vote cast for the Smallholders' party (38 percent of the total) and half of the Social Democratic vote (8.7 percent), representing 46.7 percent of all votes cast. The populist-agrarian approach was probably supported by the remaining one-third of the Smallholder vote (19 percent) and the full National Peasant party vote (7 percent), for a total of 26 percent. Finally, the Communist-industrial formula was probably supported by the remaining half of the Social Democratic vote (8.7 percent) and the full Communist party vote (17 percent), for a total of 25.7 percent. Considering the first path evolutionary and the other two revolutionary, the figures therefore indicate that the voting public was rather evenly divided between evolutionary and revolutionary change, with 46.7 percent of the electorate opting for the former and the majority (51.7 percent) for the latter. (See tables 2.5 and 2.6 for the actual results of the elections and for our extrapolated calculations.)

These calculations are based on the following assumptions: *First*, neither the Communist party nor the National Peasant party was divided on the question of development; the former supported the Communist-industrial formula, the latter the populist-agrarian approach. *Second*, not unlike Socialist parties in other parts of the world, the Social Democratic party was evenly divided between supporters of evolutionary and revolutionary change, some approving the deliberate pace of bourgeois-democratic development, others opting for rapid industrialization advocated primarily by the Communists. *Third*, the solid majority or about two-thirds of the supporters of the Smallholders' party endorsed the bourgeois-democratic path of measured modernization, independent agriculture, and democratic procedure, while the remaining minority approved the more radical solutions contained in the populist-agrarian formula.

If so, two questions may be raised: Why did that one-third minority of Smallholders, who were populist-oriented, vote for the Smallholders' party and not for the populist National Peasant party? And why did the more radical half of the Socialists vote for the Social Democratic party and not for the Communist party?

The answer to both questions is that the election was not decided on the issue of development alone. Specifically, the Smallholders' party won the

44. I am grateful to the late Professor Henry L. Roberts, former director of Columbia University's Institute on East Central Europe, for his permission to study the rich data collected by Columbia's Research Project on Hungary.

Table 2.5   Actual Results of 1945 Hungarian Elections

Party	% total vote
Smallholders' party (SP)	57.0
Social Democratic party (SDP)	17.4
Communist party (CP)	17.0
National Peasant party (NPP)	7.0
Others	1.6
	100.0

Source: Sándor Balogh, *Parlamenti és pártharcok Magyarországon, 1945–1947* [Parliamentary and Party Struggles in Hungary, 1945–1947] (Budapest, 1975), p. 98.

election primarily because of the prevailing belief that its leaders would more firmly resist Soviet pressures than those of the other parties. More than any other single factor, apprehension over Soviet domination assured the victory of the Smallholders' party. In addition, there were many who did not want to "waste" their vote on the National Peasant party despite their known populist preference and who voted for the Smallholders' party instead, because the latter was more a "governing party" than the somewhat disjointed populist National Peasant party. As to the reluctance of some Socialists to vote directly for the Communist party, that was due to their unwillingness to endorse the Communists' slavishly pro-Soviet orientation and their presumed if as yet unstated desire for political hegemony. These voters seemed satisfied that the left wing of their own Social Democratic party would press for rapid modernization without succumbing to foreign rule or political dictatorship.

To sum up, the preceding analysis of the 1945 elections points to a more widespread popular acceptance of revolutionary change in the economic and social realms than previously assumed: a slight majority of the electorate was favorably inclined toward either the Communist-industrial or the populist-agrarian model of radical development.[45] In fact, the choice under the circumstances was reduced to one between industrial and

45. Additional evidence confirming the conclusions reached here includes a study prepared in December 1945 by the respected Hungarian Institute of Public Opinion. In an extraordinary and quite surprising display of support for radical change, 67 percent of the respondents said that they favored the nationalization of factories (with 32 percent opposed and one percent "don't know/no answer"), while 75 percent favored the nationalization of banks (with 23 percent opposed and one percent "don't know/no answer"). Results reported by Robert Blumstock, "Public Opinion in Hungary," in Walter Connor, Zvi Gitelman et al., *Public Opinion in European Socialist Systems* (New York: Praeger, 1977), p. 140. It should be noted, however, that these results reflected prevailing European sentiments.

Table 2.6   Extrapolation of Results of 1945 Hungarian Elections:
Presumed Support for Three Paths of Development

Models of development	SP vote (% total)	SDP vote (% total)	CP vote (% total)	NPP vote (% total)	Evolution or revolution?
Bourgeois-democratic	38.0	8.7	—	—	46.7
Populist-agrarian	19.0	—	—	7.0 ⎫ ←→ 51.7
Communist-industrial	—	8.7	17.0	— ⎭
Totals	57.0	17.4	17.0	7.0	98.4

agrarian socialism. That the former prevailed was due not only to the Communist party's professional leadership, but also to the inadequacy of populist socialism as a developmental formula at this particular juncture, the eclecticism of populist ideology, and the divided agrarian movement. Last, but certainly most importantly, the Soviet Union provided its determined support to those pursuing revolutionary change in the direction of industrial socialism.

Summing Up

In Hungary as elsewhere, the processes of modernization were uneven. Initial progress after 1867, mainly in terms of industrialization, was followed by the syncretic reaction of the 1920s when the political system sought to curtail the pace of modernization. Tension and discontent built up at this time burst into the open after the economic crisis, resulting in unprecedented economic growth and the further intrusion of modernity just prior to and during World War II. The impact of rapid change, in turn, created a revolutionary situation embraced by the populist and Communist movements.

Moreover, and despite overwhelming public opposition to the Communist party's hidden political agenda, the cause of revolutionary social and economic change enjoyed widespread, perhaps majority, support; only the direction of such change remained in doubt. Of the two available revolutionary alternatives, the Communists' offered industrial socialism, while the populists' stressed social equality, some sort of agrarian socialism, nationalism, and anti-urbanization. In their opposition to urbanization and heavy industrialization, the populists sought to circumvent the processes of modernization, while the Communists were prepared to carry on with the timely tasks of industrialization and modernization.

The stage for some sort of basic economic and social change having been set and with the "dysfunctions"[46] of revolution in evidence, competing revolutionary ideologies thus appeared on the scene. The final trigger or "accelerator" to "catalyze . . . the already existent revolutionary levels of dysfunctions"[47] was then provided by the Soviet Union. The catalyzer rather than the creator of revolutionary change, it naturally opted for the Communist path of development.

46. Harry Eckstein, "On the Etiology of Internal Wars," *History and Theory* 4 (1954): 140.

47. Chalmers Johnson, *Revolution and the Social System* (Stanford, Calif.: Hoover Institution Press, 1964), p. 12.

3

Features of Postwar Coalitions

Between 1944 and 1948 most parliamentary governments in Europe, East and West, were composed of representatives of different political parties. They were "coalition" governments in the broad sense of the term, meaning that the several political parties participating in the activities of such governments agreed to coordinate their policies in the pursuit of certain immediate objectives.[1] Partners and competitors at the same time, these parties formed coalitions because under prevailing external and internal conditions none of them could effectively govern alone. At least formally, then, they resembled both some of the prewar European coalitions as well as those in existence in Western Europe, Latin America, and elsewhere at the present time.

The basic similarity notwithstanding, the postwar European coalition governments still differed from others in the following respects:

First, they came into being under the influence of international agreements and great power pressure, backed by the presence of foreign troops. Elections, when held, only followed the formation of the first provisional

1. In the *International Encyclopedia of the Social Sciences*, vol. 2 (New York: Macmillan and the Free Press, 1968), 524–34, William H. Riker identifies a coalition in the "broad" or "ordinary" sense as "a parliamentary or political grouping less permanent than a party or a faction or an interest group" (p. 524). William A. Gamson provides (p. 530) a far narrower definition, suggesting that a coalition means "the *joint use of resources to determine the outcome of a decision*, where a resource is some weight such that some critical quantity of it in the control of two or more parties to the decision is both necessary and sufficient to determine its outcome. Participants will be said to be using their resources jointly only if they coordinate their deployment of resources with respect to some decision. That is what is meant by saying that they have formed a coalition." For a critical review of the literature on coalition theories, see Eric C. Browne, *Coalition Theories: A Logical and Empirical Critique* (Beverly Hills, Calif.: Sage Publications, 1973).

governments, and the distribution of cabinet portfolios reflected international expectations.

Second, the other source of the postwar coalitions was a genuine domestic socioeconomic consensus within the European polities, including opposition to the reemergence of the old order and the affirmation of such objectives as economic reconstruction and the fostering of social mobility.

Third, the postwar coalitions were almost invariably all-party formations, governments of "national unity," with the real or potential opposition coopted—at times successfully, at times unsuccessfully—into an all-inclusive political framework.[2]

Fourth, and paradoxically, the all-party coalitions nevertheless did not prevent—on the contrary, they soon encouraged—political fragmentation. Despite unity statements, interparty antagonisms as well as intraparty feuds and highly contentious factionalism almost immediately came to the surface. Uncertain of the proper evaluation of, and reaction to, Communist goals, some of the non-Communist parties and leaders pursued a policy of reasonable accommodation with their local Communist parties, while others pursued a policy of firm resistance from the beginning because of the long ideological distance between the Communists and themselves.

Although these four features characterized all the coalition governments of Europe, the ultimate political outcome in the two halves of the continent turned out to be very different indeed. By 1947 or 1948 the non-Communist parties of Eastern Europe were excluded from political life, while in Western Europe the Communists, though debarred from the coalitions, could still actively continue to compete for power and influence. Put another way, the East European all-party coalitions gave way to de facto Communist one-party hegemony just as the all-party coalitions of Western Europe gave way to competitive coalitions without Communist participation. The difference between one-party hegemony in Eastern Europe and the still-competitive polities of Western Europe thus reflected the

2. Cf. Lawrence C. Dodd, *Coalitions in Parliamentary Government* (Princeton, N.J.: Princeton University Press, 1976); Sven Groennings, E. W. Kelley, Michael Leiserson, eds., *The Study of Coalition Behavior: Theoretical Perspectives and Cases from Four Continents* (New York: Holt, Rinehart and Winston, 1970). The slim scholarly literature on the nature of all-party coalition formations includes Alex Vulpuis, *Die Allparteinregierung* (Berlin: Metzner, 1957) and Peter H. Merkl, "Coalition Politics in West Germany," in Groennings et al., eds., *Study of Coalition Behavior*, pp. 13–42. Merkl's chapter provides a brief discussion of the formation of the "great" or "grand" coalition in the Federal Republic in 1966; the government had the support of 447 of the 497 deputies in the Bundestag. In the mid-1980s Israel was also governed by such a "grand" coalition.

difference between Soviet political values on the one hand and those of the United States and its European allies on the other.

It is not the purpose of this chapter to document or analyze the process of takeovers or discuss the eventual demise of the European all-party coalitions as manifested by 1947–48. Rather, the main purpose here is to explore the four characteristics of the all-party coalitions in Eastern Europe and to find out what if anything may the East European coalitions reveal about the nature of such all-party coalitions in which there is considerable ideological distance among the participating parties. Given the continuing Western fascination with "coalition governments of reconciliation" in rapidly changing and politically unstable countries, from Nicaragua to Afghanistan, do the postwar all-party coalitions of Eastern Europe offer any guidance about the durability of such all-party coalitions in other polities?

International Influences

Knowing what had happened in Eastern and in East Central Europe by 1947 or 1948, it is altogether easy to look back and assign a high degree of foresight, certainty, and consistency to Soviet planning and policy. After all, there is the conspicuous evidence of the seemingly methodical process of takeovers, beginning with the era of "genuine coalition," followed by the era of "bogus coalition," and ending in "monolithic control" by Communist parties (see table 3.3). Or, according to another interpretation, the process included the phase of "liberation" (1944–45), then the phases of "retribution" (1945–46) and "engineered disruption" (1946–47), culminating in Communist "monolithic control."[3] There is also the oft-quoted evidence, reported by Milovan Djilas, of Stalin's statement with respect to the political map of postwar Europe: "This war is not as in the past; whoever occupies a territory also imposes on it his own social system. Everyone imposes his own system as far as his army can reach. It cannot be otherwise."[4] In retrospect, to repeat, the evidence may be interpreted to point to a highly purposeful and determined Soviet commitment to one-party hegemony everywhere and at any price.

This interpretation leaves a few perplexing questions unanswered. As of

3. The most widely accepted first schema was offered by Hugh Seton-Watson in his *The East European Revolution* (New York: Praeger, 1956), the second by Andrew Gyorgy of George Washington University.

4. Milovan Djilas, *Conversations with Stalin* (New York: Harcourt, Brace & World, 1962), p. 114.

1944 or 1945, or even later, how could hundreds of non-Communist politicians fail to see the sign on the wall? How could they and many Western leaders as well assume that the nature of the Soviet interest varied from country to country—that while the eventual Soviet domination of, say, Bulgaria was likely, the same could not be said of Czechoslovakia? Conversely, how could most of them assume, as they did, that the Soviet Union would miss or postpone its historic opportunity and support broadly based coalition governments in the intermediate zone of East Central Europe and perhaps elsewhere as well for years to come?

To answer these difficult questions, one should acknowledge the prevalence of wishful thinking about Soviet goals and praise the Communists' political tactics. Yet in order to understand and appreciate the perceptions of non-Communists *at that time*, the answer should also take into account that the Soviet Union did not have an early, all-encompassing grand design and that its commitment to broad coalition governments in several of the countries of East Central Europe was genuine. For, as shown in chapter 1, Stalin's outlook was more tentative and flexible than often assumed; the Soviet Union did not appear to have a single policy toward all of Eastern and East Central Europe.[5] Divided Germany was a special case, of course. Given its extraordinary geopolitical significance and occasional expressions of U.S. and British concerns, so was Poland. Yugoslavia was also different because it was not liberated by Soviet forces. As for Romania and Bulgaria, it was evident by late 1944 that Moscow was determined to impose its system of values on them; yet it was not self-evident at the time that the same fate would await Hungary and Czechoslo-

---

5. Cf. William O. McCagg, Jr., *Stalin Embattled, 1943–1948* (Detroit: Wayne State University Press, 1978) and Vojtech Mastny, *Russia's Road to the Cold War: Diplomacy, Warfare, and the Politics of Communism, 1941–1945* (New York: Columbia University Press, 1979). Mastny's point of view (p. xvii) is worth quoting:

The point at issue is Moscow's presumed "grand strategy" in 1941–1945, that is the selection and pursuit of its long-term objectives during and immediately after the war against Germany. What was the vision of the postwar world that inspired Soviet actions at that time? What were the Russian aims in east central Europe especially, the area where both world wars and also the Cold War originated? How were those aims related to the historic Russian interests there? And how did the results measure up to the expectations?

A few standard assumptions have been common to Western authors of both the traditional and the revisionist variety: Stalin's determination to regain the territorial acquisitions he had achieved during his pact with Hitler, his quest for a division of Europe into spheres of influence, his desire to establish dependent regimes in neighboring countries. Yet such readings of Stalin's aspirations, though not necessarily wrong, may be misleading. *While plausible with the benefit of hindsight, they do not always conform to the contemporary evidence without important qualifications.* (Italics added.)

vakia as well. In short, as Adam Ulam observed, "Soviet policies responded to specific circumstances and to the wider repercussions of Soviet thrusts in this or that area."[6]

As the Red Army liberated most of Czechoslovakia and all of Poland, Hungary, Romania, and Bulgaria, Moscow could have installed Communist governments almost everywhere at once. But, at least at the beginning, Soviet planning entailed little more than the imperative of forming coalition governments of national unity. Beyond that, Soviet policy was given to improvisation. While Stalin hoped to increase Soviet influence everywhere in Europe and hence his remark to Djilas should not be dismissed, his hopes should not be confused with his expectations. As a flexible, pragmatic, and calculating man of realpolitik, he could not assume that the United States and especially Great Britain would tolerate the forceful Sovietization of all of Eastern and East Central Europe.[7] As a Marxist, he

6. Adam Ulam, *Expansion and Coexistence* (New York: Praeger, 1968), p. 345.

7. Stalin's pragmatism in Bulgaria, for example, was witnessed by a British observer in Sofia:

in many cases the local leaders were caught by surprise when [Stalin] suddenly changed course. An event which I personally witnessed will illustrate this. In August 1945, the Allied Control Commission in Bulgaria was discussing the advisability of the Bulgarians holding a general election on a single list. The British and American delegates on the Commission opposed a single list as being "undemocratic," while the Russians supported it as the only "democratic" method of holding an election. Since Stalin always worked at night, all other Soviet officials also had to work at night, so the sessions of the Commission began at 8:00 P.M. and lasted until 4:00 A.M. On this occasion the discussions started on a Wednesday evening and the elections were due to be held the following Sunday. The discussions on Wednesday, Thursday, and Friday proved fruitless, and we assembled again, much dispirited, on Saturday evening at 8:00 P.M. to listen once more to the Soviet argument in favor of a single list. The Russian side of the negotiations was conducted by the Soviet Commander in Chief in Bulgaria, Colonel-General (later Marshal of the Soviet Union) S. S. Biryuzov. He was obviously trying to drag out the discussions until the polling booths opened at 7:00 A.M. on Sunday morning so that nothing could be done about the matter, because the population would already be voting for or against the single list of candidates. But at 1:30 A.M. the telephone rang in the anteroom of the Russian general's office, and he sent his aide, a major, to answer it. When the major lifted the telephone to his ear, he stood there, as though struck dumb. The general thought his aide had become ill, so he strode over in a masterly fashion to the phone and seized it. Immediately he came smartly to attention, and stood upright for about five minutes while we could hear a voice crackling over the line. Then he said, "Yes, Comrade Stalin," and came back to us to declare: "As is well known, the Soviet government has always opposed the holding of general elections on a single list. The elections will be postponed until a more democratic method can be found." The Bulgarian prime minister was then sent for, told that the elections were to be put off, and the polling booths to be closed.

Malcolm Mackintosh, "Stalin's Policies towards Eastern Europe: The General Picture," in

could not assume that prevailing social and economic conditions every-where in the eastern half of Europe were then, or would soon be, condu-cive to or "ripe" for Communist transformation. Whatever his ultimate objectives, then, the only immediate, clearly identifiable, specific, Soviet commitment was to the formation of broadly based coalition governments in Eastern and in East Central Europe.

The apparent tentativeness of Soviet goals influenced official thinking in Washington and London, too.[8] As early as 1942, several subcommittees of the U.S. Advisory Committee on Postwar Foreign Policy addressed the issue of the postwar European political order. It appears that one of Washington's concerns was the question of postwar boundaries between the Soviet Union and its European neighbors. The Advisory Committee also considered the creation of an East European federation (presumably in order to mitigate the age-old problem of nationality conflicts after the war), and several discussions were held about the role of exiled govern-ments in the postwar era. As far as can be determined, however, none of these issues was resolved. As Lynn E. Davis concludes, members of the Advisory Committee did not have

> a clear idea of what postwar Eastern Europe would look like, politically,
> territorially, or economically. They hoped that the Atlantic Charter
> principles would be implemented, but they came to no definition of
> possible alternative futures for Eastern Europe. Implicitly, at least,
> they seemed ready to await Soviet initiatives and then respond. They
> never determined what would and would not be acceptable in terms
> of Soviet initiatives. They certainly never considered the promotion
> by the United States of its own solution for the future of Eastern
> Europe whether it be United States enforcement of the holding of
> free elections or United States imposition of nonaligned or buffer
> states in this region of the world.[9]

It seems, therefore, that what the United States was looking for at that time was the implementation of the Atlantic Charter and the ideal of self-determination, that is, representative government through free elections. In practice, given chaotic conditions after the war and hence the

Thomas T. Hammond, ed., *The Anatomy of Communist Takeovers* (New Haven: Yale Univer-sity Press, 1975), pp. 229–43. The quotation above appears on pp. 239–40.

8. This paragraph is based on Lynn Etheridge Davis, *The Cold War Begins: Soviet-American Conflict Over Eastern Europe* (Princeton, N.J.: Princeton University Press, 1974), pp. 72–76. On British policy, see Elisabeth Barker, *British Policy in South-East Europe in the Second World War* (London: Macmillan, 1976).

9. Davis, ibid., p. 76.

impossibility of holding elections right away, U.S. policy thus also amounted to the promotion of broad coalition governments.

The British were obviously more skeptical of long-term Soviet objectives. Unlike President Roosevelt, Prime Minister Churchill thought—and negotiated with Moscow—in balance-of-power terms. Yet even the British

> did not realize quite how powerless they were in the face of the Red Army's advance westwards and Stalin's determination to establish total political monopoly in all areas conquered by the Red Army. In this failure to understand Stalin the British can be charged with naiveté, blindness, even arrogance. But the pressing needs of war-time alliance and lingering fears of a second Soviet-German deal were powerful impulses to wishful thinking and to the ignoring of danger signals. The British hoped that, while the Soviet Union's security requirements would prevail in countries near its borders, *there could be some kind of Anglo-Soviet influence-sharing, matched by power-sharing inside those countries between liberals and the Left, between peasant parties, social democrats and Communists.* This idea turned out to be a pipe-dream, but it was not shameful.[10]

It was this general "idea" that Churchill sought to translate into reality via his 1944 "percentage agreement" with Stalin (see table 1.1). Once again, the goal was power-sharing or coalition governments in the countries that came up for discussion (Greece, Yugoslavia, Hungary, Bulgaria, and Romania).

At the February 1945 Yalta conference, too, the same "idea" prevailed. Concerning Poland, the "Big Three" (Roosevelt, Churchill, and Stalin) called for the establishment of a "Polish Provisional Government of National Unity," organized on a broad "democratic basis with the inclusion of democratic leaders from Poland itself and from Poles abroad." "This Polish Provisional Government of National Unity," the Big Three declared, "shall be pledged to the holding of free and unfettered elections as soon as possible on the basis of universal suffrage and secret ballot. In these elections all democratic and anti-Nazi parties shall have the right to take part and to put forward candidates."[11]

As for Yugoslavia, the Big Three recommended that the 1944 Tito-Šubašić Agreement (see chapter 1) "should immediately be put into effect and a new Government formed on the basis of the Agreement." In addition,

10. Barker, *British Policy*, pp. 267–68. (Italics added.)
11. The Yalta agreements are reprinted in Diane Shaver Clemens, *Yalta* (London: Oxford University Press, 1970), pp. 293–311.

the new government so created "should declare" that the country's legislative body (AVNOJ) "will be extended to include members of the last Yugoslav Skupština [prewar Serbian assembly] who have not compromised themselves by collaboration with the enemy."[12] The Big Three's endorsement of such a broad Yugoslav coalition government was thus based on a previous agreement, which specified that the postwar cabinet was to include six members of the Šubašić government and twelve members of Tito's National Committee.[13]

Czechoslovakia's was a different story—with the same ending. Unlike Šubašić who was clearly London's man in Yugoslavia, the head of the Czechoslovak Government-in-Exile, Eduard Beneš, had maintained excellent relations with London, Washington, and Moscow as well. He also benefited from the fact that Czechoslovakia had had a representative form of democracy in the interwar period and that it was liberated by both Soviet and American troops. Therefore, it was taken for granted all along that Czechoslovakia would continue to have a multiparty, coalition government; there was no need to discuss the country's political future at any of the formal international conferences. Beneš, a cautious and clever negotiator, nonetheless held extensive personal discussions with all three allied leaders,[14] and obtained their informal approval for the composition of the first provisional government established in the Slovak city of Košice in the spring of 1945. Needless to say, it too was a coalition government made up of representatives of several political parties.

Indeed, all of the interim governments that came into being in both Eastern and in East Central Europe after World War II invariably responded to and formally reflected international agreements and pressures. As specified by the Yalta "Declaration on Liberated Europe," they were expected to be "broadly representative of all democratic elements in the population." Although, in practice, some of them were more representative (i.e., Czechoslovakia) than others (i.e., Yugoslavia) and although the West and Moscow had different interpretations of the meaning of "representative government," for now all three allies found it convenient to press for the establishment of broadly based coalition governments. The coalition formula was the classical "easy solution." The United States liked the emphasis on "representative" governments; the British thought the "percentage

12. Ibid., p. 307.
13. Cf. Davis, *The Cold War Begins*, pp. 335–58, and Robert Lee Wolff, *The Balkans in Our Time* (Cambridge: Harvard University Press, 1956), pp. 223–33 and pp. 267–74.
14. For a fascinating account of the Beneš-Stalin discussion, see Vojtech Mastny, "The Beneš-Stalin-Molotov Conversations in December 1943: New Documents," *Jarbucher für Geschichte Osteuropas* 20 (1972): 367–402.

agreement" and Yalta might give them more influence in the Balkans than their military position in the area would have justified; and the Russians, who were suspicious of the British and hence circumspect, obtained the stamp of Western approval for the legitimate inclusion of Communists in the coalition governments. Strange bedfellows as the allies were, they now gave birth to governments of even stranger bedfellows in the eastern half of the European continent.

Domestic Consensus

While the great powers made their decisions, deals, and recommendations, indigenous political forces in Eastern and in East Central Europe did likewise. Already in 1943 a cooperative agreement was concluded between various Czechoslovak political figures, including President Beneš, and representatives of the Czechoslovak Communist party. In Hungary the tiny home Communist party reached a similar accord with the Smallholders' party and the Social Democrats in the fall of 1944. Unrealistic as it may have been, there was the Tito-Šubašić deal in Yugoslavia. Also in 1944, as the war was coming to an end, a common program and subsequently an anti-Fascist coalition surfaced in Romania and Bulgaria, too. Only in Poland did the two major contending forces during the war—the Soviet-backed "Lublin Committee" and the London-based Government-in-Exile —fail to get together; however, by June 1945, foreign pressure eventually produced a "government of national unity" even for that deeply divided country.

The agreements were based on the political reality of the moment. As Soviet forces were liberating much of Europe, there could be no question about the key role Communists were to play in the political life of all East European countries. It was also apparent, however, that they could not govern alone, for with the exception of Czechoslovakia, as table 3.1 shows, the Communists completely lacked popular appeal. Conversely, the Soviet Union, sensitive to its Western allies' perception of the legitimacy of the emerging political order in Eastern Europe, insisted on the inclusion of non-Communists in the various governments.

If geopolitical necessity was thus an important source of the initial tendency toward internal cooperation, so was the prevailing domestic socioeconomic consensus about the immediate tasks ahead. Although —because of the subsequent disintegration of the coalition governments and the establishment of Communist political hegemony—the generally cooperative spirit of 1944—45 has been largely forgotten, such a domestic-programmatic consensus did exist in Czechoslovakia, Hungary, and to a

Table 3.1   Communist Party Membership in Eastern Europe, 1944–1948

Country	Date	Number of members	Percentages of population
Bulgaria	9/1944	25,000	
	10/1944	50,000	
	1/1945	254,140	
	12/1946	490,000	
	6/1947	510,000	7.1
	12/1948	496,000	6.9
Czechoslovakia	3/1946	1,081,544	
	9/1947	1,172,000	9.4
	12/1947	1,281,131	
	2/1948	1,400,000	
	5/1948	2,150,000	
Poland	7/1944	20,000	
	12/1944	32,000	
	4/1945	301,695	
	12/1945	235,300	
	6/1946	347,105	
	12/1946	555,888	
	5/1947	823,340	3.3
	12/1947	820,786	
	6/1948	997,024	
	9/1948	1,006,873	
Hungary	12/1944	2,500	
	2/1945	30,000	
	5/1945	150,000	
	7/1945	226,577	
	10/1945	508,801	5.7
	1/1946	608,728	
	9/1946	653,300	6.7
	1/1947	670,818	
	3/1947	708,646	
	12/1947	864,000	
	6/1948	887,472	9.6
Romania	8/1944	2,000	
	10/1945	256,000	
	9/1947	710,000	4.4
	2/1948	806,000	5.0

Source: Adapted from Emil Borsi, *Az európai népi demokratikus forradalmak* [The European People's Democratic Revolutions] (Budapest, 1975), pp. 47–52, and from various East European yearbooks.

lesser extent in Bulgaria, Romania, and perhaps even in Poland and Yugo-slavia as well. It rested on the disintegration of the old order and on the opportunity to build a new one. There was an all but unanimous commit-ment to the primacy of reconstruction on the basis of united, concerted action. In the countries where it had not been done (especially Hungary and Poland), there was full support for the implementation of land reform, which was both long overdue and immensely popular. There was agree-ment in principle that the privileges of the past should be erased, educa-tional opportunity made available to all, and social mobility fostered. There was, for now, a shared view about building a "mixed" economy along agrarian-socialist or social-democratic lines. Finally, it was widely recognized that the coming transformation of society would likely necessi-tate radical, if not revolutionary, measures.

To that extent, it was also understood that the expected socioeconomic transformation would require a political order different from Western-style pluralist democracy. Seldom defined in precise terms, the "new democracy," "people's democracy," or "popular democracy" labels implied a political system devoted mainly to *substantive*, that is, socioeconomic, concerns. True, there was even a limited consensus about such political matters as the punishment of war criminals, and everyone paid lip service to political liberties and the benefits of free and competitive political processes. But, under chaotic conditions, all parties, despite their apprehension about Communism, sought to stress what united them: the burning socioeco-nomic issues of food supply, housing, health care, transportation, and public order.

Thus, the immediate task of reconstruction, combined with interna-tional pressures, produced an uneasy domestic consensus throughout the region during the last months of, and immediately after, the war. That consensus was short-lived: it barely, if ever, existed in Yugoslavia or Poland, and it survived for only a couple of years in Czechoslovakia and Hungary. Where it did last, both Communists and non-Communists supported it because they hoped to gain time and eventually improve their relative power positions. Those non-Communists who helped uphold the domestic consensus, and hence the coalition, did so in the expectation of forthcom-ing changes in international alignments leading to the withdrawal of Soviet forces. The Communists, in turn, also needed time in order to make themselves palatable to their own people and thus avoid the possibil-ity of defeat by a premature move toward hegemony.

Call it deception, temporary abnegation, or political tactics, the Communists' professed democratic platform was nonetheless a significant circumstance behind the domestic consensus. "Socialism cannot be built now," Polish party ideologist Hilary Minc stated in Lublin on August 5, 1944, "because first we need a long-lasting peace and our government's policies need to get recognition not only from the Soviet Union, as is the case at present, but also from the USA and UK. The USSR will accept no other policies in Poland. . . . Even when the war is over, reconstruction will only be possible with a national front."[15] Party leader Władysław Gomułka echoed that view when he asserted that, "We completely reject the accusation made against us by the reactionaries that we will impose a one-party system. We do not want a one-party system and we are not moving toward it."[16] The same reasoning was reflected in Czechoslovak party leader Klement Gottwald's comment to a closed meeting of Slovak functionaries after his return from Moscow: "We cannot govern on our own, and neither can they [non-Communists]. They cannot govern without us, and neither can we without them."[17] The former secretary general of the Comintern, Bulgarian leader Georgi Dimitrov, stated at the November 7, 1945, anniversary celebration of the Bolshevik Revolution in Moscow, of all places, that the "assertion that the Communists want to seize full power . . . is a malicious legend and slander. It is not true that the Communists want to have a single-party government."[18]

In Hungary the coalition formula ran into resistance from an unexpected source—from many of the home Communists, who found the Muscovites' party line too conciliatory. They wanted "socialism now." At a party *aktiv* in Szeged on November 19, 1944, for example, several home Communists heatedly argued for the immediate establishment of the dictatorship of the proletariat. Some even remarked that the conciliatory line advocated by the Muscovites must stem from their "bourgeois mentality." The answer came from Révai who had just arrived from Moscow: "England and America would not recognize a Communist government. Those who want socialism and the dictatorship of the proletariat make the anti-

15. As quoted in Anton Polonsky and Bolesław Drukier, eds., *The Beginnings of Communist Rule in Poland: December 1943–June 1945* (London: Routledge & Kegan Paul, 1980), p. 263. For a vivid account of how the Comintern prepared foreign Communists for their postwar role in Germany and in Eastern Europe, see also Wolfgang Leonhard, *Child of the Revolution* (Chicago: Regnery Gateway, 1958), especially chap. 5.

16. As quoted in Nicholas Bethell, *Gomułka: His Poland, His Communism* (New York: Holt, Rinehart and Winston, 1969), p. 122.

17. As quoted in Michael Kraus, "Communist Behavior in Coalition Governments: Czechoslovakia 1945–1948," a paper delivered at the 1978 National Convention of the American Association for the Advancement of Slavic Studies, p. 9.

18. *Izvestia*, November 13, 1945.

German policy more difficult."[19] On another occasion Gerő exclaimed: "Some Communists think that the order of the day in Hungary is the establishment of socialism. That is not the position of the Hungarian Communist party. It is not a correct viewpoint to urge the construction of socialism on the rubble of defeat."[20] On still another occasion, Révai was even more emphatic: "I declare that we do not regard the national collaboration [of the several political parties] as a passing, political coalition, as a tactical chess move, but rather as a long-lasting alliance."[21]

The policy of such "national collaboration" entailed a deliberate attempt to keep the Hungarian Communist party in the background. For example, the first Muscovite to follow the Red Army to Hungary, Zoltán Vas, was specifically instructed to "implement the Party's objectives through other people . . . even through other parties."[22] One of the eleven secret instructions given to a few party cadres on November 12, 1944, stated that, "Leaders of the party shall not thrust themselves into prominence: whenever possible, the party's objectives must be implemented through others, many times through another party."[23] That is why, as mentioned in chapter 1, Vas kept certain prominent public figures out of the Communist party. When Ferenc Erdei of the populist National Peasant party approached him with the idea of joining the Communist party, Vas told him to stay where he was.

Such deceitful maneuverings notwithstanding, the Communists' professions of "national collaboration" through coalition governments convinced

19. As quoted in Mihály Korom, *Magyarország ideiglenes nemzeti kormánya és a fegyverszünet (1944–1945)* [Hungary's Provisional National Government and the Armistice (1944–1945)] (Budapest, 1981), p. 286. It is a fair guess that the majority of the home Communists remained critical of the Muscovites' support for the coalitionary approach for at least a few months. For example, at the party's first national conference held in Budapest on May 20, 1945, Rákosi devoted about one-fourth of his long speech to attacking "left-wing sectarianism," calling it the party's "most serious problem." While the remaining three-fourths of his speech was interrupted thirty-two times by applause or other forms of approval, his audience applauded only once when he discussed various manifestations of left-wing deviations in the party. On the other hand, no home Communist criticized the "conciliatory" party line in open session by then. In fact, the leading home Communist of the day, László Rajk, went out of his way to express support for Rákosi and the Moscow-approved approach, though his speech was rumored to have been written for him by a member of Rákosi's entourage. Rákosi's speech was reprinted in his *A magyar jövőért* [For the Hungarian Future], (Budapest, 1950), pp. 528–59.

20. As quoted in Bennett Kovrig, *Communism in Hungary: From Kun to Kádár* (Stanford: Hoover Institution Press, 1979), p. 157.

21. *Délmagyarország*, December 5, 1944.

22. Related to me by Zoltán Vas.

23. Archives of the [Hungarian] Institute of Party History, KI-II/858.

most non-Communist leaders in the region that the Communists' goals were tentative and their tactics flexible. Hence almost all who were asked to join the coalitions decided to do so. Wrong as they proved to be, their perception at that time was not based on wishful thinking alone; the evidence, to repeat, pointed to the absence of a definitive Soviet grand design for the region as a whole. For one minor example, as late as March 1946 the authoritative Soviet journal *Bolshevik* conspicuously failed to list Czechoslovakia, Hungary, and even Poland among the new "people's democracies."[24] In any case, political retirement seemed neither useful nor realistic because the region's place in the emerging European political order was still unclear and its place in the Soviet orbit did not yet appear to be a foregone conclusion.

Despite their reservations and fears about the Communists' ultimate plans, then, the majority of non-Communist politicians decided to participate in the coalitions. While some of them were opportunists who could not live without the perquisites of power, most of them joined because they sought to position themselves for a future they fervently hoped to shape. Their calculation was that when the war was over, or when the peace treaties with the ex-enemy states were signed, or when the Red Army was withdrawn, the United States and Great Britain would take a stronger interest in the region's affairs. Therefore, they tried to gain time at almost any cost—lend their names to the new regimes and survive politically—so that they would have sufficient influence to make a difference when the opportunity presented itself. In the meantime, they could and did forge alliances with the Communists primarily because, by and large, they shared the Communists' avowed socioeconomic objectives.

The All-Party Coalition

Formally, the new governments were all-inclusive in Romania, Hungary, Bulgaria, and Czechoslovakia. In the three former cases, high-ranking military officers who had turned against Hitler's Germany at the last minute were co-opted into the postwar coalition governments.

In Romania the first cabinet under General Constantin Sănătescu (August 23, 1944–November 2, 1944) was dominated by generals, with the leader of each of the so-called "Historical parties" (National Peasant, Liberal, and Social Democratic) and the Communist party included in the government as ministers without portfolio. The second Sănătescu cabinet

24. Boris Ponomarev, "Demokraticheskie preobrazovania v osvobozhdennykh strankh Evropy" [Democratic Transformation in the Liberated Countries of Europe], *Bolshevik* 22, no. 6 (March 1946), p. 121.

(November 4, 1944–December 2, 1944), in which the four party leaders continued to serve as ministers without portfolio, was made up of eleven representatives of the three "historical parties" and one Communist, as well as General Sănătescu as premier. When Sănătescu was replaced by another general, Nicolae Rădescu, the composition of the cabinet remained more or less unchanged until March 1945, when the sham or bogus coalition under the premiership of Petru Groza took over. But from August 1944 to March 1945, an all-party government existed in Romania even as the Russians and the Romanian Communists worked hard to undermine it both from within and without.

In Hungary the tenure of the Provisional Government lasted from December 22, 1944, to November 15, 1945. As described in chapter 1, the cabinet was also headed by a general and it included two other military officers; all three had served the old regime. At least formally, two Communists, two Social Democrats, two Smallholders, one National Peasant, and one unaffiliated shared the remaining portfolios. After the November 1945 elections (see tables 2.5 and 3.2), the two Smallholder-led coalition governments under the premierships of Zoltán Tildy and Ferenc Nagy (November 15, 1945–May 31, 1947) included representatives of the four major parties, reflecting the results of the elections.

In Bulgaria a link with the past was provided by the inclusion of four leaders of the semimilitary *Zveno* ("The Link") group in the new government formed in September 1944. Authoritarian by temperament, skeptical of parliamentary institutions and party politics, but not unfriendly toward the Soviet Union, Zveno was useful in organizing Bulgaria's reentry into the war on the Allies' side and in giving the impression of continuity and legitimacy. One of its leading figures, Kimon Georgiev, was premier, until September 1946, of the coalition government in which, formally at least, non-Communists outnumbered Communist ministers by a margin of three to one. As elsewhere in Eastern and East Central Europe, the Zveno, Agrarian, and Social Democratic portfolios in the cabinet were gradually assumed by more pliable leaders, such as Kimon Georgiev himself (who replaced General Damian Velchev as head of Zveno), Alexander Obbov (who replaced Nikola Petkov as leader of the Agrarian Union), and the pro-Communist Dimiter Neikov (who replaced Krustu Pastukhov, Grigor Cheshmedzhiev, and Kosta Lulchev in the leadership of the Social Democratic party). All in all, the Bulgarian government was an all-party formation more in name than substance—as in Romania and as it became somewhat later in Hungary.

In Czechoslovakia, where the "old regime" had consisted of genuine democrats—rather than military leaders with an authoritarian or semi-

Table 3.2   Parliamentary Elections in Eastern Europe, 1944–1948

Country	Date	Parties/"Fronts"	Number of seats	(Percentages of total)
Bulgaria	11/18/1945	Fatherland Front	279	(all)
	10/27/1946	Fatherland Front	364	(79)
	[competitive]	Agrarians (Petkov)	92	(20)
		Social Democrats (Lulchev)	6	(1)
Czechoslovakia	5/26/1946	Czech & Slovak Communists	114	(38)
	[free]	Czech National Socialists	55	(18)
		People's party	47	(16)
		Slovak Democrats	43	(14)
		Social Democrats	38	(13)
		Others	3	(1)
Hungary	11/4/1945	Smallholders	245	(60)
	[free]	Communists	70	(17)
		Social Democrats	69	(17)
		National Peasants	23	(6)
		Citizen's Democrats	2	—
	8/31/1947	Communists	100	(24)
	[competitive]	Smallholders	68	(17)
		Social Democrats	67	(16)
		National Peasants	36	(9)
		Government Front total	271	(66)
		Democratic People's party (Barankovics)	60	(15)
		Hungarian Independents (Pfeiffer)	49	(12)
		Independent Hungarian Democrats (Balogh)	18	(4)
		Others	13	(3)
		Opposition total	140	(34)
Poland	1/19/1946	Government Front	394	(89)
		Other pro-front parties	22	(5)
		Polish Peasant party (Mikołajczyk)	28	(6)

Table 3.2   (continued)

Country	Date	Parties/"Fronts"	Number of seats (Percentages of total)	
Romania	11/19/1946	Government Front	377	(91)
		National Peasants		
		(Maniu)	32	(8)
		Others	5	(1)
	3/28/1948	Government Front	405	(98)
		Liberals (Brătianu)	7	(2)
		National Peasants		
		(Maniu)	2	—

Source: Adapted from Borsi, *Az európai népi demokratikus*, pp. 65–71, and from various East European yearbooks.

Fascist past—as well as the only large and legal Communist party in the region, the post-1945 "new regime" reflected genuine continuity with the past, with the venerable Beneš as president of the Republic. Although there were free elections in the spring of 1946, the distribution of cabinet portfolios remained essentially unchanged between April 1945 and the February 1948 Communist coup d'état. No significant elements were left out of the government, which, in Beneš's words, rejected the "purely political conception of democracy in a liberalistic sense" and instead understood it "as a system in the economic and social sense also." Despite the apparent continuity in party representation in the prewar and postwar governments, Beneš also declared that, "Our house must be rebuilt both politically and socially, with a new content, new people, and often with new institutions," and that "political democracy will have to develop systematically and consistently into a so-called economic and social democracy."[25] This general orientation, which was intended to make Czechoslovakia a "bridge" between East and West, was supported not only by Beneš's own National Socialists, but by the Social Democrats, the Slovak Democratic party, and the initially very soft-spoken Communist leaders as well.

Thus, following Seton-Watson's schema (see table 3.3), the era of "genuine coalition" may be said to have existed in Czechoslovakia for about three years, in Hungary for about two and a half years, in Romania for six months, and in Bulgaria perhaps for only four months. The period of "bogus coalition" followed—with more accommodating

25. Both quotes in Paul E. Zinner, *Communist Strategy and Tactics in Czechoslovakia, 1918–1948* (New York: Praeger, 1963), pp. 104–5.

Table 3.3 Seton-Watson's "Stages" of East European Politics, 1944–48

Country	Genuine coalition	Bogus coalition	Monolithic Communist party rule
Romania	August 1944– March 1945	March 1945– November 1947	November 1947–
Bulgaria	September 1944– January 1945	January 1945– July 1948	July 1948–
Hungary	December 1944– May 1947	May 1947– December 1948	December 1948–
Czechoslovakia	April 1945– February 1948		February 1948–
Yugoslavia		March 1945– September 1945	September 1945–
Poland		June 1945– October 1947	October 1947–

Source: Hugh Seton-Watson, *The East European Revolution* (New York, Praeger, 1956), passim.

non-Communists still in the government—for two and a half years in Bulgaria and Romania (till the fall of 1947) and for about one year in Hungary (till late 1948). Czechoslovakia, as Seton-Watson notes, "leaped" from the "genuine coalition" phase to monolithic Communist rule after the 1948 coup.[26]

As for Yugoslavia, the few non-Communist members of the government formed in March 1945 were altogether left out of the decision-making process and never allowed to have their parties properly organized. Even the short period of "bogus coalition," which was heavily dominated by Tito's forces, came to a not unexpected end in September 1945 with the resignation of Foreign Minister Šubašić. It seems that Tito, who came to power on his own, did not feel obliged to provide for continuity with the past; he considered his one-party rule legitimate. The inclusion of Šubašić, Milan Grol, and a few others from London for a few months was but an empty gesture to the British for their assistance during the war and to the Russians who thought that a one-party government in Yugoslavia would needlessly exacerbate their relations with the British and the Americans.

Finally, Poland was sui generis. On the one hand—as in Romania, Hungary, Bulgaria, and Czechoslovakia—the Polish government formed in June 1945 was nominally all-inclusive, with several of the political

26. Seton-Watson, *East European Revolution*, p. 171.

parties of the past represented in it. Although the National Democratic party, which had been one of the major parties before the war, was excluded from participation, the coalition was still composed of five parties: Mikołajczyk's People's (Peasant) party, the Polish Socialist party, the Democratic party, the Christian Labor party, and the Polish Workers' (Communist) party. On the other hand, the Communists, as in Yugoslavia, fully dominated the government from the beginning. Indeed, the actual division in the government was not between Communists and non-Communists, but between the "Lublin" Poles who were both pro-Soviet and pro-Communist and the "London" Poles. With sixteen of the twenty-one ministries held by members of the Lublin group, the government was a bogus coalition from the start — with Mikołajczyk, almost single-handedly, putting forth a non-Communist point of view for two years. This "coalition," in turn, was to give way to the establishment of monolithic Communist rule in the fall of 1947.

Thus, with the notable exceptions of Yugoslavia and Poland, the postwar governments of Eastern and East Central Europe all *began* as genuine coalitions. During this phase, they were characterized as follows:

> Several political parties, differing in social basis, ideology and long-term programme, and possessing each its own party organization, combined on a common short-term programme, which nominally included a purge of Fascists, fairly radical social reforms, political freedom and a foreign policy friendly to both the U.S.S.R. and the Western Powers. Real freedom of speech and meeting existed, and there was little political censorship except on one subject — the U.S.S.R. Not only might Soviet policy not be criticised, but it was hardly possible to write anything about any aspect of Russia which did not coincide with the official Soviet line. But this seemed a small price to pay. Apart from this, a wide variety of opinions, representing various political views and social categories, could be freely expressed. Nevertheless, already during the first stage, the Communists seized control of most of the "levers of power" — in particular the security police, the army general staff and the publicity machine.[27]

Wherever such genuine coalitions existed, they were followed in a few months (Bulgaria and Romania) or in a couple of years (Hungary and Czechoslovakia) by the phase of the bogus coalition, which was aptly characterized by Seton-Watson as follows:

27. Ibid., pp. 169–70.

The governments still contain non-Communist parties, but these are represented by men chosen no longer by the party membership but by the Communists. The essential feature of this stage is that the peasant parties, and any bourgeois parties who may have been tolerated at the beginning, are driven into opposition. In this stage opposition is still tolerated but becomes increasingly difficult. Opposition newspapers may be published, but their distribution becomes dangerous in the capital and almost impossible outside it. Censorship is exercised not only by the government but also by the Communist-controlled printers' trade unions, which "indignantly refuse to print reactionary calumnies against the people's authorities." Opposition meetings are broken up by lorryloads of Communist toughs, while the police "objectively" take no action against aggressors or aggressed.[28]

What the preceding discussion suggests is that the all-party coalition, genuine or bogus, was a formula that, imposed from without, turned out to be an unworkable political necessity. Neither variety lasted very long in either Eastern or even in East Central Europe—whether by comparison to the durability of the coalition in nearby Austria that lasted over two decades, or by absolute European standards.[29] The reason for their early demise had to do primarily with such external factors as ever-increasing Soviet pressures and, until mid-1947 when it was too late, the absence of Western support to non-Communist elements. Early control by the Communist parties of key ministries, particularly those of internal affairs and defense, was the major domestic factor hastening the disappearance of the postwar, all-party coalitions.

Political Fragmentation

Yet the decay and eventual collapse of these coalitions were also a function of their inherent structural deficiencies. Of these deficiencies, the coalitions' oversized quality was of particular importance.

Lawrence C. Dodd identifies three general types of coalitional status: (1) the greater than minimum winning status: "oversized" coalitions from which "at least one party could be subtracted" and yet "the cabinet's majority status [is still] sustained"; (2) the minimum winning status: coalitions which "do not contain any party that could be subtracted" without losing their winning status and hence the most durable coalitions;

28. Ibid., p. 170.
29. Dodd, *Coalitions*, esp. pp. 195–204.

and (3) the less than minimum winning status: "undersized" coalitions with no "reliable parliamentary majority."[30]

Clearly, every all-party government that came into being in the shadow of Soviet power possessed qualities Dodd ascribes to the first general type. They all had far greater than minimum winning status; they were over-sized and thus nondurable, primarily because the coalitions included parties, or factions within parties, which were easily expendable. "If this [the expendable] party is omitted from the cabinet," Dodd explains, "some or all of the other coalition partners will gain in the sense that they will obtain new ministerial positions formerly controlled by the expendable party(-ies). Realizing this, the various parties within the coalition act to reduce the size of the cabinet by removing at least one party."[31]

But which party or parties were expendable in the postwar all-party coalitions of Eastern and East Central Europe?

Formally, the evidence (see table 3.2) points to the Communist parties, none of which could even come close to winning a parliamentary majority on their own. Further analysis (implied by the composition of cabinets as shown in table 3.4) suggests that the Communist parties were in a minority even *within* their own creation, the all-encompassing "fronts" as well (the Fatherland Front in Bulgaria and the Government Front in Poland and Romania). Moreover, the Communist party was certainly "the odd man out" in the coalitions as the ideological distance between the Communists and others was considerably greater than it was among the non-Communist parties. Thus, had the cabinets reflected only the ideological makeup of parliaments, the Communists would have been expendable.

The reason it did not happen this way can be explained by two considerations. The obvious one is that, given the proximity of the Soviet Union and the Red Army, it was unrealistic and even unthinkable to exclude the Communists from the coalitions. (In the one known case when the "unthinkable" almost happened—in Hungary after the 1945 elections—the second echelon of the Smallholder leadership urged the formation of an all-Smallholder government. The party's top leaders rejected the idea, not only because they figured that it would be unacceptable to Moscow but also because they did not want to assume the burden of responsibility for the country's economic recovery and political fate all by themselves.)

The less obvious reason why the Communist parties were not expendable had to do with the extremely high level of dissension and factionalism within all non-Communist parties. Instead of uniting in the face of the gradually increasing Communist challenge to the status quo (as signified

30. Ibid., pp. 42–43.
31. Ibid., p. 50.

Table 3.4   Formal Distribution of Portfolios in
East European Coalition Governments, 1944–1948

Country	Period	Communists/ Others	Number of government portfolios (percentages of total)	
Bulgaria	9/9/44–	Communist party	4	(25)
	3/31/46	Others	12	(75)
	3/31/46–	Communist party	4	(25)
	11/22/46	Others	12	(75)
	11/22/46–	Communist party	10	(50)
	12/11/47	Others	10	(50)
	12/11/47–	Communist party	12	(60)
	7/20/49	Others	8	(40)
Czechoslovakia	4/4/45–	Czech and Slovak		
	7/8/46	Communists	8	(32)
		Others	17	(68)
	7/8/46–	Czech and Slovak		
	2/25/48	Communists	9	(41)
		Others	13	(59)
	2/25/48–	Czech and Slovak		
		Communists	11	(58)
		Others	8	(42)
Hungary	12/22/44–	Communist party	3	(25)
	11/15/45	Others	9	(75)
	11/15/45–	Communist party	4	(22)
	2/1/46	Others	14	(78)
	2/1/46–	Communist party	4	(21)
	5/31/47	Others	15	(79)
	5/31/47–	Communist party	4	(24)
	9/24/47	Others	13	(76)
	9/24/47–	Communist party	6	(38)
	12/10/48	Others	10	(62)
Poland	7/21/44–	Workers' party	5	(33)
	12/31/44	Others	10	(67)
	12/31/44–	Workers' party	5	(29)
	6/28/45	Others	12	(71)
	6/28/45–	Lublin Committee	16	(76)
	2/6/47	Others	5	(24)
Romania	8/23/44–	Communist party	1	(8)
	11/4/44	Others	12	(92)

Table 3.4   (continued)

Country	Period	Communists/ Others	Number of government portfolios (percentages of total)	
	11/4/44– 3/6/45	National Democratic Front	11	(85)
		Others	2	(15)
	3/6/45– 3/29/46	Communist party	3	(20)
		Others	12	(80)
	3/29/46– 11/29/46	Communist party	4	(25)
		Others	12	(75)
	11/29/46– 4/13/48	Communist party	4	(33)
		Others	8	(67)
	4/13/48– 12/24/48	Workers' party	12	(67)
		Others	6	(33)
Yugoslavia	3/7/45– 9/45	National Committee (Tito)	23	(82)
		Others	5	(18)

Source: Adapted from Borsi, *Az európai népi demokratikus*, pp. 74–79, and from various East European yearbooks.

by the all-party coalitions) and thus seeking to isolate or otherwise weaken the challenger, the non-Communist parties allowed their own political differences, personal rivalries, and petty jealousies to overcome their common interest. Simply put, they tended to consider another non-Communist party or another faction within their own non-Communist party expendable, not the Communist party. Their inability to join forces in defense of the coalitional status quo thus enhanced the Communists' "positional advantage" (as Paul E. Zinner put it) and sealed their own political fate. In Czechoslovakia, for example, where the Communist party shared power with four non-Communist parties:

> The National Socialists were antagonistic toward the Slovak Democrats, because of their separatist tendencies. Obversely, the Slovak Democrats considered the National Socialists the foremost exponents of the hated policy of "Czechization." There was friction between the National Socialists and the People's Party, because of the former's outspoken anticlerical attitude, and because these parties vied for the favors of the same constituency. The National Socialists and Social Democrats were continually at loggerheads. Their traditional rivalry was exacerbated by postwar conditions. To some extent, they too were contending for the favors of the same constituency, and the

National Socialists exerted great pressure to wean away the moderate
wing of the Social Democratic Party. . . . The conflicts . . . prevented
the formation of anything approaching a coherent anti-Communist
front."[32]

For an illustration of intraparty divisions, the quite typical case of
the Polish Social Democrats (PPS)—who joined the Communists (PPR)
and the Peasant party in the postwar coalition—is deserving of detailed
description:

> The PPS was the least homogeneous of the three main political parties.
> On the one hand, there was the core of founding members from the
> old RPPS, led by [Edward] Osobka-Morawski, who could be counted
> on to collaborate with the Communists. On the other hand, there
> was the large number of recruits who joined the party after the
> Congress of September 1944, many of whom were influenced in
> doing so by the nationalist traditions of the old PPS and by the hope
> that a strong Socialist party might provide an alternative to
> Communism. These new arrivals were divided roughly into three
> main groups. To the right were members of the old PPS from the
> underground, led by the veteran trade-unionist, Zygmunt Zulawski.
> They were fundamentally anti-Communist, realized the need for
> coming to an understanding with the PPR and the Soviet authorities,
> but hoped to maintain the identity of the PPS as a moderating
> influence. In October 1945 an attempt by Zulawski to found a
> separate Social Democratic Party was frustrated by the Communists
> and the National Council. A compromise was reached in December,
> when the Zulawski group was given eleven seats on the executive
> council of the PPS. But within a year Zulawski himself, who rivalled
> Mikołajczyk in determination, had left the Party. In the centre was a
> large body of moderates who accepted the inevitability of collabora-
> tion with the Communists, considered a united front of left-wing
> parties desirable to prevent reaction, and trusted in the numerical
> strength of the Socialists to make their influence felt. This group was
> the most variegated and fluid of the three and contained many
> opportunists. Finally, there was the left wing, which scarcely differed
> from the former members of the RPPS except in being newcomers.
> Chief amongst them was Józef Cyrankiewicz, who had come under
> Communist influence while still in a concentration camp and who
> became secretary-general of the PPS in July 1945. A man of consider-
> able intellectual ability, with a keen sense of his own interests, he

32. Zinner, *Communist Strategy*, p. 116.

played an important part in the process by which the PPS and the PPR were finally merged into one party.[33]

Of course, the more such interparty and intraparty antagonisms grew, the more the oversized coalitions worked in favor of the Communists. To begin with, because of their positional advantage and despite their minority standing, the Communists were the only ones who were not expendable; their participation in the coalition was predetermined. Moreover, since they needed non-Communist allies to keep at least the appearance of a broadly based government, many non-Communists positioned themselves in such a way as to be kept by the most likely ultimate winner—the Communist party. Yet, to the extent the Communists continued to need non-Communist participation in the cabinet, all non-Communists were not expendable either, only almost all of them. Knowing this, many of the more opportunistic non-Communist parties, factions, or individuals—the so-called fellow travelers—turned against their own parties or colleagues in order to prove their utility to the Communists.

Hence both the "size principle" and the notion that oversized coalitions are nondurable were operative in postwar Eastern and East Central Europe, except that the Communist parties had two decisive advantages. The first was the external backing of the Soviet Union, of course, and the second was their greater internal ideological cohesion.[34] Put another way, the breakup of the coalitions was made possible in part by the self-destruction of the non-Communist elements, as much as it was due to the Communists' determination, skill, and cohesion. Because they were too divided and because of their fervent desire to avoid a civil war or direct Soviet military intervention, such decent democrats as Beneš and Tildy—and, of course, opportunists like Groza and Cyrankiewicz—shied away from applying equally the coalitional rules of conduct: in order to gain time and survive, they were reluctant to encroach on Communist prerogatives, while the Communist parties could and did provoke internal turmoil in the other

33. Richard Hiscocks, *Poland: Bridge to the Abyss?* (London: Oxford University Press, 1963), pp. 99–100.

34. This is not meant to imply the absence of political differences and especially personal rivalries in the Communist parties. In Poland and Romania, there were differences between the Muscovites and the home Communists. In Czechoslovakia and Hungary, too, there were early debates about the pace of the Communist parties' approach to power. Personal rivalries were very much in evidence everywhere. As to substance, most home Communists could not understand why their ultimate goals had to be postponed. With the possible exception of the "Pătrășcanu affair" in Romania, however, the issue was quickly resolved everywhere in favor of the Muscovites' orientation. Compared to the seemingly permanent feuds that characterized the non-Communist parties, then, the Communist parties possessed considerable internal cohesion.

parties.[35] Many non-Communist leaders came to believe that if they were to stay on they could influence the political system from within. After all, their alternative was political exile or worse, and, given the way the oversized coalition worked, they knew that there would always be others to fill the quota of non-Communists in the emerging political order.

Implications and Conclusions

The coalition governments of national unity born after World War II in Eastern and East Central Europe contained the seeds of their own decay. They were given birth by an international alliance that was about to collapse. The initial domestic unity of purpose began to fade away as soon as, or even before, Fascism was defeated and economic reconstruction achieved. The oversized coalitions were structurally conducive to easy Communist manipulation. In the Balkans and in Poland, Moscow's commitment to Sovietization was all but total, while in Czechoslovakia and Hungary the lack of effective countervailing power, domestic and international, gave the Communist side an unexpectedly early opportunity to get its way by 1947–48.

Elsewhere in Europe, however, the Communist parties allowed themselves to be eased out of the broad postwar coalition governments soon after they had joined them—in France, Italy, Belgium, Luxembourg, Austria, Norway, Denmark, Iceland, Greece, and Finland. Later on, Communist parties helped keep the Social Democrats in power in Sweden and the Christian Democrats in Italy. Throughout Western Europe, Communists continued to participate in the management of municipal governments in hundreds of cities and towns. Of all these countries, only in Greece did the Communist party make an overt move toward political hegemony. That the others did not does not mean that they did not wish to or that they might not do so in the future; but the record indicates that in the face of effective countervailing power—be that the strength of cohesive domestic democratic forces or the fear of external reaction—Communist parties quite consistently opt for a cautious course and for what seems politically feasible under the circumstances, thus accepting

35. In a carefully phrased memorandum he sent abroad surreptitiously in the fall of 1946, when he was Hungary's president, Tildy defended his position this way: "The coalition's dispersal would constitute a revolution . . . which would inevitably rip the country into two parts. The bitter internal struggle would make our people suffer and perish, and it would also open our gates to such external influence that would destroy the opportunity for the development of Hungarian national existence for a long time." Zoltán Tildy, "Irány és teendők" [Direction and Tasks], *Uj Látóhatár* (Munich) 13, no. 1 (January–February, 1962): 72–79.

either minority status in coalition governments or oppositional status (more or less) within the rules of constitutional conduct.

Therefore, the entry of Communists into coalition governments does not "lead" to Communist takeovers. It is a mistake to focus exclusively on the Communists' "ultimate" objectives; surely they, like others, seek more power. It is a mistake to assume that Communists will emerge, more or less automatically, as the eventual victors of coalition infighting; winning does not happen automatically in politics. And it is a mistake to identify all those who enter into coalition agreements with the Communist parties as collaborators or even fellow travelers; in Western Europe, they were the ones who succeeded in co-opting the Communists rather than the other way around. That was the way it happened throughout Western Europe after World War II, and that is the way it has worked out in France and elsewhere even in the mid-1980s.[36]

The lesson from the postwar experience of Eastern and East Central Europe is that, given the ideological distance between the Communist and the non-Communist parties, the Communists are always difficult and frequently deceitful coalition partners. Their internal cohesion and self-discipline can also give them a decisive edge over their competitors. Although the structural weakness of all-party coalitions certainly did not determine the ultimate collapse of these governments, it helped the Communists' cause, fostering factionalism and dissension in the ranks of other parties. Finally, the positional advantage they derived from international conditions provided them with certain resources, material and psychological, that the West consistently denied to their non-Communist opponents. All in all, then, as the all-party coalitions of Eastern and East Central Europe fell apart because they no longer reflected the political needs and alignments that were operative at the time of their birth, the main lesson for other polities is that all-party coalitions with Communist participation can only endure if the domestic and international circumstances that produced them in the first place endure as well.[37]

36. For different conclusions, see Gerhart Niemeyer, "Communists in Coalition Governments," in Frank R. Barnett et al., eds., Peace and War in the Modern Age: Premises, Myths, and Realities (Garden City, N.Y.: Doubleday, 1965), pp. 179–95.

37. Afghanistan is a recent case in point. As the New York Times reported on January 20, 1986, dozens of non-Communists, including a religious leader or two, were "allowed to join the Afghan Government in an attempt to broaden its popular support." Clearly, they are presently needed to create the impression that the country is not run by pro-Soviet forces alone. If these forces overcome popular resistance to nebulous authority—that is, when the domestic circumstances that produced this "coalition" are no longer in evidence—then these non-Communists, having outlived their usefulness, will no doubt disappear from the political scene.

4

A Note on Communists and the Jewish Question

Even more so than in Romania and Poland, people of Jewish origin led the Hungarian Communist party and the notorious, Communist-dominated political police for over a decade after World War II. Why was that so? Did the "average Jew" also support the Communist party? Was József Cardinal Mindszenty on target with his reported complaint that while "Christian Hungary" in 1943–44 had done what it could to protect the country's Jewish population, "Jewish-Communist Hungary" after 1945 failed to return the favor?

That so many of the top leaders of the Hungarian Communist party were of Jewish origin requires no documentation. Of course, they did not observe religious holidays or Jewish traditions. Indeed, their rejection of the tradition of their parents and grandparents, followed by their joining the Communist movement, suggests the need to deny familial ties; Révai's notorious early poem in which he forcefully expressed the wish for his parents to drop dead speaks for itself. Their adoption of Hungaricized names also suggests the need to assume a new identity; after all, Rákosi used to be Róth, Gerő used to be Singer, Farkas used to be Wolf, Vas —whose grandfather was a rabbi—used to be Weinberger, Gábor Péter, the sadistic chief of the political police, used to be Benő Auspitz, Sándor Nógrádi used to be Grűnberger, Márton Horváth used to be Schiller, and so on. That approximately 70 to 80 percent of the leadership of the political police known by its dreaded acronyms ÁVO and then ÁVH —department heads and other higher ups—was Jewish[1] also symbolized

1. Estimate given by Róbert Gábor (see chap. 1, n. 13). Prior to his escape to the United States in the fall of 1947, Gábor had cooperated with the most secret of all U.S. intelligence services called the Secret Intelligence Branch—nicknamed "The Pond"—by providing extensive information on the personnel, organizational structure, and activities of the dreaded "Department for the Defense of the State" (ÁVO). A copy of his report on

a psychological break with thousands of years of gentle Jewish tradition
—both compensating for the presumed weaknesses of their forefathers and
assuming a new identity.

Jewish participation in the activities of the Hungarian Communist
movement and of the ÁVO stemmed from two sources. First, the appeal of
radicalism and of a harmonious society to Jewish intellectuals everywhere,
including Western Europe and North America, was apparently particularly great in Hungary because of some of the peculiarities of Hungarian
history (see chapter 2). As a result, many of the top leaders of the
Hungarian Communist movement were Jews. Of the fifteen members
of the first Central Committee of the Communists' party of Hungary,
founded in 1918, at least ten were Jewish. About three-fourths of the 200
high officials of the 1919 Hungarian Soviet Republic or Commune were
Jewish. From Béla Kun to Gerő, every secretary general of the Communist
party was Jewish. Thus, most of the reliable cadres available after 1944–45
were of Jewish background, and this applied not only to the Muscovites
but to the home Communists as well. Second, among Jews who joined the
movement after World War II many did so because of recent experiences in
concentration camps and labor battalions. They sought to avenge the
recent past, believing that the Soviet Union and the Hungarian Communist party, having distinguished themselves in the struggle against Fascism in general and Nazi Germany in particular, would support their
claim for retribution. For Jews in the middle echelons of the party and in
the ÁVO, the unstated motto seemed to be "Never Again!"

The resulting anti-Semitism in postwar Hungary differed from earlier
expressions of Hungarian anti-Semitism in that it was now largely, though
not exclusively, directed against "the new Jew"—tough, unforgiving,
revengeful—and against "Jewish political authority" as symbolized by the
Communist party.

The Soviet leaders had been aware of the implications of such a development when they sought to exclude Jews from the Provisional Government.
It should be recalled that Molotov, whose wife had been exiled by Stalin
because she was Jewish, had told members of the Hungarian armistice
delegation in November 1944 to include Muscovites, but not Jews, in the
new postwar government. "Jews must be counted out," he stated matter-of-
factly. Reflecting Soviet policy, Rákosi (who was in Moscow at the time)
immediately wrote Vas (who was already in Hungary) that he should not
count on being a member of the party's top leadership for the time being

ÁVO, prepared immediately after his departure from Hungary, was lent to me by Mr.
Gábor.

because the "Christian Imre Nagy" had to be added to the (Jewish) foursome—Rákosi himself, as well as Gerő, Révai, and Farkas.[2] Further exemplifying Soviet policy, after the 1945 elections, according to Vas, Marshal Voroshilov personally decided against the appointment of Farkas as minister of internal affairs, "suggesting" Nagy instead. Making an obscure distinction, Moscow nevertheless allowed that Jewish-born "foursome" to run the party for a decade; there were times between 1945 and 1956 when the majority of the Politburo was of Jewish background.[3]

Though others perceived them as Jews, these leaders of the Hungarian Communist party did not or did not want to see themselves that way —indeed, they tried to hide their identity. True, Hungarian Jews, unlike their counterparts in Russia, Poland, and Romania, had always tended to assimilate; in very large numbers, they had adopted Hungarian-sounding names. But Rákosi and his colleagues were not merely assimilated Jews; they pretended not to be or ever to have been Jewish. For one small example, Rákosi even tried to shed his urban accent lest his audience identify him with Jews or with the "Jewish" city of Budapest. Trying to speak the folksy language of the countryside, he inserted many a Hungarian proverb into his speeches. For his part, Révai asserted his Hungarianness by being an early and strong promoter of populist literature, the content of which was deeply nationalist and occasionally anti-Semitic.

The Hungarian Communist party did not openly embrace anti-Semitism, of course, but its demagogic outbursts against so-called black marketeers was but a veiled appeal for the support of Fascist and anti-Semitic small-fry. During the course of a couple of ugly anti-Semitic incidents in 1946 in the cities of Kunmadaras and Miskolc, the Communist press spoke with understanding of the "people's anger" against the (Jewish) merchants.

---

2. Rákosi's letter to Vas, the content of which has been confirmed to me by Mr. Vas, is quoted in Mihály Korom's unpublished doctoral dissertation (see chap. 1, n. 30), pp. 103–4 and p. 303. Significantly, Korom's book (see chap. 1, n. 11), though based on his dissertation, fails to mention the Soviet leaders' concern about the Hungarian Communist party's Jewish leadership.

3. Of the eleven members of the 1945 Politburo, for example, at least six were of Jewish origin. Thus, it is likely that Moscow did not really seek to exclude Jews from the leadership of the party, only limit their number. Stalin might have assumed that "rootless Jews" could be more easily controlled than "Christian" Hungarians. Moscow appeared to be more consistently opposed to Jews occupying high *government* positions than *party* positions. For a pioneering study demonstrating the role played by members of different minorities, including especially Jews, in the establishment of Communist regimes in Eastern Europe, see R. V. Burks, *The Dynamics of Communism in Eastern Europe* (Princeton, N.J.: Princeton University Press, 1961). For Soviet attitudes toward Hungary's Communist leaders of Jewish origin in the 1950s, see chap. 6, below.

Encouraging the mobs, Rákosi himself stated: "There is a place in a democracy for spontaneous acts of the masses, and it is only right that the people should take justice into their own hands."[4] While the more principled Social Democratic party and two small urban parties, the Citizen's Democrats and the Hungarian Radicals, were prepared to risk their popularity by distinguishing between Jews and black marketeers, the Communists were not. The same three parties, but not the Communists, also promptly criticized anti-Semitic remarks made every now and then by such populist leaders of the National Peasant party as Péter Veres and József Darvas.[5]

Before the elections in 1945, the Communist party went so far as to attract small-time Hungarian Fascists, including members of the pro-Nazi Arrow Cross party, to the Communist party. Who gave the order for this effort and how many such ex-Fascists were so recruited is unknown, but it is known that it was done and how it was done. Very simply, a potential recruit was told by a provincial party secretary or a Communist member of the political police that his past would be forgotten—that he would not be tried for wartime activities—if he signed an affidavit stating that he regretted his past and that he would support the policies of the Communist party from then on.[6]

The recruitment drive was partly successful, especially among unskilled industrial workers. A comparison of the results of the 1945 parliamentary elections with those of 1939 shows that an exceptionally large number of voters supporting the Communist party in 1945 had voted for the Arrow Cross party in 1939. This was demonstrably the case in the working-class

4. As quoted in Paul Lendvai, *Anti-Semitism Without Jews* (New York: Doubleday, 1971), p. 306. For further details, see George Garai, *The Policy toward the Jews, Zionism, and Israel of the Hungarian Communist Party, 1945–1953* (Ph.D. diss., London School of Economics and Political Science, 1979).

5. For example, during the election campaign of 1945 Veres told his audience in the town of Hajdúszoboszló that the National Peasant party he chaired "does not want any aliens: neither Swabians nor Jews." József Darvas, another nominal leader of that party but in reality a secret member of the Communist party, noted that, "There is a stratum here which demands for itself privileges on account of its past sufferings. If by reason of suffering anybody has the right to get compensation, then it is the working people of Hungary. In the past we condemned racial persecution, now we do not recognize racial privileges." *Magyar Nemzet*, August 31, 1945. The same daily, which was loosely associated with the Smallholders' party, went even further by publishing an unsigned letter to the editor: "In what way can they [the Jews] be said to have suffered when they returned home [from concentration camps and labor battalions] much fatter than when they had left? . . . There are certainly more Jews in this country today than before they were taken away for a holiday." Ibid., September 6, 1945.

6. A blank copy of such an affidavit, which appears to be genuine, is in my possession.

district of Csepel, an industrial town on the outskirts of Budapest that the Communists proudly called "Red Csepel" in 1945—the same town Arrow Cross "greenshirts" had equally proudly proclaimed as "Green Csepel" in 1939.[7] In some areas, then, the effort paid off as the Fascist small-fry, thoroughly intimidated if not convinced, signed up and even voted for the Hungarian Communist party. In other areas of the country, however, the recruitment drive only swelled the party's membership roster. For when the results of the 1945 elections were counted, it turned out that in a few east Hungarian districts the Communists received fewer votes than they had members—an embarrassing reminder of the circumstances under which the Communist party had drafted new recruits.

Evidence of the Communist party's cynical approach to, and manipulation of, the issue of anti-Semitism also includes its (Jewish) leaders' casual comments and behavior. For an anecdotal example, Rákosi once called in for consultation one of the younger home Communist leaders, Géza Losonczy. In a country where it was, and remains, customary to identify someone as "one of us" or "one of them" (Jewish or non-Jewish), Losonczy was obviously of non-Jewish background. Rákosi wanted Losonczy to undertake a different assignment in the cultural realm, making his case by advancing a few derogatory comments about "all the Jews" occupying high cultural positions in the country and expecting Losonczy to appreciate his anti-Semitic sentiment. Losonczy, who otherwise admired Rákosi at that time and hence accepted the new assignment, was still neither amused nor impressed.[8] For another example, at a Central Committee meeting on October 11, 1945, where the disappointing results of the just-concluded municipal elections were evaluated and preparations for the forthcoming parliamentary elections were made, Gerő allowed—in the unpublished part of his remarks—that "rich Jews" should be blamed (among others) for the Communist party's difficulties and problems.[9]

There is no definitive reason why these Communist leaders behaved the way they did. One complex psychological interpretation is that they toler-

7. For a block-by-block, quantitative study of the 1939 elections in Csepel, see György Ránki, "The Fascist Vote in Budapest in 1939," in S. U. Larsen et al., eds., *Who Were the Fascists?* (Oslo: Universitetforlaget, 1980). Ránki, a preeminent Marxist historian in Hungary, reports a "positive correlation" between the percentage of workers and the percentage of votes cast for the Arrow Cross party (p. 402). On the 1945 elections, see data in Ferenc Gáspár, ed., *Források Budapest történetéhez 1945–1950* [Sources on the History of Budapest 1945–1950] (Budapest, 1973), pp. 172–82.

8. The Rákosi-Losonczy conversation (date uncertain, but probably mid-1946) was related to me by one of the late Losonczy's closest friends and comrades.

9. Extensive summaries of the minutes of this important Central Committee session are in my possession.

Table 4.1   November 1945 Election Results in Three
Budapest Districts Compared to Voting Results Elsewhere

Party	Combined vote of 5th, 6th, and 7th districts (%)		Budapest (%)	Greater Budapest (%)	National (%)
Smallholders	69,153	(38.2)	50.5	47.5	57
Social Democrats	53,156	(29.4)	23.7	26.3	17.4
Communists	45,513	(24.1)	19.6	21	17
Citizen's Democrats	10,116	(5.6)	3.9	3.1	1.7
National Peasants	2,804	(1.5)	1.6	1.5	6.8
Hungarian Radicals	2,168	(1.2)	0.7	0.6	0.1
	180,910	(100)			

Source: Adapted from Ferenc Gáspár, ed., *Források Budapest történetéhez* [Sources for Budapest's History] (Budapest, 1973), pp. 181–82.

ated and even sparked a new wave of anti-Semitism in order to fulfill two contradictory needs at once: the need to punish their parents and grandparents for the "shame" of being Jewish and the concurrent need to punish themselves for the thought of wanting to break with their families' past. A less complex interpretation is that they were so committed to the quest for power—and so fanatical—that they would do anything to advance their goal and thus demonstrate to Stalin, the new father figure, that they were worthy of his respect.

But what about the "average Jew?" It is known that in 1945–46 at least half of the Jewish population in Budapest sought to leave Hungary, hoping to reach either the United States or Palestine.[10] That unsurprising sentiment aside, was the same Hungarian Communist party that could attract part of the old Arrow Cross vote also able to obtain Jewish support?

Although there is no precise way to determine how Jews voted in the 1945 parliamentary elections, it is possible to extrapolate the "Jewish vote" on the basis of the voting pattern in the three mid-town districts of Budapest—the fifth, the sixth, and the seventh—which had an unusually large number of Jewish residents. As table 4.1 shows, 180,910 votes

10. Survey by the Hungarian Institute of Public Opinion, as reported by Robert Blumstock, "Public Opinion in Hungary," in Walter Connor, Zvi Y. Gitelman et al., eds., *Public Opinion in European Socialist Systems* (New York: Praeger, 1977), p. 142.

were cast in these districts. Of these votes, the Smallholders' party received 69,153 (38.2 percent of the total); the Social Democratic party 53,156 (29.4 percent); the Communist party 43,513 (24.1 percent); and the Citizen's Democratic party 10,116 (5.6 percent).[11]

When the voting pattern in the three districts is compared to the results in Budapest, Greater Budapest, or the country as a whole, the conclusion is clear: these heavily Jewish, middle-class districts essentially reflected the city-wide voting pattern—with some interesting, though minor differences. Specifically, a comparison of results in the three districts with those in Budapest shows that (a) the liberal Citizen's Democratic party obtained 44 percent *more* votes in these districts than it did in Budapest as a whole; (b) the Social Democrats and the Communists received 24 and 23 percent *more*, respectively; while (c) the Smallholders' party, which did not do as well in the capital city as it did in the countryside, received 24.5 percent *fewer* votes in the three districts than it did even in Budapest.

Assuming that the Jewish vote is reflected in the results of the inner districts, it seems that many Jews felt attracted to the one clearly liberal, Western-oriented, bourgeois party on the political scene, the small Citizen's Democratic party, and they also felt "safe" with the Social Democrats and the Communists as well. All three of these parties put up at least one, and some ran several, Jewish candidates for election, while Jews were all but absent from the Smallholders' list of candidates. For the Hungarian Jewry, the Smallholders thus presumably came to represent the past, not the Arrow Cross or Nazism, of course, but the Horthy regime and its more genteel anti-Semitism in the interwar period. After all, some of the leaders of the Smallholders' party—including President Zoltán Tildy whose future son-in-law turned out to be Jewish—voted for anti-Jewish legislation in the late 1930s. More importantly, the Smallholders' party was simply not an urban party, and for that reason, too, the Jewish vote went elsewhere.

Of all the votes cast in the country, perhaps one in four or one in five Jews voted for the Communists, at most 25,000 to 30,000 of the 110,000 or so adults who survived the holocaust. Depending on one's perspective, this may seem a *large* number given what was known about the Nazi-Soviet pact; what the Communists did to attract small-time Arrow Crossists to their party; and, above all, what the Hungarian Communist party failed to do to counter anti-Semitic outbursts. Moreover, in view of the

11. The "Jewish vote" is extrapolated from the actual figures as reported in Gáspár, *Források Budapest történetéhez*.

fact that "45 percent of the gainfully employed Jews were independent businessmen in industry and commerce, or belonged to the liberal professions,"[12] Jewish economic interests also militated against the Communist party. On the other hand, however, the number of Jews voting for the Communists may seem *small* given what *all* Jews felt: that if it had not been for the Red Army, they would not have survived. Hence, Jews who supported the Communist party did so because they were grateful to the Soviet Union for being alive.[13]

It appears, then, that proportionally not many more Jews, if any, stood behind the Communist party than did the rest of the urban population. Therefore, Cardinal Mindszenty's remark about "Jewish-Communist Hungary" was not particularly well-founded; it was also perplexing because the cardinal had approached the Jewish question during the war with restraint and even some empathy. Hence his remark should be seen as a reflection of widespread popular sentiments blaming the Jewish-born Communist leaders for the Sovietization of Hungary. Of course, *these* sentiments were well-founded. But so was the feeling of the "average Jew" who blamed the same Jewish-born Communist leaders for the new wave of postwar anti-Semitism; after all, these leaders perpetuated and exacerbated that old and odious division between Christians and Jews in Hungarian society by adding new fuel to an old fire.

12. Lendvai, *Anti-Semitism*, p. 309.

13. Cf. István Bibó, "A zsidókérdés Magyarországon" [The Jewish Question in Hungary], in Bibó, *Harmadik Út* [The Third Road] (London: Magyar Könyves Céh, 1960), pp. 227–354. Written in 1948, Bibó's scholarly study on Hungarian anti-Semitism before, during, and after World War II remains a unique example of judicious and occasionally even brilliant analysis. Under prevailing circumstances, it was also quite courageous of Bibó to assert that, "Neither captivity during the war, nor internment, nor police brutality can compare to what happened to the Jews. . . . Mentioning any of those [hardships] under the same breath with the massacre of the Jews is nothing but either frivolous or malicious" (pp. 250–51). See also Péter Hanák, ed., *Zsidókérdés, asszimiláció, antiszemitizmus* [Jewish Question, Assimilation, Anti-Semitism] (Budapest, 1984) and an informative collection entitled *Zsidóság az 1945 utáni Magyarországon* [Jewry in Post-1945 Hungary] (Paris: Magyar Füzetek, 1984).

5

The End in Szklarska Poreba

By the time the founding meeting of the Cominform got under way on September 21, 1947, in Szklarska Poreba—a stunning resort high in the mountains of Polish Silesia—Stalin's differentiated plan for postwar Europe had ceased to produce new gains for the Soviet Union. Both the Popular Front strategy of domestic cooperation through coalitions with non-Communist parties in Western and in East Central Europe as well as the Popular Front strategy of international cooperation with the West had outlived their usefulness.

Gone was the spirit of 1943 or 1944 when an influential American magazine like *Life* could draw political conclusions from its nebulous assertion that the Russians "look like Americans, dress like Americans, and think like Americans." Gone were the days when *Reader's Digest*, of all magazines, would publish the condensed version of former U.S. ambassador Joseph E. Davies's extraordinarily naive, pro-Soviet memoirs. Who could even remember the time, three short years earlier, when respectable people in the West used to explain away Stalin's "occasional stubbornness" by claiming that he was but the victim of faceless bureaucrats in the Politburo? Indeed, the once prevalent American image of a benign and trustworthy Uncle Joe had been replaced by a widely perceived reality called the Soviet totalitarian menace.

The cold war was under way. The West, which had construed the various wartime agreements and deals to mean that Soviet presence on the continent would end after the cessation of hostilities or at least after the conclusion of the peace treaties, had lost hope for continued cooperation. For his part, Stalin felt that the West had neither appreciated nor reciprocated for the restraint he believed was inherent in his differentiated postwar policies. Although he had tried to hold back the West European Communist parties and although he had even allowed free elections in

Hungary and Czechoslovakia—no doubt to divert attention from the rapid seizure of power in Poland, Romania, and Bulgaria—the West had failed to take notice of the subtle difference in his approach to the three "regions" of Western, East Central, and Eastern Europe. From Stalin's perspective, the West was presently repudiating those wartime deals that, in his view, had entitled Moscow to maintain a sphere of "control" in Eastern Europe and a sphere of "influence" in East Central Europe in exchange for Communist "restraint" in Western Europe.

While by his own standards Stalin had pursued a calibrated policy, what the West saw was Communist insurgency in Greece, rapid takeovers in Poland, Romania, and Bulgaria, and gradual moves toward the seizure of power elsewhere. Despite his carefully designed "Polish trade-off," then, Stalin could no longer deflect Western resistance to what the West had come to perceive as a general Communist offensive *everywhere* in Europe.

Thus, with the Grand Alliance shattered—and given the removal of Communists from the governments of Western Europe and the still-incomplete takeovers in East Central Europe—it was time for Stalin to initiate drastic changes in policy. He made the founding meeting of the Cominform the turning point in his approach toward the West and toward the international Communist movement, and it was at this crucial meeting that he began to lay the groundwork for a sinister move against Yugoslavia, too.

When the delegates representing nine European Communist parties arrived in Szklarska Poreba, a small health and winter-sports resort some five thousand feet high up in the Sudetan Mountains of Polish Silesia, they were ready to form a new advisory or coordinating body called Cominform. By the time they arrived, the organizers had hastily emptied the resort of vacationers; only policemen on duty stayed on to guard the arriving veterans of the international Communist movement. The Polish hosts were represented by Władysław Gomułka and Hilary Minc, the Yugoslavs by Eduard Kardelj and Milovan Djilas, the French by Jacques Duclos and Étienne Fajon, the Italians by Luigi Longo and Eugenio Reale, the Czechoslovaks by Rudolf Slánský and Štefan Baštovanský, the Hungarians by József Révai and Mihály Farkas, the Romanians by Ana Pauker and Gheorghe Gheorghiu-Dej, and the Bulgarians by Vlko Chervenko and Vladimir Poptomov.

The setting could not have been more impressive, the welcome more generous. From the top of the mountain nearby, the delegates could survey the breathtaking Polish landscape below and even parts of neighboring Czechoslovakia and the Soviet zone of Germany as well. The buildings were surrounded by a stately park measuring some five or six hundred yards across; the rooms, though not particularly elegant, were spacious and comfortable. There was plenty of caviar and vodka, not to mention the eight to ten dishes served for every lunch and dinner. There were lavish gifts for the delegates, too: a fine camera one day, a pair of pajamas another.

What the delegates soon learned was that Stalin had decided to replace the Popular Front strategy of the recent past with a more rigid left strategy of militancy against the West and against the Communists' coalition partners in all European countries. The official reason for this change notwithstanding, some, probably correctly, speculated that the new party line had something to do with the specter of "incipient diversity" in international Communism, Stalin's fear of the Communist parties' increasing autonomism.[1] In any case, the change did not take place from one day to the next, of course; Stalin had been concerned about the apparent erosion of Communist revolutionary élan for some time. The celebrated April 1945 article by Jacques Duclos might have been the first sign that Stalin was having second thoughts about the Popular Front approach. In that Moscow-inspired article, Duclos had specifically and sharply criticized the American Communist party for "revisionism" and attacked its leader, Earl Browder, for antiparty behavior.[2] It seemed likely at the time

1. The term is borrowed from Joseph R. Starobin. See his essay ("Origins of the Cold War," *Foreign Affairs* 47, no. 4 [July 1969]: 681–96) in which he offers the following conclusion:

> The origins of the cold war lie deeper, however, than any analysis of Russia's own interest. Nor can they be understood only in terms of an attempt to prevent economic recovery and political stability in Western Europe. The cold war's origins must be found in a dimension larger than the requirements of Soviet internal mobilization or the thrust of its foreign policy; they lie in the attempt to overcome the incipient diversity within a system of [Communist] states and parties, among whom the changes produced by the war had outmoded earlier ideological and political premises. The conditions for the transformation of a monolithic movement had matured and ripened. The sources of the cold war lie in communism's unsuccessful attempt to adjust to this reality, followed by its own abortion of this attempt. For Stalin the cold war was a vast tug-of-war with the West, whereby not only internal objectives could be realized but the international movement subordinated; its constituent parts went along—bewildered but believing—on the assumption that, in doing so, they would survive and prosper. . . . Thus, the cold war arose from the failure of a movement to master its inner difficulties and choose its alternatives.

2. The Duclos article was originally published in *Cahiers du communisme*, no. 6 (1945): 21–38. The English translation appeared in the New York *Daily Worker* on May 24, 1945, under the title: "On the Dissolution of the Communist Party of the United States." Significantly, the end of the coalition-seeking approach was recognized by American Communists only *after* the founding meeting of the Cominform. In a statement, the party declared: "The present political situation in the United States is such that the Communist Party should not affiliate." *Political Affairs*, December 1947, pp. 1141–42.

that Duclos—and Stalin—had only meant to signal their displeasure at the *excessive zeal* with which Communists were carrying out Moscow's calibrated policies.

It was in Szklarska Poreba where Stalin definitely signaled a dramatic turn in international Communism—from right to left, from gradualism to militancy. For, by the autumn of 1947, his early doubts had crystallized. In Western Europe the Communist parties had allowed themselves to be removed from their countries' governments. In East Central Europe the gradualism he had devised for this area was thwarted by the Yugoslavs who, contrary to his vision, had seized power too soon; it was frustrated by the Finns and the Austrians whose quest for power had failed altogether; and it was even foiled by the Czechoslovaks and the Hungarians who had not moved soon enough to consolidate their power. In Eastern Europe Stalin had reason to be satisfied with what was happening; yet even here he could find the Gomułka-wing in Poland too pertinacious, too intractable, somewhat independent.

To present the rather abrupt change in policy without giving the impression that he had been wrong or inconsistent, Stalin needed the Yugoslav Communists' assistance. Then, as always, the Soviet party insisted on being consistently correct, and Stalin of course was infallible. If so, how could the two Soviet representatives at the Cominform meeting, Andrei Zhdanov and Georgi Malenkov, put forth Stalin's militant line without criticizing Stalin's previous gradualist line? And how could they prevent the Yugoslavs, who had advocated such a militant line all along, from asking the embarrassing question as to why Stalin had to wait so long to shelve his "capitulationist" Popular Front ideas? Would not Tito's representatives, Eduard Kardelj and Milovan Djilas, claim to have been "consistently correct"?

To protect Stalin's authority, Zhdanov employed the simple device of shifting blame for the gradualist sins of the recent past by pretending that it was the Communists of Western and East Central Europe who had failed to implement Stalin's policies correctly and hence it was they, not Stalin, who were at fault.

The more complex device Zhdanov employed aimed at the entrapment of the Yugoslav Communists. The two Yugoslav delegates had been asked to come to the Cominform meeting a day or two before the opening session in order to consult with the Soviet representatives. Hoping to use the occasion to discuss a couple of misunderstandings between the two parties, Kardelj and Djilas were happy to oblige. And what they learned and what they were asked to do were both surprising and satisfying: at long last, Stalin was ready to turn against the gradualist right in international Communism and he asked for the Yugoslavs' support. Would the Yugoslav comrades criticize the "insufficiently militant" Communist parties of Western and East Central Europe for relying on parliamentary methods to gain power, for trusting Social Democrats, for failing to see through imperialist designs?

Kardelj and Djilas did not understand in time that Stalin's cordiality toward the Yugoslav party would be short-lived, and that there was a price to be paid for the harsh attacks they were urged to deliver. For in a deceitful political scheme strikingly similar to his tactics during the factional struggles of the 1920s,[3] Stalin, through his representatives, presently instigated the Yugoslav left to censure the gradualist right, all the while contemplating the next round when he would use the right, by then properly humbled, to bring the self-righteous and stubborn Yugoslavs under control.[4] When, several months later, Kardelj and Djilas finally realized that in preparation for the 1948 confrontation Stalin had turned them loose to "create a gulf" between the Yugoslav party and the others, and that Stalin was thus planting the seeds of bitter hostility toward the Yugoslavs among Communists everywhere,[5] it was too late. Most participants left Szklarska Poreba with a sense of brooding resentment against the humiliation inflicted on them by Kardelj and Djilas, and when in 1948 the time came to retaliate they would be as vehement and zealous in their denunciation of the Yugoslavs as Kardelj and Djilas had been of them.

An Acrimonious Gathering

From official accounts published afterward, the outside world could learn some of what happened at the founding meeting of the Cominform, but not much.

3. At that time, Stalin had first allied himself with Bukharin and others on the right to oust Trotsky, Zinoviev, and others on the left, but shortly thereafter he had the remnants of the left help him remove his erstwhile ally and their former antagonist, Bukharin.

4. I am indebted to Robert C. Tucker for suggesting this as a possible interpretation of Stalin's motives. Subsequently, I asked Milovan Djilas in an interview held in Belgrade in the summer of 1980 if he thought, in retrospect, that he and Kardelj had been trapped by Stalin. Djilas told me that he and his colleagues in the Yugoslav Politburo had discussed this possibility at several meetings in 1948. In the absence of firm evidence one way or another, they could only speculate, but of all the Yugoslav leaders it was especially Tito who believed that Stalin was devious enough to set them up in order to isolate them in the movement. "And Tito knew Stalin well," Djilas added.

5. Vladimir Dedijer, *Tito* (New York: Simon and Schuster, 1953), p. 295, where Dedijer also notes: "It was no accident that Yugoslavia was given top place at the first [Cominform] meeting. The intention was to bind her as tightly as possible to this organization in order to facilitate the blow that was to follow."

Zhdanov's "two-camp" speech received the most attention, and his message was clear: the era of cooperation between the Soviet Union and the West had come to an end. His reasoning was simple: "The more the war recedes into the past," he declared, "the more distinct becomes . . . the division of political forces operating in the international arena into two major camps: the imperialist and anti-democratic camp on the one hand and the anti-imperialist and democratic camp on the other." Although Soviet foreign policy was still to be based on long-term coexistence between socialism and capitalism, Zhdanov no longer expected the West to reciprocate.

He identified the Truman Doctrine and the Marshall Plan as extreme manifestations of American imperialism, steps reflecting aggressive military and strategic intent as well as a commitment to economic expansion and ideological warfare. Supported by Great Britain and France, American imperialism was said to aim at the enslavement of Europe—making it a "49th state"—and at unleashing a new war against the Soviet Union. According to Zhdanov, the United States was also aided by right wing Social Democrats—such as British Prime Minister Clement R. Atlee and Foreign Secretary Ernest Bevin, French Premier Paul Ramadier, the German opposition leader Kurt Schumacher, Austrian President Karl Renner and Vice Premier Adolf Schaerf, and Italian Socialist leader Guiseppe Saragat—all of whom he now classified as turncoats and traitors "pushing their countries on the road to vassal-like dependence on the USA." Still, Zhdanov concluded, progressive forces led by the Soviet Union would prevail because they were united against imperialist expansion, and because they knew that any concession similar to Western appeasement of Hitler's Germany in Munich would only prompt the imperialists to engage in "even more shameless and aggressive" actions.[6]

6. The official report on the conference is *Informatsionnoe soveshchanie predstavitelei nekotorykh v Polshe v kontse sentyabrya 1947 goda* (Moscow, 1948); Zhdanov's speech appears on pp. 13–48. The most complete unofficial account is by one of the Italian delegates, Eugenio Reale, who left the Italian Communist party after the Soviet intervention in Hungary in 1956; see his *Avec Jacques Duclos au banc des accusés* (Paris: Plon, 1958). See also Lilly Marcou, *Le Kominform* (Paris: Presses de la Fondation Nationales des Sciences Politiques, 1977); Adam B. Ulam, *Titoism and the Cominform* (Cambridge: Harvard University Press, 1952); and William O. McCagg, Jr. "Domestic Politics and Soviet Foreign Policy at the Cominform Conference in 1947," *Slavic and Soviet Series* (Tel-Aviv) 2, no. 1 (Spring 1977): 1–30. Reale subsequently added to his initial account in "The Founding of the Cominform," in Milorad M. Drachkovitch and Branko Lazitch, eds. *The Comintern: Historical Highlights* (New York: Praeger, 1966), pp. 253–68. Another important delegate, Milovan Djilas, was kind enough to make available to me his recollections of the 1947 meeting; his memorandum is dated October 1, 1973.

In the West it was not particularly difficult to decipher the cold war message of Szklarska Poreba, all the more so because the militant language of the conference was promptly translated into widespread demonstrations and strikes throughout Western Europe. By the end of October, Italy's violent strikes claimed twenty-two lives, 154 others were wounded, and 118 anti-Communist clubs were damaged or destroyed. In France the first large-scale strike since World War II, organized by the Communists, took place in November; Duclos declared that France was rapidly becoming a satellite of the "Anglo-Saxons" and called for a new offensive against American expansionism.[7] Such militant actions and bellicose statements, combined with what was then known of the conference proceedings, confirmed the initial Western impression of increased Soviet hostility toward the West, particularly the United States. It was also believed, given the Soviet view of the existence of two unalterably opposed camps and the centrality of Europe in Soviet thinking, that Moscow's political and possibly even military offensive would be waged on the central front, in Europe.

Yet the official record of the conference concealed as much as it revealed. As the unofficial accounts of the conference would subsequently reveal, the delegates may have attended one of the most acrimonious gatherings in the stormy history of the world Communist movement. Especially the French and the Italians were subjected to bitter accusations, while criticism of the Czechoslovak and the Hungarian Communist parties, and of the Gomułka-wing in Poland, was more muted and rather circuitous. Heckling some of the speakers was the order of the day. Even Duclos was rudely and repeatedly interrupted by the Yugoslavs, the Russians, and the Romanians. Ana Pauker accused him and the Italian Longo of "parliamentary pirouetting." Zhdanov also turned on Duclos: "Do you not believe, Comrade Duclos, that the people would have understood the situation better if you had said that the Communist party was an opposition party? This expression has not occurred in either Thorez's or your speeches since May. If the Communist party observes that it has taken the wrong road, it must openly confess its mistake; this you have not done!" Malenkov joined the rumpus: "We would like Duclos to state his conclusions clearly, to tell

7. As quoted in *World Communist Movement: Selective Chronology 1918–1957* (Washington, D.C.: GPO, 1963), p. 309. As late as November 1946, French Communist party leader Maurice Thorez still upheld the validity of the Popular Front approach to power when he stated: "The progress of democracy around the world . . . makes it possible to visualize the march toward socialism by other paths than those followed by the Russian Communists. . . . The French Workers' party that we propose to constitute by fusing the Communists and the Socialists would be the guide to our new and popular democracy." *Times* (London), November 18, 1946.

us just what errors were committed by the leadership of the French Communist party."[8] Djilas denounced the two West European Communist parties for "political and ideological liberalism," adding that the French Communists had underestimated the Gaullist danger posed by the man who was known to be Churchill's "agent."[9] Zhdanov interrupted Luigi Longo: "You, Italian comrades, are bigger parliamentarians than [Premier] de Gasperi himself. You are the biggest political party, and yet they throw you out of the government."[10]

Humiliated and angry, Duclos at one point left the meeting, sat by himself on a bench in the park, and would not talk to anyone. Back at the conference hall, his voice still trembling, he admitted his party's "opportunism" and apologized to his inquisitors. So did Longo for the Italian party. In fact, Longo went so far as to ask Kardelj and Djilas, by far his most vocal critics, to explain their position privately and in greater detail. When they did, with Kardelj stressing the old Yugoslav view that a "fetish of coalitionism" had been infecting the Communist movement, Longo responded by reassuring the Yugoslavs that the Italian Communist party had not embraced reformism, social democracy, or liberalism and that therefore it had not deprived itself of proper revolutionary fervor. In any case, Longo added, the Italian Communist party had only followed Moscow's instructions.

With the obligatory and rather pitiful self-criticism behind them, Duclos and Longo left for home to implement the new party line. Puzzled, confused, and probably angry, they must have wondered why they had to accept rebuke for policies that had been initiated, approved, and promoted by Stalin himself.

The Turn of the East Europeans

Although the collusive Soviet-Yugoslav condemnation of the French and Italian parties and Zhdanov's "two-camp" speech were the two featured events in Szklarska Poreba, the sideshow was not without interest either. Three other parties—the Polish, the Czechoslovak and the Hungarian—had some difficulty explaining why they had continued to uphold the concept of peaceful transition to socialism for so long, why they still tolerated the existence of other political parties at this late date, why they failed to press for a radical economic program on the Soviet pattern.

Speaking for the Polish party, Gomułka turned out to be the only

8. Both quotations are in Reale, "Founding of the Cominform," p. 266.
9. Ibid.
10. Dedijer, *Tito*, p. 296.

delegate at the conference to express reservations about the proposed militant approach, about the very formation of the Cominform, and about adopting a strategy common to all Communist parties. In open session, he stubbornly repeated the view that political circumstances in Poland still called for Communist cooperation with, rather than the absorption of, the Polish Socialists' quite accommodating left wing. Neither the official record nor the unofficial accounts indicate how the other delegates responded to these by now outdated ideas, but Gomułka is known to have left the gathering skeptical about the new line in international Communism. In Warsaw he continued to argue "that the PPR [the Polish Communist party] would be wrong to vote for collectivization." When his Politburo colleagues failed to go along, Gomułka sought to circumvent their authority by claiming that "the Politburo should refer such an issue to the party's Central Committee."[11] An unreconstructed believer in the "Polish road" to socialism, Gomułka lost and was soon dismissed as his party's secretary general and placed under house arrest.

Unlike the openly divided Polish party, the Czechoslovak Communist party was apparently united behind the Cominform resolutions. Yet, because of the party's gradualist past, some of its leaders were very much on the defensive. Party chairman Gottwald was particularly concerned that his own close identification with the coalition-seeking, parliamentary approach would diminish his political authority. To end the era of "parliamentary pirouetting," and "in their anxiety about the fate of the revolution,"[12] Gottwald and his supporters went so far as to consider the immediate introduction of the hegemonic Yugoslav political order. Without Moscow having told them as yet exactly what to do, but having seen Soviet-Yugoslav collusion in Szklarska Poreba, they figured they should now emulate the Yugoslav system. An American counterintelligence agent was told by "informants from the Czechoslovak security police (STB) and army intelligence (OZB)" *for the first time in September 1947*—at the time of the constituent Cominform meeting—that a "takeover was bound to come, probably in early spring."[13]

While preparing for the seizure of power, an "extremely distrustful attitude"[14] developed within the Czechoslovak party. Circumstantial evi-

11. *Nowe Drogi*, September–October 1948: 40 ff.

12. Karel Kaplan as quoted in Pavel Tigrid, "The Prague Coup of 1948: The Elegant Takeover," in Thomas T. Hammond, ed., *The Anatomy of Communist Takeovers* (New Haven: Yale University Press, 1975), p. 408.

13. Claire Sterling, *The Masaryk Case: The Murder of Democracy in Czechoslovakia* (Boston: David R. Godine, 1982), p. 162.

14. Tigrid, "Prague Coup," p. 408.

dence suggests the possibility that a few party leaders—such as Julius Ďuriš, Antonin Zápotocký, Communists in the security apparatus, and perhaps even General Secretary Slánský—might have felt vindicated now by the more militant approach that they were suspected to have favored for some time.[15] True or not, Gottwald began to act in a highly defensive way, compensating for his gradualist orientation and trying hard to prove his loyalty to Stalin anew. That is why he sought to do what he presumed Stalin expected of him—to emulate the Yugoslav system.

After the Stalin-Tito break in mid-1948, Gottwald made still another turn to reflect the *latest* Soviet-ordained party line. He began to make preparations for an extensive and violent purge in his party, a purge whose main victim would be the "Titoist" Slánský himself.[16] Having so maneuvered to preempt the militant orientation by employing a scheme worthy of Stalin's schemes, Gottwald succeeded in making himself his party's unchallenged leader in the dark years of Stalinist intransigence to come.

As to the Hungarian Communist party, its predicament at, and after, Szklarska Poreba was similar to that of the Czechoslovak Communists. Its delegates had left Budapest for the conference on short notice, not knowing what to expect. If anything, they had reason to believe that the Hungarian Communists' record of the previous three years would earn them accolades from their foreign comrades. After all, the Hungarian party had applied consummate skill to the implementation of the Popular Front strategy. Operating in a hostile—anti-Soviet and anti-Communist—environment comparable only to Poland's and Romania's, the Hungarian Communists had still managed to become a dominant force in the country. In their dealing with the non-Communist parties, Secretary General Rákosi and ideologist Révai in particular possessed an uncanny knack of knowing when to be accommodating and when to be unyielding, when to rely on parliamentary methods and when to resort to intimidation and even terror, when to make concessions and when to threaten to make public an embarrassing story about a stubborn opponent's past.

After the Muscovite leadership convinced the home Communists of the need to shelve their militancy for the time being—a process that was completed by the spring of 1945—there were no differences over strategy or even tactics within the Hungarian Communist party, certainly none

15. For a fascinating account of factional infighting in the Czechoslovak Communist party on the eve of the February 1948 coup, see an unpublished, mimeographed study dated March 1979 by Karel Kaplan, "The Rise of a Monopoly of Power in the Hands of the Communist Party of Czechoslovakia, 1948–1949." Kaplan had complete access to Czechoslovak party archives during the "Prague Spring" of 1968.

16. Sterling, *Masaryk Case*, p. 219.

that were significant. True, it was widely rumored that the leading home Communist on the left, László Rajk, would have preferred to move along on the road to power more rapidly, and that the veteran literary critic and philosopher on the right, György Lukács, would have preferred a cultural orientation more closely attuned to Hungary's European tradition. But at least until the winter of 1947–48, and hence during the course of Hungary's democratic interlude, the leadership was both united and disciplined, and its commitment to the Popular Front strategy of gaining power over an extended period of time was all but absolute.

Yet so difficult was the balancing act the Communists were expected to perform, and so complex was the task of shaping a political order they concurrently sought to support and subvert, that there were times during the democratic interlude when all the Communists could do was to emulate their coalitionary partners/opponents—and play for time! As Zoltán Vas sums up his and his comrades' sense of uncertainty (in the unpublished version of his extraordinarily candid memoirs), they were unsure *even in 1946* whether "Stalin might not let Hungary come under the political influence of the [Western] allies in exchange for Soviet demands on Poland and Germany."[17] Indeed, Marshal Kliment E. Voroshilov told Soviet staffers of the Allied Control Commission *at the very end of 1946* that they should get ready to leave Budapest on short notice in case a final decision is made for the Soviet forces to evacuate Hungary.[18]

To be sure, the Communists had resorted to some harsh measures before the founding meeting of the Cominform in Szklarska Poreba. Early in 1947, they implicated Béla Kovács, the Smallholders' popular secretary general, in a so-called antidemocratic conspiracy, and the major political crisis they created that summer brought down the Smallholder-led government of Ferenc Nagy. On the eve of the Cominform gathering, on September 16, 1947, the party's Politburo began to prepare guidelines for the

17. Mr. Vas, who died in 1983 at the age of eighty, was kind enough to allow me to read the uncensored version of his memoirs.

18. This stunning piece of information was related to the historian Péter Gosztonyi by Tibor Szamuely, who served Voroshilov in his capacity as an NKVD or Soviet secret police lieutenant. According to Szamuely, Voroshilov also told his staff that, "Hungary will be a bourgeois democracy and therefore it is necessary to make important preparations. The task for 'Chekists,' among others, is to place in the government apparatus and social organizations such people who have not compromised themselves with the Soviet occupying forces as yet and who could be trusted in the future." Szamuely added: "At the beginning of 1947—perhaps in February?—further preparations were cancelled by headquarters. . . . I still don't know which agreement in world politics prompted Stalin not to evacuate Hungary in the end." Szamuely died in 1972 in London. *Irodalmi Ujság* (Paris), January 15-February 1, 1973.

"fusion" of the Communist and Social Democratic parties.[19] Still, much of what transpired at Szklarska Poreba took the Hungarian party by surprise. In his first speech at the conference itself, Révai still argued that the Hungarian political system was a "mixture made up of elements of the people's democracy and bourgeois democracy" and that it was uncertain as yet which of the two elements would prevail.[20] In a retrospective article written two years later, Révai candidly acknowledged his party's predicament during the democratic interlude:

At most we were feeling our way in the right direction. The Party didn't possess a unified, clarified, elaborated attitude in respect to the character of the People's Democracy and its future development. We must point this out, exercising self-criticism. And we must emphasize the fact that we received the decisive stimulation and assistance for the clarification of our future development from the Communist (Bolshevik) Party of the Soviet Union, from the teaching of comrade Stalin. The two sessions of the Cominform, the first in the fall of 1947, the second in the summer of 1948, were of fundamental help for us. The first taught us that the People's Democracy couldn't halt at any but the final stage of its destruction of the capitalistic elements. . . .[21]

Indeed, it was only after Zhdanov had classified Hungary as one of the people's democracies at Szklarska Poreba that the Hungarian delegation began to understand that the new militant line, the end of the Popular Front era, required a fundamental change in the party's policies at home. By the time he made his second speech, Révai sought to make it appear as if the Hungarian Communists had had "everything under control." Instead of pointing out that even in the recently concluded August elections the non-Communist parties had gained 78 percent of the vote, he boasted of the successful infiltration of the tiny National Peasant party (which could muster only 8 percent of the vote in 1947 and 7 percent in 1945): "It acts under our guidance," Révai declared. "The secretary [presumably Secre-

19. Erzsébet Strassenreiter, "Adalékok a magyarországi munkásegység történetéhez és az egységes munkáspárt létrejöttéhez" [On the History of Workers' Unity and of the Creation of the United Workers' Party], in Károly Suri, ed., *A munkásegység fejlődése Somogy megyében 1944–1948* [The Development of Workers' Unity in Somogy County 1944–1948] (Kaposvár, 1979), p. 61.

20. J. Révai, "O deyatelnosti TsK Vengerskoi kommunisticheskoi partii," in *Informatsionnoe soveshchanie*, pp. 256–79.

21. J. Révai, "The Character of a 'People's Democracy,'" *Foreign Affairs*, October 1949: 143–52.

tary General Erdei] is a Communist; one of the two ministers representing it in the government [presumably Darvas] is a Communist. Fifteen of its 32 deputies are Communists, eight are sympathizers."[22] With respect to Zoltán Pfeiffer's anti-Communist Hungarian Independence party, which had been created on the ruins of the Smallholders' party in mid-1947, Révai could only promise future action: "The destruction of Pfeiffer's party is indispensable," he tried to assure his comrades at the conference. "We shall use the police to carry it out."[23]

With Full Speed Ahead

When he returned to Budapest, Révai concluded in a secret memorandum to the Politburo that the Cominform had made "significant changes in the political and tactical direction of the Comintern's 7th Congress."[24] Although he sought to minimize the direct implications of this "significant change" for the Hungarian party in order to justify the gradualist sins of the recent past, his memorandum was full of self-critical remarks: the party was said to lack a firm ideological basis for its programs and policies, it overestimated the function of "parliamentary combinations," and it was given to "practicism." In order to fulfill its new mission, Révai urged the party to adopt six new steps: revision of the party's coalition strategy; reexamination of economic policy with a view toward supplanting the role of the bourgeoisie; changes in state administration and in the army's organizational structure; measures to raise the party's "militant spirit"; improvements in the work of the trade unions to avoid "bureaucratic degeneration"; and a thorough reorientation of ideological work to provide a theoretical basis for the implementation of all the other tasks and to explain anew the evolution of the country's political system since 1944.[25]

At one of many debates in the Politburo later that year, on December 10, 1947, Imre Nagy, apparently alone, argued against the new militancy. Couched in obtuse Marxist language, his main point was that external

22. Reale, "Founding of the Cominform," p. 255.

23. Ibid.

24. As quoted in Bálint Szabó, *Népi demokrácia és forradalomelmélet* [People's Democracy and Revolutionary Theory] (Budapest, 1974), p. 222. For another summary of Révai's report, see Ágnes Ságvári, *Népfront és koalíció Magyarországon 1936–1948* [Popular Front and Coalition in Hungary 1936–1948] (Budapest, 1967), pp. 272 ff. András Hegedüs, the future Stalinist prime minister who was then a rising star in the party bureaucracy, relates that Révai personally told him that he (Révai) and his colleagues were "very surprised by this whole turn of events in [September] 1947." András Hegedüs, *Élet egy eszme árnyékában* [Life in the Shadow of an Ideal] (Vienna: Zoltán Zsille, 1985), p. 71.

25. Szabó, *Népi demokrácia*, p. 220.

developments by themselves were not sufficient to prompt the adoption of radical internal measures; that the thorough nationalization of Hungary's economy was not warranted by prevailing socioeconomic conditions. He maintained that although the "industrial working class" (i.e., the Hungarian Communist party) had obtained a leading role in the country's political life, the economy remained predominantly capitalist and that fact was the decisive characteristic of Hungary's economic and hence political order (rather than international circumstances). In short, Nagy continued to hold on to the pre-Cominform view that the Hungarian transitional system was a "mixture" of the old and the new, a view that had been the Hungarian party line all along and that had been put forth by Révai as late as the beginning of the Szklarska Poreba gathering. But Nagy's position was by now untimely and therefore inoperative.

The post-Cominform majority view—the new party line—was summed up by Gerő, who served as chairman of one of the two commissions that the Politburo appointed to study the lessons of the Cominform meeting:

> As a result of domestic and international developments and contrary to our previous conceptions, a new and serious forward step is possible in the nationalization of industry and, in part, of commerce. As is known, our original plan was to effect nationalization gradually. . . . In my view, it would be a mistake to adhere to the original schedule and not to take advantage of the favorable circumstances.[26]

In another speech, Gerő stated that Hungary "had crossed the Rubicon between bourgeois democracy and people's democracy." János Kádár, then one of the party's secretaries, echoed that opinion when he asserted that the country had "caught up" with its neighbors in Eastern Europe. Rákosi, in sharp contrast to his earlier view according to which the stage of "people's democracy" did not yet denote the construction of "socialism," presently redefined the term suggesting that the building of a people's democracy was identical with the building of socialism, after all.

These statements and ideological revisions were accompanied by harsh measures in the political realm.

First, the results of the August 1947 elections were de facto revoked by the party's decision to encourage non-Communist politicians to leave the country—or cooperate with the new bogus coalition. Dozens if not hun-

---

26. Gerő's report to the Politburo is quoted in Iván T. Berend, *Ujjáépités és a nagytőke elleni harc Magyarországon 1945–1948* [Reconstruction and the Struggle Against Big Capital in Hungary 1945–1948] (Budapest, 1962), p. 373.

dreds of prominent political figures were thus forced to leave for the West in October–November; others signed up to serve the Communist regime.[27]

Second, as the centrist leaders of the Social Democratic party were among those who escaped, the Communists called for the "unification" of the two so-called working-class parties (which took place in mid-1948).

The third political development in the aftermath of the founding meeting of the Cominform had to do with the intensification of infighting within the Communist party leadership itself. It seems that Rákosi perceived a potential challenge to his authority less from the gradualist Imre Nagy, who was not given to political infighting and who was reportedly protected by Moscow, than from László Rajk, another Politburo member and then minister of internal affairs. For, not unlike Ďuriš and Zápotocký in Czechoslovakia, Rajk had been suspected by Rákosi to have favored a more militant approach since 1945; according to one account, Rajk and a few other home Communists had "considered the coalition 'corrupt,' and they craved a cleaner break with the past than Rákosi was offering."[28]

Although there is no evidence that he actually did so, Rajk *could* claim to have held the "correct" militant position all along and hence he was a potential threat to Rákosi, who had pursued the coalitionary games with gusto and, hence, felt vulnerable. A consummate master of political intrigues, Rákosi accordingly allowed, perhaps encouraged, Gábor Péter, the political police chief and thus Rajk's subordinate, to accuse Rajk at a closed leadership meeting in December 1947 of "anti-Party and anti-regime behavior;" at the same time Politburo member Farkas joined in with the equally incredible claim that, because of Rajk, "[the ministry of]

27. In the mid-1980s a Hungarian scholarly journal confirmed that while after the Cominform meeting the Communist party still professed to support the multiparty system, Rákosi was working hard toward its effective disappearance—by force if necessary. Speaking to a group of Communist functionaries in March 1948, for example, he explicitly anticipated the "liquidation" of several parties. ". . . We are going to make sure that the remaining reactionaries disappear from the scene," he said, ominously. Rákosi is quoted in Lajos Izsák, "Rákosi, Révai, Rajk a többpártrendszer felszámolásáról" [Rákosi, Révai, Rajk on the Liquidation of the Multi-Party System], *História* 6, no. 3 (1984): 34. Toward the end of 1947 a secret superagency called *kollégiumi testület* was created in the ministry of internal affairs "to assure the implementation of the Communist Party's guidelines." It was headed by László Rajk, the minister, and its five members were all leading party cadres. The apparent purpose of the superagency was to circumvent the authority of a few officials still in the ministry who were not party members or who were otherwise not considered to be fully reliable. See Béla Rácz, "A Belügyminisztérium ujjászervezése" [The Reorganization of the Ministry of Internal Affairs], *Levéltári Közlemények* 60, no. 1 (1970): 89–130.

28. William O. McCagg, Jr., *Stalin Embattled 1943–1948* (Detroit: Wayne State University Press, 1978), p. 268.

Internal Affairs was not in the Party's hand."[29] Next month Farkas went so far as to call Rajk an "enemy."[30] All this was said behind closed doors, of course. But in the autumn of 1948 Rajk was transferred to the ministry of foreign affairs. In May 1949, he was arrested as a Titoist, tortured, sentenced, and killed. His real crime was that his more militant sentiments had been perceived or presumed before either Stalin or Rákosi would come to regard them as timely—and he paid for them with his life.

It spoke well for Rákosi's political acumen that he had as effectively implemented the Stalinist policy of gradualism before Szklarska Poreba as he did the Stalinist policy of militancy and confrontationism after Szklarska Poreba. In the winter of 1947–48 he reduced the Hungarian coalition into a bogus coalition, a Communist political order in which a few nominally non-Communist figureheads served in order to cover up the dramatic change—the watershed—that took place in the party's policies after the Cominform's constituent meeting. The Hungarian Communists' solemn declaration made three short years earlier—"we do not regard the national collaboration [of the several political parties] as a passing, political coalition, as a tactical chess move, but rather a long-lasting alliance"—turned out to be a lie.

29. As quoted in Erzsébet Strassenreiter and Péter Sipos, *Rajk László* [László Rajk] (Budapest, 1974), p. 185.

30. Ibid.

PART TWO

Revolution and Reform

6

Moscow and Imre Nagy, 1953–1956

There are several unmarked graves in the northeast corner of one of Budapest's many cemeteries. On appropriate anniversaries, a few mourners —family and friends—come by and stand there. Occasionally, they bring flowers. Because the authorities have refused to confirm it, the visitors only suspect that three of the martyrs of the 1956 Hungarian revolution are buried there.[1] The three are Imre Nagy, prime minister and leader of the revolution, General Pál Maléter, his young and brave defense chief, and Miklós Gimes, one of Nagy's associates, a particularly gifted journalist. They were tried together and executed in 1958.

For Hungarians who remember him or know of him, Nagy was a rare politician. With his large and thick mustache, innocent, round face, inevitable pince-nez, and jovial demeanor, he looked, and was, straightforward and trustworthy. Though only sixty in 1956, his associates affectionately referred to him as *az öreg*, the old man, or as *Imre bácsi*, Uncle Imre. For that small group of young anti-Stalinist, reform-minded Communists who had surrounded him for a few short years before 1956—writers, journalists, and other political and intellectual hangers-on—Nagy was both a genuine father figure and the last hope for socialism with a human face. During the revolution, when suddenly everything seemed possible, he became the last hope for freedom and independence for all Hungarians. For before it was all over he had realized the dream of ten million Hungarians by withdrawing Hungary from the Warsaw Pact and reconstituting the postwar, multiparty coalition government.

Of course, his associates helped. The most astute anti-Stalinists from his original entourage—Géza Losonczy, Ferenc Donáth, and Miklós

---

1. Béla Lipták, "Searching for the Grave of Imre Nagy," *Wall Street Journal*, October 9, 1985, p. 33.

Vásárhelyi—eventually opened his eyes to the nature and scope of what was happening. Zoltán Tildy, the veteran Smallholder leader and postwar president of the Republic, emerged from eight years of house arrest to become his calm, de facto deputy. But Imre Nagy was both the leader and the symbol of the 1956 Hungarian revolution. And when he died for it in 1958, he did so without denying what he had done and without recanting what he had stood for.[2] A genuine hero, he belongs on the pedestal where his compatriots have put him.

Yet it is one of those paradoxes of political life in Eastern Europe that, until the last days of this short-lived revolution, *Nagy was also the man Moscow counted on, and could count on, to save its cause in Hungary.* Indeed, from the time of the first demonstration on October 23 to October 31, Nagy could only envisage a Hungarian future based on Soviet tutelage. With Soviet consent, he sought to make order by promising "reforms," assuming that the promise of such reforms would end the uprising.

Nagy's first turning point came on October 28 when he reached the conclusion that the *party* had to be changed, too. He had come to understand—and the Kremlin concurred—that the time for reform had passed, and hence his all but impossible historic mission was to reconcile Soviet power-political interests with those of a new—somewhat independent and somewhat pluralistic—Hungarian political order. He consulted with Anastas Mikoyan and Mikhail A. Suslov, the two Politburo members who were in Budapest, and with Yuri V. Andropov, the Soviet ambassador to Hungary, to gain their approval for the transfer of the functions of the hapless Central Committee to a new, six-member party Presidium. So anxious was Nagy not to circumvent Moscow that he called the Kremlin from Andropov's office that morning to obtain confirmation of the *authorization* he had just received from the Soviet representatives in Budapest. Whether he spoke with Nikita S. Khrushchev or someone else is not known, but he was told to make the change. Two days later, on October 30, when the new party leadership proved unable to impose order, Nagy was ready to meet one of the revolution's major demands by establishing a pluralistic political system. Before making his decision, he (and his deputy Tildy) once again asked for—and received—Mikoyan's approval for the creation of a genuine, four-party coalition government. In short, Nagy knew or thought he knew during the first hectic week of

2. Even the Hungarian government's White Book, which most tendentiously quotes from Nagy's testimony during the trial, suggests his stubborn determination. See *Nagy Imre és bűntársai ellenforradalmi összeesküvése* [The Counterrevolutionary Conspiracy of Imre Nagy and His Accomplices], (Budapest, n.d. [1958]).

the revolution what the Soviet Union wanted him to do "to save the cause of socialism" in Hungary and he acted accordingly.

Only his second turning point, which came on November 1, signified a parting of the ways between Nagy and Moscow. Soviet troops having reentered Hungary the night before, Nagy realized that morning that the Kremlin was no longer interested in finding a political solution to the crisis under his leadership. He felt betrayed. In vain had he consulted with the Kremlin; in vain had he gained Soviet approval for every major measure he had adopted between October 23 and October 31. The party was over. From the loyal Muscovite he had been all his life, this is when Nagy became a Hungarian revolutionary. On November 1, acting for the first time *without* Soviet concurrence, his government declared Hungary's withdrawal from the Warsaw Pact and the country's neutrality. On November 4, when its troops reached the capital, the Soviet Union overthrew the Nagy government and crushed the revolution.

My purpose in this chapter is neither to describe the revolution nor to judge Nagy's performance. In keeping with this book's theme, my interest is in drawing attention to the apparent flexibility, confusion, *and* duplicity in Soviet conduct and to the crucial impact of Kremlin infighting on Hungarian politics before and during the revolution.

From Moscow to Moscow

Except for a short absence from late 1949 to early 1951, Imre Nagy was a full member of the Hungarian Communist party's Politburo from 1944 to 1953. Having spent almost fifteen years in the Soviet Union as the party's expert on agriculture, he returned from Moscow to play a not insignificant role in the execution of the 1945 land reform. In 1945–46 he served as minister of internal affairs for a few months, but when he proved too gentle for that assignment he was asked to relinquish his post and take up another. As related previously, he is known to have expressed reservations about the scope and tempo of change in agriculture in the winter of 1947–48, and of the collectivization campaign in 1949, but then—as minister of crop collection for a few months—he was put in charge of implementing the very policies he had questioned. In 1952 he became a deputy prime minister with responsibility for agriculture. During all these years, however, he was never an influential decisionmaker.

Although Nagy publicly supported whatever the Hungarian Communist party decided to do, and although he exercised "self-criticism" whenever the Politburo majority considered his views erroneous, his colleagues disliked him from the beginning, and Rákosi as well as Gerő were said to have hated him.[3] If so, given Rákosi's extraordinary powers, how could Nagy keep his seat on the Politburo all these years and why was Rajk rather than the occasionally "difficult" Nagy chosen to be the "leader" of a "Titoist conspiracy" and sentenced to death? The only reasonable answer, confirmed by the then pro-Rákosi acolyte Zoltán Vas, was that Nagy had been protected by the Kremlin. It was probably especially Malenkov and Beria who considered Nagy a reliable and loyal party man. What is certain is that Nagy had early and important supporters in Moscow, perhaps Stalin himself, who had imposed him on Rákosi at the end of 1944. It should be recalled that at that time Rákosi, then still in Moscow, informed Vas that the "Christian" Nagy and not the "Jewish" Vas had been chosen to be the fifth highest-ranking member of the Politburo after the (Jewish) foursome of Rákosi, Gerő, Farkas, and Révai. Having been so installed by Moscow, Nagy survived—literally—through the dark years of Hungarian Stalinism, too, because he was a Muscovite and because somebody, somewhere in the Kremlin, looked after him and for this reason Rákosi did not dare to touch him.

Soviet confidence in Nagy was conclusively demonstrated in 1953, after Stalin's death in March and just before the outbreak of the June 17 riots in East Berlin. On short notice, the Kremlin invited a group of Hungarian leaders to Moscow for a meeting on June 13–14, specifying the precise composition of the delegation.[4] The group included Rákosi and Gerő, but not Farkas and Révai—a curious signal. Others who were told to appear were Nagy, then a deputy prime minister, István Dobi, the nonparty figurehead of the Presidential Council, and four younger party leaders (András Hegedüs, Béla Szalai, István Hidas, and Rudolf Földvári). According to Hegedüs, there might have been some tension between the new Soviet leaders and the Hungarians prior to the June meeting, but —even though he was a Politburo member—he did not know what it was about. There was no discussion of differences during the flight from Budapest to Moscow; he was in the dark as to what to expect. Because both he and Nagy were specialists in agriculture, it occurred to him that they might receive some "helpful criticism" from the Soviet comrades

3. Information by Zoltán Vas.
4. Except for Beria's reference to Rákosi having become "the Jewish king of Hungary" (see note 5, below), all quotes in this summary of the June 13–14, 1953, meeting in the Kremlin are drawn from the published accounts of two participants, Imre Nagy and András Hegedüs. See Imre Nagy, *On Communism: In Defense of the New Course* (New York: Praeger, 1957), and András Hegedüs, *Élet egy eszme árnyékában* [Life in the Shadow of an Ideal] (Vienna: Zoltán Zsille, 1985), especially pp. 188–97.

about that. If so, Hegedüs says, he looked forward to it. But agriculture was not a major item on the agenda.

The Soviet delegation included every important member of the post-Stalin Soviet Politburo: Malenkov, Khrushchev, Beria, Molotov, Bulganin, Mikoyan, Lazar Kaganovich, as well as Marshal Voroshilov, the Kremlin's veteran Hungarian expert. In no uncertain terms they let the Hungarians know that the Soviet Union was deeply dissatisfied with Rákosi's leadership and that he must give up either his position as prime minister or his position as the party's first secretary; he held too much power. The Hungarian economy was on the verge of collapse. The collectivization campaign had gone too far. The purges had decimated the party. Obviously well-informed, Beria even wanted to know why the wife of ÁVO chief Gábor Péter, Rákosi's personal secretary, was among those recently arrested. In reply, according to Hegedüs, Rákosi mumbled something about Stalin having told him that Péter was a CIA agent. Beria lost his cool: "As an old Bolshevik, you Rákosi must know that we really know how to break someone's back!"

From Nagy's account it appears that at one point the Soviet leaders called Rákosi aside for what turned into a particularly nasty, personal confrontation. For a starter, Beria accused Rákosi of trying to become "the Jewish king of Hungary." Referring to "Turkish sultans, Hapsburg emperors, Tartar kings, and Polish princes" who had all once ruled Hungary, Beria warned: "But, as far as we know, Hungary has never had a Jewish king. Apparently, this is what you have become. Well, you can be sure that we won't allow it."[5] At the same meeting, as related to Nagy by Malenkov, "We asked [Rákosi], 'Whom do you recommend as your deputy?' He could name no one. He had objections to everyone whose name was mentioned; he had something against everyone. Everyone was suspect except him alone. This appalled us very much." Nagy was also told by Molotov that Rákosi had "wanted a Premier [prime minister] who would have no voice in the making of decisions." Later, at a plenary session, the Soviet leaders "proposed" Nagy's appointment as prime minister and Gerő's and Hegedüs's appointment as Nagy's deputies. There and then, they also changed the composition of the Politburo, from which Farkas and Révai were left out for reasons neither requested nor given.

Nagy's appointment was all the more significant because it was not yet clear whether he as prime minister or Rákosi as the party's first secretary would be #1. In the Soviet Union, the head of the government, Malenkov,

5. Tamás Aczél and Tibor Méray, *The Revolt of the Mind: A Case History of Intellectual Resistance Behind the Iron Curtain* (New York: Praeger, 1959), p. 159.

was #1. For that reason, according to Hegedüs, Rákosi feared that his demotion was even more serious than it turned out to be. As they left one of the conference rooms in the protocol-conscious Kremlin, Rákosi was politely prompted by Nagy to be the first Hungarian to step outside. But, as Hegedüs was shocked to witness, Rákosi pushed Nagy ahead: "You go [first], Imre, you're the leader now."

The New Course Nagy was told to pursue as prime minister[6] received only perfunctory support from Rákosi, who was put on the defensive by every new measure announced by Nagy—about agriculture, about the new emphasis on light industry, or about the rehabilitation of political prisoners. After all, he was in charge when those "mistakes" had been made. For almost two years, then, Rákosi kept returning to Moscow for permission to reverse the reformist course—and to oust Nagy. On one such occasion, according to Nagy,[7] Khrushchev said: "Rákosi is responsible for the arrests. Therefore he does not want to release these people. He knows that he is guilty and will compromise himself." On another occasion, Khrushchev was said to have complained that, "The detainees are being released slowly. This is Rákosi's fault, because he hasn't taken the matter in hand. Rákosi alludes to the fact that his nerves are bad. Nerves don't count." When Rákosi tried to use the news of the ouster of Beria, presumably one of Nagy's supporters, to discredit Nagy, Khrushchev rebuffed the pro-Rákosi forces: "They can't hide behind Beria as Rákosi is trying to do. We were there, too, when these errors were ascertained, every one of us!" Malenkov echoed that view: "The faults we noted in June are being

---

6. This chapter does not attempt to treat the reforms enacted during the New Course and the intellectual ferment of 1953–56. For details, see Nagy, *On Communism*, and numerous scholarly and journalistic accounts including Miklós Molnár and László Nagy, *Imre Nagy: Réformateur ou révolutionnaire?* (Geneva: Droz, 1959); Tibor Méray, *Thirteen Days that Shook the Kremlin: Imre Nagy and the Hungarian Revolution* (New York: Praeger, 1959); and Aczél and Méray, *Revolt of the Mind*. For a comprehensive and elegant scholarly treatment of this subject—as, indeed, so many other subjects treated in this book—see Bennett Kovrig, *Communism in Hungary: From Kun to Kádár* (Stanford, Calif.: Hoover Institution Press, 1979), pp. 267–98. Two key documents from 1953 surfaced only in 1985 in a Hungarian *samizdat* publication in Budapest called *Hírmondó*. One, translated into English by Bill Lomax, is Nagy's previously suppressed speech to the Hungarian party's Central Committee on June 27, 1953; see "Imre Nagy's Secret Speech," *Labour Focus on Eastern Europe* 8, no. 1 (Summer 1985): 3–16. The other is the resolution of the same Central Committee session, passed on June 28, 1953, but withheld from the public; see "A júniusi határozat" [The June Resolution], *Irodalmi Ujság* (Paris) 36, no. 3 (1985): 11–14. Significantly, Nagy's 1953 "secret speech" to the Central Committee indirectly confirms Nagy's and Hegedüs's subsequent accounts of what the Soviet leaders so vividly said during the June 13–14 confrontation in the Kremlin.

7. All quotes in this paragraph are from Nagy, *On Communism*.

remedied very slowly. Rákosi has not taken the lead in remedying the faults." Khrushchev attacked Gerő, too: "Gerő has no words of self-criticism or feeling of responsibility for the serious mistakes of the economic policy."

As the struggle within the Hungarian party continued, the Kremlin appeared to favor Nagy over Rákosi for now. Nagy appreciated the confidence of "the leading Soviet comrades," their "sincere, plain and sharp criticism, which was given in a true party spirit," "their readiness to offer fraternal help," and "the great trust which they extended toward us."[8] In reality, that "trust" appeared to be limited; after all, both Rákosi and Gerő were allowed to retain their most important positions despite all that they had done. "I have to keep Rákosi . . . because in Hungary the whole structure will collapse if he goes," Khrushchev argued.[9] Yet, to the extent the Soviet leadership preferred Nagy, it was for good reasons. He was a Muscovite. He was not Jewish. He could speak Russian well. He was a loyal supporter of Soviet policies, under Stalin and now under his successors as well. He had played no role in the purges. By temperament he was earnest, disciplined, and reliable, if frequently stubborn. Though an early critic of the tempo of forced collectivization, he never publicly questioned party policy once adopted. As the new Soviet leaders were about to introduce their own New Course, Nagy was very much on their new wavelength. He was the man they needed.

On the Kremlin's Waiting List

As late as October 1954 Nagy was still riding high; Gerő, after a brief vacation in Moscow, was uncharacteristically supportive of him. But Soviet signals began to change in November. Mihály Farkas, that barometer of Soviet sentiments, was the first to reflect the new line: "There is no New Course . . . it is rightist to pursue it . . . the old road must be pursued, only some mistakes to be corrected."[10] In charge of culture and the press at the time, Farkas accordingly dismissed several leading Nagy supporters from the editorial staff of *Szabad Nép* on December 16.

Rákosi had just returned from a Soviet vacation, too. Having learned there of the new Soviet party line against the New Course and against right-wing deviationism, and looking for an opportunity to discredit Nagy, Rákosi began to say—behind closed doors as yet—that in Hungary,

---

8. "Imre Nagy's Secret Speech," p. 5.

9. As quoted in George Mikes, *The Hungarian Revolution* (London: Deutsch, 1957), p. 61.

10. Ferenc A. Váli, *Rift and Revolt in Hungary: Nationalism versus Communism* (Cambridge: Harvard University Press, 1961), p. 155.

too, right-wing deviationism had become the main danger. He said that it was an error to have favored light industry and to have allowed collective farms to disband. By so identifying Nagy's policies with the just-discovered "errors" of the recent past, Rákosi anticipated the charges Khrushchev would make against *his* as yet unnamed opponent (Malenkov) at the end of January.

It was against the background of the ascendancy of this newly formed anti-Malenkov coalition that an urgent invitation was sent to a group of Hungarian leaders to appear in the Kremlin on January 7, 1955. The Hungarian delegation was composed of Nagy, Rákosi, Gerő, Szalai, and Farkas. The Soviet Politburo was represented by Malenkov, Khrushchev, Mikoyan, Molotov, Kaganovich, and Bulganin. This time, Nagy was put on the carpet. Following Soviet custom, according to one source, the task of attacking him was given to his mentor Malenkov who, with a thick file in front of him, began to quote from Nagy's recent speeches and articles and then accused him of "slander against the Party," of contradicting "the Leninist principle of [democratic] centralism," of "underestimating the Party's governing role," of denying "the class struggle," of "opportunism," "chauvinism," and "demagogy." Obviously well briefed, Malenkov also cited facts and figures to show how the New Course, for which Nagy was now said to be responsible, had exacerbated Hungary's economic problems. Malenkov even knew of, and complained about, the small anti-Soviet demonstration during a Soviet-Hungarian water polo game in Budapest.[11]

It is clear in retrospect that Khrushchev, once one of the strongest supporters of Nagy and the New Course, had turned coat in order to get rid of Malenkov with the help of such Stalinist opponents of the New Course—and of Malenkov—as Kaganovich and Molotov. (Soon enough, in mid-1957, Malenkov would join Molotov and Kaganovich in an unsuccessful attempt to oust Khrushchev.) At this time, though, they all wanted to discredit Nagy in order to demonstrate the harm Malenkov's policies had supposedly done even outside the Soviet Union. As for Malenkov, he followed the usual Bolshevik formula, which required him to save himself by implementing the *anti*-Malenkov position. Malenkov was to purify himself by accepting responsibility for his, and Nagy's, advocacy of the New Course in the Soviet Union and in Hungary, a policy *everyone* in the Politburo had only recently favored. By so degrading himself, Malenkov was to be demoted but not ousted for the time being. In the summer of 1955 a

11. For a detailed account of this encounter, see Méray, *Thirteen Days*, pp. 22–28. The source for Méray's summary is not indicated, but subsequent public charges against Nagy generally confirm its accuracy.

secret Soviet memorandum was sent to the Communist leaders of Eastern Europe that clarified the meaning of and the concurrent rationalization for this Byzantine, Mafia-like affair. Seweryn Bialer, who saw it in Poland at the time, summarized the memorandum this way: "The policy of Malenkov, aside from the harm which it threatened in Soviet domestic matters, *concealed serious dangers for the countries of the People's Democracies and for the relations of the Soviet Union with these countries, an example of which is the situation in Hungary*."[12]

After Malenkov's demotion in February, Nagy's turn came in early March. His errors? "Undervaluating the leading role of the Party," "rightist opportunist deviation . . . concerning socialist industrialization," "rightist views . . . concerning the peasants," revision of "the Marxist-Leninist doctrine of the dictatorship of the proletariat," and more.[13] The only significant difference between Malenkov and Nagy was that Nagy did not exercise self-criticism and did not accept a lesser position in the government. That difference prompted Mikhail A. Suslov, the Kremlin's Hungarian specialist, to show up in Budapest to persuade Nagy to follow the "Malenkov formula." Would Comrade Nagy confess his errors? No. Would Comrade Nagy accept a lesser position in the government as Malenkov did? No.[14] In mid-April Nagy lost all his positions. He remained an ordinary party member until November 1955, when he was expelled from the party he had helped found in 1918. The day it happened, an irate Nagy told Tamás Aczél, a friend: "Look what they've done to me. . . . After so many years as a Party militant. . . . These absolute nonentities. . . . But I told them the truth. . . . I told them the truth. . . ."[15]

For now, Rákosi prevailed. He used the Malenkov affair, the way he had not been able to use the Beria affair, to take revenge for the humiliation he had suffered. For during the Beria affair Khrushchev and Malenkov had still been allies, and hence there was no need for Khrushchev to turn against Nagy and the New Course. During the Malenkov affair, however, Khrushchev needed the Stalinists to defeat Malenkov, and hence the New Course had to be reversed. Considerations of power preceded considerations of policy, and Nagy became the unwitting victim of such a very complex Kremlin free-for-all as well as Rákosi's pernicious maneuverings.

Presently, Nagy became a pensioner. He took long walks, held extensive talks with his growing number of admirers, and enjoyed his sudden,

12. Seweryn Bialer, "The Three Schools of Kremlin Policy," *New Leader*, July 29, 1957, p. 10. Emphasis added.

13. *Szabad Nép*, March 9, 1955.

14. Aczél and Méray, *Revolt of the Mind*, p. 324.

15. Méray, *Thirteen Days*, p. 41.

immense popularity. He also wrote a series of political essays and studies (which would be published in the West in 1957 under the title *On Communism*). In these studies he defended his Marxist-Leninist positions, angrily denounced Rákosi and his supporters, and respectfully praised the post-Stalin Soviet leaders' views and policies. Nagy took courage from the fact that Moscow apparently had not authorized his arrest; that in mid-1955 the Soviet Union made up with Tito's Yugoslavia, a leader and a country he admired; that the Austrian Peace Treaty, the Geneva Summit, and especially the 20th Congress of the Soviet party all pointed to change for the better, including his vindication and rehabilitation. He also took courage from an outpouring of support he received from intellectuals, mainly disillusioned Communist writers and journalists, whose "revolt of the mind" was rapidly gaining new adherents and new momentum every day.

By the summer of 1956, with the main act of the Malenkov drama and the 20th Congress behind them, and with signs of high elite tension and persistent instability in Hungary, the Soviet leaders began to take a second look at Rákosi. They were under tremendous pressure by their new friend Tito to oust him. Tito had taken the unusual and undiplomatic step of publicly and vehemently denouncing Rákosi and his cohorts: "These men," said Tito, "have their hands soaked in blood, have staged trials, given false information, sentenced innocent men to death. They have had Yugoslavia mixed up in all these trials, as in the case of the ["anti-Titoist"] Rajk trial, and they now find it difficult to admit before their own people their mistakes."[16] Tito had long despised Rákosi and favored Nagy; already in 1955 and especially in 1956 contacts were made between Yugoslavia and some of Nagy's supporters. In fact, Nagy managed to send his essays and at least one personal letter to Tito via the Yugoslav embassy in Budapest.[17]

At long last, on July 17, 1956, Mikoyan—on his way to Belgrade and as a present to Tito—stopped in Budapest to tell the Hungarian Politburo that Rákosi must go. This "wise leader" of Hungary, as he was officially called in Stalin's time, or the "bald murderer" as he was more commonly called, did not want to believe that Mikoyan was speaking for the Soviet comrades.[18] Only after Khrushchev confirmed the bad news on the phone did he resign, admitting a few of his errors and complaining of poor health. Then he left for the Soviet Union. His replacement was neither Imre Nagy nor the centrist János Kádár, but Ernő Gerő. Moscow must

16. *Documents on International Affairs, 1955* (London: Oxford University Press, 1958), p. 271.

17. Information by Miklós Vásárhelyi.

18. Váli, *Rift and Revolt in Hungary*, 234–35.

have still believed that order and stability could be restored by the Hungarian party following more or less the same policies Rákosi had pursued—without Rákosi himself.[19]

Why not Nagy? Were not the Russians having second thoughts about him, too? The first piece of evidence suggesting that they were came from a Hungarian sculptor, Zsigmond Strobl Kisfaludi, who was in Moscow at the beginning of the summer of 1956. He was commissioned to make a bust of Marshal Voroshilov. After a few drinks, Voroshilov was reported to have told the maestro: "Things do not go well in your country . . . Rákosi? A vulgar blackguard . . . And Gerő is just as worthless . . . There is only one honest man in the whole Party leadership [sic]. He is Imre Nagy."[20] Then there were other signs, too. Yuri V. Andropov, the new Soviet ambassador, kept inviting Nagy, just a pensioner, to his residence on Bajza Street for long and apparently pleasant discussions. Suslov called on him in mid-June, again offering the prime ministership if Nagy would only exercise self-criticism.[21] Returning from Belgrade, Mikoyan made another brief stopover in Budapest on July 21 to see Nagy and to assure him that it was Rákosi and not the Kremlin who had ordered his expulsion from the party. Alarmed by growing tension in Hungary, Mikoyan also asked for Nagy's help to find a way out.[22]

Thus, with Tito as a key player now and Nagy as Tito's obvious choice, the Russians were increasingly interested in Nagy and the authority he could command. But they were hesitant. On the one hand, Nagy was stubborn; he still refused to exercise self-criticism and thus follow the

19. There are contradictory reports on who was the Kremlin's first choice at this time. On the one hand, Tito reported in his famous Pula speech of November 11, 1956, that the Soviet leaders had "made it a condition [of Rákosi's removal] that Rákosi would go only if Gerő remained." See Paul E. Zinner, ed., *National Communism and Popular Revolt in Eastern Europe* (New York: Columbia University Press, 1957), p. 524. On the other hand, however, András Hegedüs reports that when Mikoyan landed in Budapest, he and Rákosi received him at the airport. In the car, on their way to the guesthouse, Mikoyan suddenly turned to Rákosi: "The Party Presidium [Politburo] thinks that in the given situation, claiming ill health, you must resign, Comrade Rákosi. Comrade Hegedüs must take over the position of the First Secretary." Hegedüs, who was cognizant of his modest talents, declined the appointment. See Hegedüs, *Élet egy eszme árnyékában*, pp. 242–45. I find Hegedüs's account quite plausible. The reason why the Kremlin would have wanted him as first secretary was self-evident: unlike Gerő, Hegedüs was neither a Muscovite nor Jewish (even though, because of his large nose, Budapest anti-Semites eagerly and not unsuccessfully spread the rumor that he was Jewish).

20. Méray, *Thirteen Days*, p. 47.

21. Hegedüs, *Élet egy eszme árnyékában*, pp. 240–41.

22. Méray, *Thirteen Days*, p. 55. Méray reports that at this meeting "Mikoyan overflowed with amiability."

"Malenkov formula." On the other hand, with Malenkov on the sidelines, Nagy no longer had to be a scapegoat for Malenkov. Therefore, what began to matter to the Kremlin *now* was that Nagy, though a nonparty pensioner, remained loyal to the Soviet Union and to the party, and he was needed. Hungary was bursting at the seams. As the day of reckoning, October 23, 1956, approached, then, Nagy—his authority to be used and his loyalty to be manipulated—was available, and he seemed to be once again at or near the top of the Kremlin's waiting list.

Nagy was finally readmitted to the party on October 13, but before that Gerő and his present deputy, János Kádár, had held further consultations with Mikoyan and Suslov, and Khrushchev had arranged for Gerő to meet "accidentally" with Tito in the Crimea.[23] There, on the condition that Nagy would be promptly rehabilitated and as a gesture of goodwill toward Khrushchev, Tito agreed to receive Gerő in Belgrade the following week. Gerő had no time to waste. In Budapest, before leaving for Belgrade to formally apologize to Tito for the Hungarian party's past behavior,[24] he worked out a compromise that called for Nagy's readmission to the party without preconditions. Thus, Nagy did not have to recant and the party did not have to admit its error for having him ousted in the first place. To his associates' dismay, Nagy accepted the formula. For however much he despised Gerő, it was more important for Nagy to demonstrate that he was a disciplined Communist. Above all, he seemed to appreciate the Soviet comrades' efforts on his behalf; he was grateful to them for letting him repair to the party he loved, the party that had endowed his life with meaning, significance, and a mission for almost forty years.

Revolution or New Course?

On October 23, when peaceful demonstrations began in support of the dramatic changes then taking place in Poland—including the elevation of Władysław Gomułka to his old position as first secretary of the Polish party—Nagy and his supporters met at Géza Losonczy's apartment to assess the situation.[25] They knew that the party would soon call on Nagy, and perhaps on his associates, too, to rejoin the regime and thereby help reestablish a measure of stability in the country. So they held a caucus; they talked politics. They seemed to agree that Nagy should accept his old

23. Veljko Mićunović, *Moscow Diary* (Garden City, N.Y.: Doubleday, 1980), pp. 116–17.
24. Hegedüs, *Élet egy eszme árnyékában*, pp. 249–50.
25. For a small segment of Losonczy's diary and other testimony about this meeting, see *Nagy Imre és bűntársai ellenforradalmi összeesküvése*, pp. 34–36. One of the participants also gave me a detailed description of what happened at Losonczy's apartment.

position as prime minister only if his worst Stalinist enemies were ousted and his adherents offered responsible assignments. They thought that Kádár, who never belonged to Nagy's group, should be the party's first secretary and Imre Mező and József Köböl, who shared some of Nagy's views, should be his deputies. From among Nagy's closest associates, Losonczy as well as Ferenc Donáth, Sándor Haraszti, and Zoltán Szántó—as well as Nagy, of course—were regarded as strong candidates for the Politburo. They also agreed on a dozen or so people, mainly writers and journalists, whom Nagy would recommend for Central Committee membership.

By nighttime, with Stalin's large statue toppled and the radio building under siege, the Hungarian revolution was under way.[26] The army, instead of following orders and attacking the crowds, handed over its weapons to the insurgents. At party headquarters, Gerő, having just returned from Belgrade, was preparing to address the country on the radio. He was constantly on the phone with the Kremlin and with Soviet ambassador Andropov. When Nagy was brought in, Gerő offered him the prime ministership. Nagy accepted the offer. Hegedüs, the current occupant, readily agreed to be demoted; he stayed on as Nagy's deputy. Hegedüs would later recall that, "We all understood that . . . there was no other political solution but Imre Nagy's entry into the government."[27] Tired and confused, Nagy asked for no further personnel changes as yet. Generally, he let Gerő take the lead. Gerő had already obtained Khrushchev's approval for Nagy's appointment.[28]

During its almost continuous series of meetings that began at midnight, the Central Committee sought to appease the insurgents and disarm the political opposition by removing a few of the worst Stalinist diehards from the Politburo and by replacing them with Nagy, with two of the less militant Nagy supporters (Köböl and Szántó), and with two centrists around Kádár (Gyula Kállai and Sándor Gáspár). Of Nagy's best friends, Losonczy was named only an alternate member of the Politburo and Donáth one of the party's secretaries under Gerő and Kádár.

Co-opted to the leadership in their absence, Losonczy and Donáth refused to take up their assignments.[29] They thought the changes were but

26. This section deals only with the Soviet Union's relationship with Nagy and with other events of "high politics" that are essential to an understanding of that relationship. For comprehensive accounts of the revolution itself, see various sources already cited in this chapter.

27. Hegedüs, *Élet egy eszme árnyékában*, 259.

28. Ibid., p. 260.

29. The following interpretation of Nagy's early behavior is based on information

cosmetic, and they found Nagy aloof and indeed unwilling to implement the understanding about personnel that they had reached at Losonczy's apartment less than twenty-four hours earlier. They were dismayed to find that Nagy lacked any understanding of—any "feel" for—what was happening outside party headquarters. They failed to convince Nagy that he must immediately turn against Gerő. They were upset that he had only reproached Gerő for the past—for having brought about this situation —but did not take issue with him about what to do next. As they saw it, Nagy was not responding to the revolution; he was reflecting the atmosphere at party headquarters.

Specifically, how could Nagy have agreed to declare martial law? How could he have failed to object to the overnight announcement, made on behalf of the Council of Ministers of which he was its designated head, that demanded all "fascist, reactionary elements" to stop their "counter-revolutionary activities"? Worse, why was Nagy silent when Gerő, in consultation with Andropov, arranged on the night of October 23 for Soviet troops stationed in the countryside to leave their barracks and offer "fraternal assistance"? As Hegedüs confirms, too,[30] Nagy was passive or agnostic, if not agreeable, on the key issues of the day, including that of requesting Soviet aid.

Nagy's agnosticism on calling for Soviet help became particularly clear when Gerő and Andropov asked Nagy to sign the formal request for it. Having been silent when the issue was discussed, Nagy simply avoided them; he walked away without saying yes or no. (In the end, with Andropov still insisting on having something in writing, *former* Prime Minister András Hegedüs signed the document. He did so on October 26, three days after the Soviet troops had been called in and hence when he was no longer the country's prime minister. The letter was predated to make it appear that it had been signed sometime on October 23, when *formally* Hegedüs was probably still the prime minister and Nagy the party-designated prime minister. Of course, the reason why Gerő and Andropov did not yet ask Hegedüs to sign it on October 23 was because at that time they were still trying to get Nagy's signature in order to compromise him.)

Nagy failed to assert himself on another, potentially crucial issue as well. On October 25, Nagy's friend Ferenc Donáth introduced a motion at

derived from Méray, *Thirteen Days*, 88 ff.; Hegedüs, *Élet egy eszme árnyékában*, pp. 260–77; and information by George Heltai, Zoltán Vas, and Miklós Vásárhelyi. For a fine description and analysis of what happened at party headquarters and of "high politics" during the revolution, see also Váli, *Rift and Revolt in Hungary*, chap. 21 (pp. 280–305).

30. Hegedüs, ibid.

a Central Committee session. Against the background of Gerő's provocative speech on the radio some thirty-six hours earlier, Donáth's moderate proposal was intended to calm the country's angry, explosive mood. In his motion, Donáth urged the party to express its understanding of the reasons for the people's fury and to identify itself with some of the popular demands. The motion was intentionally somewhat vague, but its message was quite positive and its tone conciliatory if not soothing. If passed *at this early date* and subsequently amplified, it might well have reduced the chances for the continuation of the violent confrontation under way. Incredibly, only Losonczy and Márton Horváth, the latter a political chameleon, supported Donáth's motion. When Nagy, their hero, voted against it, Donáth and Losonczy left party headquarters for home. (They returned only four days later.)

With both Mikoyan and Suslov at party headquarters on October 24–26, Nagy reverted to his *1953* political program and mentality. The fighting spirit of Imre Nagy of 1955 or early 1956 was not in evidence. Having declared martial law, Nagy went on to ask the people to trust him and to let him proceed toward the full implementation of the "June way," the 1953 New Course. New Course? Only a devoted party apparatchik could still think in terms of ending the era of the "personality cult," of correcting "past errors," of shifting economic priorities. The "enemy" was misleading the good people of Hungary? The students and workers on the streets, fighting for freedom and independence, were stunned; the party jargon was jarring and the content it conveyed was an insult. They no longer thought in terms of the party, its alien jargon, and its warring factions. Years of suppressed hostility had suddenly found expression in new expectations and demands, of which one more than any other could be heard time and again: *Ruszkik haza!* (Russians, go home!)

It was all very puzzling. While a nonparty, private citizen in 1955–56, Imre Nagy had grown considerably. His studies written at the time had shown his understanding of the growing gap between the party and the people. With insight and compassion, he had warned that if political and economic reforms were denied, the consequences could be catastrophic. He understood well that *tactical* changes, a minor concession here and "one step backward" there, would not be adequate. He demanded that the party adopt a new *strategic* direction that, based on the concept of sovereignty, would lead to equitable relations between the Soviet Union and Hungary. He took the Soviet leaders' declarations about de-Stalinization, especially those made at the 20th Congress, at face value. He had not reached the point of advocating a return to the postwar, multiparty coalition era, but in his scheme of things those who did not belong to the party would still have equal access to the country's resources and a say about the country's orientation. He seemed prepared to go beyond the creation of an old-fashioned Popular Front.

Nagy had also understood the meaning of the post-Stalin riots in East Berlin, Pilsen, Prague, and in the Hungarian industrial towns of Csepel, Ózd, and Diósgyőr. He had prophetically warned in 1955, and hence before the 20th Congress:

> The degeneration of power is seriously endangering the fate of socialism. . . . Today, probably a return to the policy of the New Course . . . could still check the growing crisis and avert catastrophe. But it is doubtful whether a return to the June principles {of 1953} would suffice as a solution tomorrow. . . . If this does not happen soon, there is a danger that the masses, having lost their faith, will reject both the June way and the Communist Party, and *it will become necessary to make a much greater retreat in order to keep the situation under control*.[31]

His pulse on the growing crisis, the Imre Nagy of 1955–56 had thus come face to face with the imperatives of reform *and* independence, though he had also believed in the possibility of shaping a Marxist, humane, and Hungarian political order within the post-Stalinist framework of the Soviet bloc.

Yet, during its first days, the revolution brought to power a Muscovite reformer of 1953—and not of 1955–56—vintage. It was almost as if Nagy did not know or did not want to know that a revolution had begun, that the people had transcended his "June way and the Communist Party," and that therefore it *had* "become necessary to make a much greater retreat." Was he a realist who understood the limits of Soviet tolerance or did he lose his nerve? Did responsibility make him waver? Did he become a victim of the siege mentality that engulfed party headquarters? Did he find Gerő's—and Mikoyan's and Suslov's and Andropov's—arguments about the dangers of "counterrevolution" so persuasive as to break ranks with his ardent supporters and forget his own prophetic warnings? The whole country wondered.

The most widely accepted explanation was that Nagy had become a prisoner of party headquarters. In a special sense, this was, and remains, a plausible explanation. For Nagy *was* a prisoner of the Communist political mentality permeating party headquarters—the prisoner of a limited ideological horizon and of intraparty intrigues—from which there was no easy

---

31. Nagy, *On Communism*, pp. 49–50. Emphasis added.

escape. His prophetic words about a coming crisis notwithstanding, Nagy could only imagine, but did not expect, something like *this* to happen. Those around him at party headquarters could not even imagine such a revolution to take place.

As Hegedüs describes the scene at party headquarters, the *basic question* was not even considered at first: Could the party make such timely and significant concessions that would satisfy all or most of the insurgents? Instead, the question on everyone's mind was this: How could the party most effectively isolate and then break down this counterrevolutionary insurgency? Thus, all of the initial speeches and measures reflected the traditional mentality of authoritarian leaders, Communist and otherwise, for whom the only question was not how to solve the problem but how to protect their power. For leaders of this kind—for Gerő and his colleagues —the answer was self-evident. First, they must use force to defeat the rebellion. Second, by first co-opting him and then making him appear to be the man in charge of breaking down the rebellion, they must discredit and then defeat Imre Nagy as well.

From the moment Mikoyan and Suslov arrived at party headquarters on October 24, unannounced and in an armored car, it was obvious that on the second point the interests of the Soviet Union and of the Gerő group diverged. The Soviet Union wanted to end the rebellion, a task for which it judged Nagy and not Gerő to be the right man. While Gerő had expected to get the job done, consolidate his and his group's hold on the levers of power, and then remove Nagy, the Soviet Union wanted Gerő out of the way now in order to restore order quickly and if possible without further violence. Mikoyan and Suslov told Gerő immediately that his speech the night before was unduly provocative and he must go.[32] A TASS report issued in Moscow also signaled the Kremlin's preference; it mentioned Nagy twice and by name. He was given credit for the declaration of martial law, which was said to have been necessary to repel "fascist thugs" and "enemy elements," and for having "called on the whole people to maintain [sic] calm and order."

With Mikoyan and Suslov in attendance, the Politburo replaced Gerő with János Kádár the next day (October 25). Nagy broke the news on the radio. He also offered amnesty to those who "immediately stop fighting and surrender their arms," and then mentioned for the first time that the government would soon initiate negotiations with the Soviet Union concerning various aspects of Soviet-Hungarian relations including the withdrawal of Soviet troops from Hungarian territory. "Under the leadership of

32. Hegedüs, *Élet egy eszme árnyékában*, p. 271.

the Party," as Nagy said, the rebellion must be ended. His policies and words had Moscow's approval.

If Nagy's announcement had been made just one day, let alone one week, earlier, it would have had an extraordinary effect. He spoke of amnesty, not counterrevolution. He called for the withdrawal of Soviet troops from Hungary, not for their "fraternal assistance." Next to him was Kádár, a victim of Stalinist purges, not Gerő, who held responsibility for Stalinist purges. True, Nagy affirmed the "leadership" of the Communist party, but what changes did he announce! Alas, as the ÁVO had just massacred over one hundred demonstrators at Parliament Square, Nagy's words fell on deaf ears. The initiated few understood that he was making some headway with the Kremlin's representatives and with the remaining diehards at party headquarters. But, as would happen again and again in the coming days, his announcement did not play well on the streets. He was a step or two behind the latest, increasingly impatient demands. At this point, for example, it was no longer sufficient to declare that the government would "initiate" negotiations about the withdrawal of Soviet troops; the streets, resounding with the rhythmic *Ruszkik haza!*, wanted him to report results. It was too little and too late.

Conversely, the popular demands made on Nagy were too many and too soon. One delegation after another kept telling him what to do and especially to be more daring. He replied, impatiently, that they should go home and implement his policies. Nagy remained a cautious reformer. Above all, he did not want to go beyond the understanding he had reached with Mikoyan and Suslov, which appeared to approximate the deal the Kremlin made with Gomułka in Poland: "wider internal autonomy for the Hungarian Party, measures of liberalization, 'domesticism' taking account of Hungarian peculiarities, discarding of compromised Stalinists, revision of trade agreements with the Soviets, and also the later withdrawal of Soviet troops." Such a compromise "would help to maintain the essence of Party rule and Soviet control, but would do away with the ostensible shortcomings and satisfy sensitivities of national feelings."[33]

This was the general idea that Mikoyan and Suslov had left behind when they returned to the Soviet Union. It is not known precisely how Moscow maintained high-level contact with Nagy while the two Soviet trouble-shooters were gone for four days, October 26–30. Presumably, there were many conversations on the phone. Of course, Ambassador Andropov was there. Most important, the Soviet troops were there. But it is clear that *until October 30 or 31 Moscow was supportive of Nagy's decisions*, includ-

---

33. Váli, *Rift and Revolt in Hungary*, p. 285.

ing the appointment of a few non-Communists to his cabinet, a move that foreshadowed the creation of a multiparty system (October 27); the formation of a more or less centrist six-member party Presidium to take over the functions of the Central Committee (October 28); and the abolishment of ÁVO (October 29). Not without some ambiguity, Moscow kept signaling its approval of what Nagy was doing. In contrast to Khrushchev's early skepticism about a political solution, voiced privately on October 24,[34] Radio Moscow presently praised the "newly formed Hungarian government headed by Imre Nagy" for having mastered the situation, adding that "the calculations of the counterrevolutionary insurgents are suffering failure."[35] At a diplomatic reception in Moscow on October 29, Soviet Foreign Minister Dmitri T. Shepilov referred to "the well-known fact" about counterrevolutionary activities, but he confirmed that the sooner these activities ceased "the sooner would the Soviet troops withdraw." At the same reception, Marshal Georgi K. Zhukov, the minister of defense, said: ". . . the situation in Hungary is improving. *A government has been formed which is enjoying our support* and the support of the Hungarian people.[36] In his memoirs Khrushchev confirms that the Kremlin vacillated between "crushing the mutiny" and "get[ting] out of Hungary": "I don't know how many times we changed our minds back and forth."[37]

It can only be surmised that, after their return to Moscow on October 26, Mikoyan and Suslov convinced the Soviet Politburo of the *possibility* that Nagy might still find a political solution to the crisis. Indeed, when they returned to Budapest on October 30 to take a second look at the

34. On October 24 Khrushchev told the Yugoslav ambassador in Moscow that, if possible, he wanted to find a political solution. "But Khrushchev gave the impression that he had no faith in such a solution." Mićunović, *Moscow Diary*, p. 127.

35. For the text of this broadcast, see Melvin J. Lasky, ed., *The Hungarian Revolution* (New York: Praeger, 1957), p. 104. The following day *Pravda* carried a similar article entitled "The Collapse of the Anti-People Adventure in Hungary" (*Pravda*, October 28, 1956), which prompted the Hungarian party daily *Szabad Nép* to take issue with the Soviet claim that a counterrevolution was taking place in Hungary. In point of fact, the *Pravda* piece, like a Radio Moscow broadcast the night before, contained an essentially positive message; even its very title referred to the *collapse* of the insurgency. The nuance is important here: at this time Soviet signals stressed the "collapse of the counterrevolution" rather than the idea that what transpired in Hungary should be classified as a "counterrevolution." For this unique and even moving rebuttal of *Pravda*, see Miklós Molnár, "Válasz a Pravdának" [Reply to Pravda], *Szabad Nép*, October 29, 1956. For an English translation, see Lasky, *Hungarian Revolution*, p. 135.

36. Ibid., pp. 132–33. Emphasis added. For the original report on the reception, see T. Popovski's account in *Borba*, October 30, 1956.

37. *Khrushchev Remembers*, translated and edited by Strobe Talbott (Boston: Little, Brown, 1970), p. 418.

situation, they were outgoing and even friendly. Hungary was following the "Polish formula." The atmosphere at party headquarters and in the Parliament building was reported to be excellent. Their discussions with Nagy, Kádár, and Tildy went exceptionally well. Mikoyan spent an hour with Tildy, who raised several issues, including the possibility of reestablishing the 1945 four-party coalition government and thus meeting one of the revolution's most important demands. Mikoyan, who had apparently anticipated the question, agreed. A jubilant Tildy immediately told József Kővágó, the Smallholder-designated Mayor of Budapest, that Mikoyan "accepted everything."[38] Indeed, Mikoyan and Suslov appeared willing to settle two other key issues as well. In their discussion with Nagy and Kádár, they agreed to the prompt withdrawal of Soviet troops and to negotiations about Hungary's withdrawal from the Warsaw Pact. An enterprising reporter from the new, revolutionary newspaper *Igazság* managed to enter party headquarters at Akadémia Street where he found himself face to face with Mikoyan and Suslov (whose presence in Budapest had not been announced). The young journalist was not told very much, but he could report that all seemed well. They smiled and they even shook *his* hand on the way out of the building.[39]

Nagy made his historic announcement on the radio at 2:28 P.M. on October 30, 1956:

> In the interest of the further democratization of the country's life, the cabinet abolishes the one-party system and places the country's government on the basis of democratic cooperation between the coalition parties as they existed in 1945. In accordance with this decision, a new national government with a smaller inner cabinet has been established, at the moment with only limited powers. The members of the new cabinet are Imre Nagy, Zoltán Tildy, Béla Kovács, Ferenc Erdei, János Kádár, Géza Losonczy, and a person to be appointed by the Social Democratic Party.

Next at the microphone was a fragile but jubilant Zoltán Tildy of the Smallholders' party, once a Calvinist minister:

> Hungarian Brothers! The will of the nation, the national revolution has prevailed. I stand before the microphone deeply moved. I don't have a prepared text, my speech may be disjointed, but with my heart overflowing with love and joy I salute the beloved youth of

38. József Kővágó, *You Are All Alone* (New York: Praeger, 1959), pp. 197–202.
39. "Szemtől-szembe Mikojánnal és Szuszlovval" [Face to Face with Mikoyan and Suslov], *Igazság*, November 1, 1956.

Hungary. . . . We are a small nation, but we want to live in this country in our Hungarian way and in freedom. I am convinced that once the peoples and leaders of the Soviet Union face not a humiliated but a free nation and its representatives, they will see how different our relationship can be, how much more understanding, respect, and affection there will be. . . . Let there be no more sacrifice, no more destruction. Let us all be faithful to ourselves, to this historic moment, let us make peace and order in our country. Rejoice my Hungarian brothers and let's get to work.[40]

For the first time since the revolution began one very long week ago, the Nagy regime was not far behind the people's demands. Although some Soviet troops were still in the country, the government could still list quite a few accomplishments. Most of the Stalinists had cleared out of party headquarters. Nagy had obtained a measure of authority. Under Pál Maléter's leadership, the Hungarian Army had restored a modicum of order. Though some of the insurgents, waiting for the Soviet troops to leave, held on to their weapons, they were beginning to line up behind the government. The "much greater retreat" Nagy had anticipated in 1955 "in order to keep the situation under control" had already been implemented —with the Kremlin's apparent approval.

Whatever suspicions Nagy may have still entertained about Soviet duplicity were dispelled later that evening. Or so it seemed at that time. For next morning's *Pravda* would carry the official declaration of the Soviet government, which no longer characterized the Hungarian situation as a "counterrevolution." "The course of events has shown," the Soviet government stated, using its customary jargon, "that the working people of Hungary . . . are rightfully raising the question of the need to eliminate the serious defects in the field of economic construction, of improving further the material well-being of the population, and of combating bureaucratic distortions in the state apparatus." The operative parts of the official declaration then stated:

> It is known that, in accordance with the Warsaw Treaty and governmental agreements, Soviet units are stationed in the Hungarian and Romanian republics. . . . With a view to ensuring the mutual security of the socialist countries, the Soviet government is ready to review with the other socialist countries of the Warsaw Treaty the question of Soviet troops stationed on the territory of the above-mentioned countries. . . . Since it considers that the further pres-

40. *Magyar Nemzet*, October 31, 1956.

ence of the Soviet Army units can serve as a cause for even greater aggravation of the situation, the Soviet government has given instructions to its military command to withdraw the Soviet Army units from Budapest as soon as this is considered necessary by the Hungarian government.[41]

The Kremlin Had Enough

This statement appeared in the morning editions of *Pravda* on October 31, 1956. It was almost certainly on that day, while Mikoyan and Suslov were still so agreeable in Budapest, that the Soviet Union decided to overthrow the Nagy government. My reading of the evidence suggests that, the initial *military* decision to mobilize the Soviet armed forces having been made prior to the publication of the *Pravda* declaration, the ultimate *political* decision to deploy the forces, invade Hungary, and overthrow the Nagy government was made early on Wednesday, October 31, in Mikoyan's and Suslov's absence.

The evidence for this contention is that (1) it was during the night of October 31 and the morning of November 1 that new Soviet troops entered the country; (2) Imre Nagy's relationship with the Russians suddenly deteriorated during the morning hours of November 1; and (3) on November 1 Khrushchev, Molotov, and Malenkov were already secretly consulting with the Polish leadership in Brest, near the Soviet-Polish border, following which Khrushchev and Malenkov went on to Bucharest the same day to brief the Romanian, Czechoslovak, and Bulgarian leaders.[42] Moreover, Khrushchev confirms that the decision to intervene was made while Mikoyan and Suslov "were not present."[43]

On Thursday, November 1, Nagy was awakened with the news of Soviet troops crossing the Soviet-Hungarian border. He tried to get in touch with the Kremlin but could not. (Mikoyan and Suslov were on a plane between Budapest and Moscow, while Khrushchev, Molotov, and Malenkov were on their way to Brest.) Nagy ordered a news blackout on the apparent Soviet invasion, the result of which were (published) rumors but few reliable facts. As many of the insurgents drew their conclusion from what they saw — the ongoing and visible evacuation of Soviet forces from Budapest — there was a curious mixture of joy and anxiety in the air. One newspaper headline captured the mood of the day: *Are They Coming or Going?*

41. *Pravda*, October 31, 1956.
42. Mićunović, *Moscow Diary*, p. 132.
43. *Khrushchev Remembers*, p. 417.

Nagy held at least five meetings with Ambassador Andropov this day. He demanded to know what was going on. After checking with the Kremlin, Andropov at one point returned to Nagy's office in the Parliament building to assure the prime minister that the Soviet government stood by its "historic" declaration of October 30 and that Soviet troops had *entered* Hungary only in order to safeguard the security of Soviet forces *leaving* Hungary. This was too much for Nagy. He bluntly warned Andropov that Hungary was prepared to declare its neutrality. When Andropov failed to return with a satisfactory reply, Nagy knew that the "Soviet comrades" had deceived him.[44] But he was no comrade any more, certainly not theirs.

Nagy called into session the executive committee of the Communist party to obtain its support for a declaration on Hungary's neutrality and for the country's withdrawal from the Warsaw Pact. Two members of the committee, György Lukács and Zoltán Szántó, as well as Sándor Haraszti, editor of the party daily and an ex officio member, expressed reservations. But the motion easily carried. Then Nagy took the proposal to his cabinet. There everybody supported him. Then Nagy made this statement on the radio a few minutes before 8:00 P.M.:

> The Hungarian National Government, imbued with profound responsibility toward the Hungarian people and history, and giving expression to the undivided will of millions of Hungarians, declares the neutrality of the Hungarian People's Republic. It is on the basis of independence and equality, and in accordance with the spirit of the UN Charter, that the Hungarian people wish to live in true friendship with their neighbors, with the Soviet Union and with all the peoples of the world. . . . Working millions of Hungary! Revolutionary determination, sacrificial work and the consolidation of order [will] protect and strengthen our homeland—the free, independent, democratic and neutral Hungary.[45]

Prior to Nagy's speech on November 1, János Kádár had disappeared from Budapest in the company of Ferenc Münnich, an old Muscovite and a former Hungarian ambassador to Moscow and Belgrade. Both had backed Nagy's moves. Kádár had been a strong and enthusiastic supporter of the formation of the multiparty system. He had voted in favor of declaring Hungary's neutrality. In a radio speech recorded earlier *that day* he had

---

44. For months to come, in Romanian exile as well as in Hungarian jails, Nagy's refrain about the Soviet leaders remained the same: "Becsaptak . . . elárultak" [They deceived me . . . they betrayed me].

45. *Magyar Nemzet*, November 2, 1956.

referred to "our glorious revolution." Earlier *that day* he had defended the cabinet's decision about neutrality and the Warsaw Pact in a confrontation with Andropov. In the presence of the whole cabinet, he was reported to have told the Soviet ambassador that if Soviet tanks were to reenter Budapest, he would personally join the armed struggle against them.[46] It can only be surmised that sometime during the day Münnich and then in the evening Kádár, too, were informed of the Soviet decision to intervene and they decided to break ranks with Nagy and the revolution.

The remaining events of November 1–4 can be summarized briefly. Most everything fell into a *pattern of duplicity*. Throughout the country, Soviet troops were in evidence everywhere; they were coming from bases in the Soviet Union and Romania. They were no longer in evidence in Budapest, however, and the Soviet Union kept assuring the Nagy government that it was still prepared to negotiate the details of their withdrawal from the whole country. Indeed, negotiations on that subject began during the day on November 3 and considerable progress was being made.[47] But on that fateful night, all pretense was gone when General Ivan Serov, the Soviet security chief, broke up the "negotiating" session and arrested all members of the Hungarian delegation. At dawn on November 4, 1956, Soviet forces, having entered Budapest overnight and occupied the Parliament building, crushed the revolution.

During the last three days before the attack on Budapest, Hungarians had allowed themselves the luxury of a bit of self-deception. Among ordinary people, optimists could still find evidence of a Soviet willingness to reach an acceptable compromise. If they were *coming*, why were they *going*? There was no panic. At least in Budapest, life was returning to something approaching normalcy. More food was available, some of the streetcars and buses were operating, several factories reopened. The city was flooded with announcements about the formation of social and political organizations and parties, and every shade of political opinion was reflected in dozens of new newspapers and weeklies. The scope of Soviet troop movements was not widely known.

46. Méray, *Thirteen Days*, p. 194.
47. Agreement was reached on the following: (1) Soviet troops will leave Hungary before January 15, 1957; (2) while the troops remain in the country, the Hungarian government will take care of their needs; (3) Hungary will repair all Soviet monuments and will bid respectful farewell to the departing Soviet troops; (4) after the two delegations consult their respective governments, they will meet at 10:00 P.M. at the headquarters of the Soviet forces stationed in Hungary [near Csepel, outside of Budapest] in order to sign an appropriate document. Béla Király, *Az első háború szocialista országok között* [The First War Between Socialist Countries] (New Brunswick: Magyar Öregdiák Szövetség/Bessenyei György Kör, 1981), p. 58.

In the Parliament building and at party headquarters, however, the facts about Soviet troop movements were well-known. One of the least appealing members of Nagy's group, Zoltán Szántó, approached the Yugoslav embassy already on Thursday, November 1, with a request for asylum. That afternoon, Münnich, Kádár, and three or four other leading Communists departed for the Soviet side. But Nagy remained calm. Judging by his activities, he may have considered it a possibility—a most remote possibility, to be sure—that the Kremlin had not yet made the final decision, or if it had the Soviet Politburo might still reverse itself. If so, what should he do, what would impress the Kremlin? First, and most important, was the consolidation of domestic order and stability. For it would be one thing for Moscow to invade a conflict-ridden country in which Communists—mainly ÁVO officers—were being killed; it would be something else to invade a peaceful country in which law and order prevailed. For this reason the government kept issuing almost desperate pleas for discipline and self-restraint. Second, Nagy had reason to believe that the Kremlin might be sensitive to world opinion. Andropov had asked him on November 1 not to turn to the United Nations; this sort of thing seemed to matter to Moscow. At the time Nagy had agreed to wait on the condition that the influx of Soviet troops would be stopped. When it did not, he responded not only by sending several appeals to the United Nations but by notifying all diplomatic missions in Budapest about the situation.

There was nothing else to do. On November 3, Nagy declined to give a press conference he had scheduled for foreign journalists; he asked Tildy and Losonczy instead to make a statement and answer questions. They made a heroic effort to project calm—and to let Moscow know that Hungary was eager to protect the "gains of socialism." That afternoon, István Bibó, a minister of state in Nagy's last cabinet, asked General Béla Király, the highest-ranking Hungarian army officer after Maléter, how long Hungary could resist. Budapest could be held for one or two days at most, Király replied, but probably only for a few hours.[48] Bibó appeared resigned. So did Nagy. He had done what he could. He had tried to satisfy the Kremlin's needs and concerns. He had been mindful of the security interests of the Soviet Union and of the Soviet bloc in Eastern Europe. He had accepted the "Polish formula" for Hungary. He had believed that the Soviet leaders wanted him to build a Hungarian-style socialist system. Only after he had Moscow's trust on October 31, or perhaps the day before that, did he choose to proceed on his own. Nagy's cautious

48. Ibid., p. 59.

patriotism prevailed when he refused to order the Hungarian Army to do battle against impossible odds.[49]

The Question of Soviet Motives

Having briefed their allies first in Brest (accompanied there by Molotov) and then in Bucharest on the impending intervention, all on November 1, and after a brief stopover in Moscow, Khrushchev and Malenkov continued their secret journey to the Yugoslav island of Brioni to see Tito. They landed in Pula at 6:00 P.M. on November 2 and arrived in Brioni at 7:00 P.M. The Yugoslav side was represented by Tito, his two closest associates, Eduard Kardelj and Aleksander Rankovic, and by Veljko Mićunović, the Yugoslav ambassador to the Soviet Union. The discussion, all about Hungary, lasted for ten hours. The Soviet leaders left for Moscow the next morning at 5:00 A.M. Mićunović kept detailed notes about the proceedings in his diary.[50]

Of the two Soviet leaders, Khrushchev seemed to carry the day. He said they came to inform the Yugoslavs "about the Soviet Union's decision" and to hear Tito's views. He ticked off four "external" and one "internal" reasons for what Moscow was about to do. They were given as the following: (1) Communists were being murdered in Hungary; (2) Nagy withdrew from the Warsaw Pact, declared neutrality, and appealed to the United Nations; (3) capitalism was about to be restored in Hungary; (4) the British-French-Israeli intervention in Suez would divert the world's attention from Soviet "assistance"; and (5) if he failed to act, Stalinist diehards and especially leaders of the Soviet Army would hold the "loss of Hungary" against the new political leadership in the Kremlin. As to implementation, Malenkov added that the Soviet armed forces were ready to act. They must go in "frontally and with great force," he said, because the Soviet Union was "completely isolated from the Hungarian people."

Factually, some of Khrushchev's reasons for the Kremlin's decision to

---

49. Nagy made the following statement on Radio Budapest at 5:19 A.M. on November 4: "This is Imre Nagy speaking, the Chairman of the Council of Ministers of the Hungarian People's Republic. Today at daybreak Soviet forces started an attack against our capital, obviously with the intention to overthrow the legal Hungarian democratic government. Our troops are fighting. The government is in its place. I notify the people of our country and the entire world of this fact." Lasky, *Hungarian Revolution*, p. 228. In point of fact, Nagy refused to order General Király to engage his troops. For their two dramatic conversations during the night of November 3, see Király, *Az első háború szocialista országok között*, pp. 62–64.

50. The following paragraph is based on Mićunović, *Moscow Diary*, pp. 130–42.

intervene seemed more justified than others. (1) Communists, especially officers of the ÁVO, were indeed tortured and killed during the early days of the revolution. Their number was small; comparable outbreaks in history had produced many more summary executions. Still, Khrushchev could have been deeply disturbed by pictures carried in the Western press of Communists being cruelly treated and in some cases hanged on lampposts. (2) Hungary formally withdrew from the Warsaw Pact, declared its neutrality, and appealed to the United Nations only after new Soviet troops had entered Hungary; indeed, the threat of intervention *caused* these measures and declarations to be adopted rather than the other way around. (3) Capitalism, perhaps on a small scale, might have returned to Hungary, especially in agriculture and the service industries. What actually happened, however, was that every political party affirmed again and again that the "gains of socialism" would not be reversed. (4) Suez was very possibly the reason for the timing of the intervention rather than the intervention itself. (5) According to Khrushchev, certain army and Stalinist elements maintained that "as long as Stalin was in command everybody obeyed," while the present group of Kremlin leaders could not even hold on to Hungary. He implied that the anti-Stalinists had to show firmness, outdo the Stalinists if necessary, in order to pursue the course of de-Stalinization. Doing nothing would only play into the hands of Molotov and Kaganovich. This was but a veiled appeal for Tito's empathy—and it was something the Yugoslavs could understand and appreciate.[51]

What can be made of Khrushchev's reasoning, of Soviet motives? To the extent that his explanation was offered in such a secret setting and to the extent that its summary—from a highly intelligent and sophisticated participant's diary—can be regarded as reliable, his points offer unusually valuable insights into the Kremlin's own assessment of the decision to intervene. That much said, it is still important to add that a decision of this magnitude is not likely to have been made on the basis of such specific reasons alone. Nor is it necessarily true that the leaders' motives were completely apparent even to themselves. Indeed, in my view, Khrushchev's

51. Of course, there must have been other Soviet considerations as well that either Khrushchev did not mention to Tito or Mićunović did not include in his *Moscow Diary*. For example, the Chinese leaders were known to have advised the Kremlin against military intervention, at least at the beginning, while the Romanians, fearful of the impact of the revolution on the large Hungarian minority in Romania, were early advocates of such an intervention. Moscow might also have taken account of the preoccupation of the United States with presidential elections that week; it might have influenced the timing of the intervention. For a sound analysis of Soviet policy, see Paul E. Zinner, *Revolution in Hungary* (New York: Columbia University Press, 1962), pp. 320–26.

explanation should be interpreted to mean that the Soviet leaders responded primarily to their sense of threat, to their fear of vulnerability, to their concern about the reputation and hence the power of the Soviet Union. As Khrushchev said in Brioni: "If we let things take their course the West would say we are either stupid or weak, and that's one and the same thing. We cannot possibly permit it, either as Communists and internationalists or as the Soviet state." This rings true; fear is a great inventor. By stating, "If we let things take their course . . . ." Khrushchev seemed to be alluding to what *might happen*. More lynchings? Capitalism? Neutralism today, NATO tomorrow? What then of the Soviet sphere in Eastern Europe, who's next to go? That these developments were or were not likely to happen did not really matter; what mattered was that they might. Therefore, the Soviet leaders had to respond by force to overcome their fear of all the uncertainties Hungary implied. Among these uncertainties, the fear of losing control over the bloc, and then being seen by the West as weak, appeared to be their most compelling reason to act.

As the Kremlin's leading anti-Stalinist, Khrushchev's power was also very much on the line. His name was synonymous with the 20th Congress, with de-Stalinization. The Hungarian revolution, which began as an intraparty struggle between Stalinists and anti-Stalinist reformers in 1953, would not have happened in the absence of the 20th Congress, in the absence of de-Stalinization, in the absence of Khrushchev. True, Khrushchev had denounced Nagy in 1955. But his colleagues knew, and Khrushchev feared that they remembered, who was ultimately responsible for de-Stalinization in Hungary. Thus the Hungarian revolution found Khrushchev politically vulnerable, so much so that he had to prove it anew that he could be firm and indeed uncompromising. As he had done in 1955, then, he once again deserted Nagy—whose anti-Stalinist views were so very close to his.

In retrospect, it is as futile to speculate about what Imre Nagy should or should not have done (or what Nikita S. Khrushchev could or could not have done had he had more political room to maneuver) as it is to bemoan the Hungarian people's lack of realism. For the Soviet intervention was only marginally related to what Nagy had done or had failed to do. It was not caused by his "provocative" declaration about neutrality and the Warsaw Pact. In fact, the opposite is true: it was the (second) Soviet intervention on the night of October 31 that prompted him, *now* a heretic and a patriot, to shed his Muscovite past and issue his historic declaration.

It is also futile, even cynical perhaps, to instruct the people about what they should or should not have done. Unrealistic as any popular uprising in Eastern Europe may be (see chapter 9), once such an uprising begins it cannot be expected to be modest, limited, prudent, and properly calibrated. Because 1956 was a response both to the complete suppression of the country's independence and to extremely harsh dictatorial rule, it was a revolution made by people for whom a hero's death had become a meaningful alternative to a coward's submission. Thus the revolution's obviously excessive demands, its lack of realism, was a function of what the Hungarian people had been denied. They only reacted to the excessive demands that had been made on them, to the lack of realism in the policies of the Kremlin and the Rákosi-Gerő regimes since about 1947–48.

As for the personal drama between Khrushchev and Nagy, the tragedy of their encounter was that while Khrushchev's behavior was circumscribed by the fears and the intricate politics of the Kremlin, Nagy's eventual resistance to it was fueled by a heretic's sense of revulsion over being betrayed.

7

Moscow and János Kádár since 1956:
An Overview

Do you *really* not know the kind of people you're dealing with? —János Kádár to
Alexander Dubček, on August 17, 1968, three days before the Soviet intervention
in Czechoslovakia. [1]

During the secret discussions that Nikita S. Khrushchev and Georgi
Malenkov held with Tito and his associates in Brioni on November 1–2,
1956, there was a good deal of talk about who, after the Soviet intervention,
should be Hungary's next leader.[2] The Kremlin's choice had been narrowed
to Ferenc Münnich and János Kádár. Khrushchev said he preferred the
seventy year old Münnich whom he knew well from the 1930s (as well as
the early 1950s, too, when Münnich served as Hungary's ambassador in
Moscow). "I could deal with him better than with Kádár," Khrushchev
recalled in his memoirs. "Münnich was a cunning and battered old wolf
who had been through the Hungarian revolution with Béla Kun. He lived
in the Soviet Union for a long time and I thought he was better prepared
than anyone else. . . ."[3]

When the Yugoslavs noted that during his visit to Belgrade in October
Kádár "had made a very good impression," Khrushchev readily agreed that
Kádár was "a good guy," too.[4] And so in the end Kádár was chosen as first
secretary of the reconstituted Hungarian Socialist Workers' party (HSWP),
which under its latest name was founded on November 1, 1956. Kádár
was chosen because of his age (forty-four); because as minister of internal

1. As quoted in Zdeněk Mlynář, *Nightfrost in Prague: The End of Humane Socialism* (New
York: Karz, 1980), p. 157.
2. Veljko Mićunović, *Moscow Diary* (Garden City, N.Y.: Doubleday, 1980), pp. 136–38.
3. *Khrushchev Remembers*, translated and edited by Strobe Talbott (Boston: Little, Brown,
1970), p. 424.
4. Mićunović, *Moscow Diary*, p. 138.

affairs (1948–50) he had showed himself able and willing to implement the early purges, some of whose victims he knew were innocent;[5] and especially because the following three years that he had spent in Mátyás Rákosi's jails (1951–54) qualified him as an anti-Stalinist. It was also helpful that Münnich did not mind becoming the power behind Kádár's throne; indeed, Münnich was reported to have recommended Kádár to the Russians.[6]

Both Münnich and particularly Kádár had strongly backed Imre Nagy's policies during the revolution. Kádár had publicly supported the reestablishment of the multiparty system; he had voted in favor of declaring Hungary's neutrality. On November 1, a few hours before he was to defect to the Russians, Kádár—in the presence of the whole cabinet—reportedly yelled at Ambassador Yuri V. Andropov: "I am a Hungarian, and if necessary I will fight your tanks with my bare hands."[7] Six days later, as the new Soviet-sponsored leader of Hungary, he was delivered in a Soviet armored car to the Parliament building in Budapest. The day was November 7, 1956, the thirty-ninth anniversary of the Bolshevik revolution.

Given the circumstances, both Kádár and the Kremlin were in a desperate bind. With a membership of 900,000 on the eve of the revolution, the party had disintegrated. According to its own figures, it had only 37,818 members as of December 1, 1956, and 101,806 members as of the end of the year.[8] Worse, no more than a handful of high-ranking Communist

5. Kádár's official biography relates that he was sure that at least one detail was untrue in the fantastic charges made against László Rajk, who was arrested in May 1949. It had to do with the prosecution's contention that Rajk had conspired with the Yugoslav minister of internal affairs, Aleksander Rankovic, "in a hunting lodge in Hungary." The official biographer quotes Kádár saying that, "Rajk was a clever man. He had learned [in the underground] not to take unnecessary risks. Why did they not meet in Yugoslavia, in complete safety?" This was the question that Kádár, in his capacity as minister of internal affairs, was supposed to have posed to Mátyás Rákosi. The biographer adds: "He told Rákosi and Co. that he did not believe that Rajk was guilty and he protested against his arrest." But then Kádár stayed on to serve as minister of internal affairs—until his own arrest in May 1951. (By contrast, Kádár's successor as minister of internal affairs, Sándor Zöld, first killed his family and then committed suicide.) For the Kádár quotes, see L. Gyurkó's "Introductory Biography" in *János Kádár: Selected Speeches and Interviews* (Budapest, 1985), pp. 74–75.

6. According to Kádár's testimony, Münnich voluntarily stepped aside because "he had been away [from Hungary] for a long time and people were less familiar with his views and actions." *Népszabadság*, January 29, 1957.

7. As quoted in William Shawcross, *Crime and Compromise: János Kádár and the Politics of Compromise Since 1956* (New York: E. P. Dutton, 1974), p. 15.

8. Iván Szenes, *A Kommunista Párt ujjászervezése Magyarországon, 1956–1957* [The Reconstruction of the Communist Party in Hungary, 1956–1957] (Budapest, 1976), pp. 54,

officials was available for the seemingly impossible mission of returning Hungary to the Soviet fold, of taming the Hungarian people. For most of those who signed up early on were either old Stalinists, like Antal Apró, Imre Dögei, and József Révai, or so-called centrists with no apparent political or administrative skills, like Gyula Kállai, István Kossa, and György Marosán. Several leading positions could not be filled for the time being.

Kádár had to start from scratch. There was no continuity with the past. The Stalinist followers of Rákosi, the dogmatists, were as unsuited as the followers of Nagy, the revisionists, to join the new leadership. For example, of the seven leaders of the HSWP as of the day of its founding on November 1, five had asked for and received asylum in the Yugoslav embassy in Budapest on November 4—until their subsequent kidnapping and exile to Romania by officers of Soviet military intelligence. They were Ferenc Donáth, Géza Losonczy, György Lukács, Imre Nagy, and Zoltán Szántó. The sixth man, Sándor Kopácsi, was arrested personally by General Ivan Serov, head of the KGB, before he could reach the Yugoslav embassy.[9] Thus the only person from the party's original leadership to stay on was János Kádár.

The circumstances of his power were further defined by what Kádár claimed had to be done, which was the liquidation of the revolution's leaders, young and old. Because of the revengeful and vindictive Red Terror of 1957–58, too, then, Kádár was a hated man. Was it 99.8 or 99.9 percent of the population that considered him a traitor? The words commonly used to describe him cannot be reproduced in this book. Many also remembered Kádár bubbling over "our glorious revolution," only to turn around and help defeat the "counterrevolution." Did he not learn anything in Rákosi's jails? Even if he could not help Imre Nagy whose fate was presumably sealed in Moscow, a likely but far from certain proposition, why did he not use his influence to save Miklós Gimes, Pál Maléter, and

76. Szenes believes the official figure of 37,818 to be too low; he thinks it was closer to 50–60,000.

9. Although the Hungarian government guaranteed the Nagy group's safety, five of the leaders of the HSWP were arrested and abducted minutes after they left the Yugoslav embassy on November 22, 1956, by officers of Soviet military intelligence. Nagy was tried and executed in 1958. Losonczy died in jail. Donáth received a twelve year prison sentence in 1958 and was released in 1960. György Lukács and Zoltán Szántó returned from Romanian exile to Budapest in 1957. Lukács, who was readmitted to the party in 1967, then lived in forced retirement until his death in 1971, while Szántó turned into a prosecution witness at the Nagy trial. As for Kopácsi, he was sentenced to life imprisonment in 1958, released in 1963, and allowed to join his daughter in Canada. Hence, of the seven founding members of the HSWP only Kádár and Szántó betrayed the revolution.

József Szilágyi from the firing squad? Particularly puzzling was Kádár's apparent lack of interest in the "lesser" case of Ferenc Donáth (who received a twelve-year prison term), since Donáth had been Kádár's alter ego and good friend in the Communist movement during World War II and then his prison-mate in the early 1950s. Having come to the Kremlin's aid when there were few applicants for the job of taming Hungary's will, Kádár was not without leverage. If so, why did he fail to use the leverage to save the lives of his friends and comrades, or at least arrange for a few suspended sentences?[10]

That was three decades ago.

In these three decades, Kádár has grown to become the senior statesman of Hungary and indeed of Eastern Europe. His countrymen, still known for their anti-Soviet and anti-Communist sentiments, widely regard him as a clever and broad-minded leader of considerable political skills; even his critics call Hungary the best barrack in the Soviet camp. His regime is the envy of most East Europeans. Not without reservations, his audience in Moscow appears satisfied too: from Khrushchev to Mikhail S. Gorbachev, all Soviet leaders have applauded him, calling Kádár an "excellent statesman, Party leader, and an outstanding personality in the international labor [Communist] movement."[11] In the West, Kádár's Hungary has come to be described as the homeland of "goulash Communism," a prosperous country where rule by persuasion has replaced rule by coercion and where a tolerant regime has outfoxed the Kremlin in order to realize the 1956 revolution's more realistic demands and expectations. After a visit to Budapest in 1985, Secretary of State George P. Shultz was moved to note that Kádár was a "wise man" to whom it was "well worth listening."[12]

Occasional exaggerations aside, both Kádár and the "Kádárization" of Hungary—the person, the process, and the product—are indeed remarkable phenomena. Since Kádár restored order, consolidated his authority, and terminated the terror of the post-1956 era, he has managed to leave that past behind, embark on a path of reform, and deliver a political tour

10. Kádár was both defensive and aggressive in his comments about the Nagy trial. After the public learned about the harsh sentences, he was said to have told a group of his followers: "Comrades, because we entered on this course on November 4, it was necessary to go to the very end." As quoted in Bennett Kovrig, *Communism in Hungary: From Kun to Kádár* (Stanford, Calif.: Hoover Institution Press, 1979), p. 337. However, according to stories circulating in Budapest, Kádár may have been instrumental in reducing Kopácsi's death sentence to life imprisonment in 1958 and in allowing Kopácsi to leave Hungary in 1963.

11. *Pravda*, April 13, 1964.

12. *New York Times*, December 17, 1985.

de force. In purely Hungarian terms, his three decades in power constitute a milestone. In terms of Hungary's impact on the bloc, "Kádárization" may not be transferable as a complete or distinct socialist "model" for export, but it has nonetheless become an example for others—even for China—to take into account.

My purpose in this overview is to (1) discuss the essential features of "Kádárization," (2) explain the sources of the "Kádár mystique," and (3) analyze the predicament Kádár's Hungary has brought on the Kremlin.

What's "Kádárization"?

"Kádárization" is both a product and a process. The product is reform in the political and economic realms. The process is Kádár's style of decision-making and the way he relates to his constituents at home and abroad.

Political aspects.   The Kádár regime has instituted few political reforms. Elections to Parliament and to local councils have been modified to allow for two or more officially endorsed candidates to run for office. The resulting competition between members of the political elite can be very interesting—for example, several unpopular trade union leaders and HSWP county secretaries have emerged with diminished authority after the 1985 elections—but the elections, though contested, do not amount to structural change. Rather, they signify a modicum of public participation in the ongoing struggle among different factions within the party itself. Nor have there been changes in the way the party selects its leaders; "democratic centralism" continues to prevail. In practice, Kádár chooses his associates.

In the absence of structural changes, what differences exist between the Kádár regime and other one-party Communist polities? Perhaps the most important difference is that Kádár's Hungary has set limited political objectives for itself. It seeks less the enthusiastic or even active support of the population than its passive tolerance. Mindful of the tragic experiences of 1956, it tries to shape but it does not attempt to change a defeated people. As Kádár put it: "People do not exist so that we may test Marxism on them." The result is a largely depoliticized society, with the overwhelming majority concerned with private pursuits and only an apparently tiny group, the "democratic opposition," concerned with public issues. In contrast to similar groups in the neighboring countries, however, even the democratic opposition has called for further reforms rather than for systemic transformation. Hence the public mood, like the regime's, is grudgingly accommodating—as reflected in the resigned observation that Hungary has come to have the best it can have "under the circumstances."

The HSWP's politics are a function of its nuanced approach to what it calls "continuing contradictions" in Hungarian society. Behind the ideological code words is the recognition of two essential facts of life (and hence the contradiction): that while the means of production remain largely under state control, only a small proportion of the Hungarian population identifies itself with socialism, especially Soviet-style socialism. That being the case, the regime regards it futile and possibly catastrophic—as 1956 showed—to proceed on the assumption that the beliefs and ideologies of yesterday have disappeared. "There was a time," Kádár once noted, "when we saw reality not as it was but as we would have liked it. We have cured ourself of this delusion." Accordingly, the party maintains that it is "normal" to hold religious beliefs, to enjoy Western music, to expect material incentives for good performance. The long-term ideal remains the much-heralded "socialist man" who is unselfishly dedicated to that which is good for society, but in the meantime the system accepts and works with a population considerably less perfect than the ideal type.

This political mentality has found expression in a variety of ideological formulations. One is Kádár's "alliance policy"—witness his motto, "he who is not against us is with us"—and another is his conviction that the regime can afford to and indeed must rely on persuasion. As he explained in 1964:

> If a person does not have sufficient gumption to acquire knowledge of the somewhat more strenuous and time-consuming method of persuasion, and if his leadership skill stops at the recipe of "expel-jail," he cannot get on in public life any longer today and still less in the future. We shall fight against such people. After all, it is necessary to remember what caused the difficult situation in 1956. . . . It began with suspicion. But every rational person must understand that *a whole nation cannot be suspect*. Our starting point is that the people are our people, that we are here for them, and that when the people put us [sic] in a responsible post they do so for the reason that we should work for them.[13]

Kádár reiterated this view in 1980:

> So we have power, we have strength, and we can maintain law and order. But I still say we should not rely on this to maintain order in our society; instead we should rely on political work and persuasion. Believe me, an experience we once gained in underground work is still valid: only the people we have convinced are really, wholeheart-

13. *Népszabadság*, March 21, 1964. Emphasis added.

edly and fully with us. What a convinced person is able to do for a good cause cannot be done by command, by briefing and least of all by threats. For the implementation of our policy we must continue to rely on persuading people.[14]

Another formula reflecting the Kádár regime's mentality is the putative three-tier "interest structure" in the Hungarian polity today. It has come to be taken for granted that the "collective interest" is not the only legitimate interest in a socialist society; on the contrary, theoreticians speak of the legitimacy of individual and group interests as well. "When making decisions," wrote József Bognár, a prominent economist, "the government pays attention to the groups affected by them. . . . Alternatives and different interests are taken into account before making important decisions. . . ."[15]

Perhaps the least abstract Kádárist formula is the distinction applied to culture and by implication to political orientations as well. As stated and to a great extent practiced, too, the regime distinguishes between those views it will *support*, those it will *tolerate*, and those it will *prohibit*. (The three words in Hungarian all begin with a "t"—*támogatott, tűrt, tiltott*—and hence this is known as the "three t's" of Kádár's Hungary.) The distinction captures the essential feature of the Kádár regime's political mentality: that, as other Communist systems, there are things it likes and hence supports and there are things it does not like and hence prohibits; however, unlike other Communist systems, it tolerates rather than prohibits expressions of less-than-hostile views.[16] As the corresponding English acronym for the "three t's" is "STP," Iván Völgyes made the perceptive and witty observation that this approach served as the "lubricant" of the Kádár system.[17]

Because of such supervised steam-letting, the Kádár regime has not had to rely heavily on the political police to enforce its authority. There are few if any political prisoners in the country; a particular "troublemaker" may

14. *János Kádár: Selected Speeches and Interviews*, pp. 450–51.

15. József Bognár, "Initiative and Equilibrium: Major Political and Economic Issues in Hungary," *New Hungarian Quarterly* 11, no. 37 (Spring 1970), p. 27.

16. One of the actual results of this policy is that some periodicals tend to be much less conformist in both substance and style than others. For two of many examples, the monthly *Valóság* [Reality] frequently offers comprehensive and largely unbiased analyses of prevailing conditions in Hungarian society, while *Heti Világgazdaság* [Weekly World Economy]—patterned on the London *Economist*—provides a good deal of reliable economic information.

17. Iván Völgyes, "Politics, Ideology and Culture: The STP's of Life in Communist Eastern Europe," *Social Science Journal*, October 1976, pp. 93–102.

spend a few hours or overnight at a police station, but he is unlikely to be tried and even more unlikely to be sent to jail. ~~Religion is neither supported nor prohibited; it is tolerated~~. Everyday life is also affected by the relative ease with which citizens can travel abroad. True, the so very highly prized passport to the West is not a right that has been granted—but it is readily given. ("Let Hungarians see for themselves the so-called 'Paradise of the West,'" said Kádár in 1980, "and to be happy once they get back here."[18]) As to family reunification cases, there are occasional delays but no known final denials. What *is* prohibited, of course, is hostile political activity that is perceived to aim at undermining the regime's authority. Also prohibited is anything, talk or action, that either the Soviet Union or Hungary's neighbors might find provocative or offensive.[19] These are the identifiable limits of the regime's tolerance—limits that are seldom tested.

Of course, "Kádárization" is more than relative political tolerance by a benevolent, paternalistic dictatorship; it is also Kádár's own political style. Unlike his predecessors—Rákosi, Gerő, and Nagy—Kádár is neither a theoretician nor an intellectual; in the Western meaning of the term, he is a populist. Although he makes frequent references to Marxism, the fine points of theory and ideology do not seem to interest him. Especially when he speaks extemporaneously, his stories, anecdotes, and metaphors are always simple, if not simplistic, and for that reason they are easily understood by all. Even in the stately atmosphere of a party Congress, for example, he makes his points in the following—folksy—way:

> Recently I was on a visit in the eighth district of Budapest. In the conference room of the party committee, where our conversations took place, there was a portrait of Lenin on the wall. As time passed, I told the comrades that something was missing from that wall—a clock. For at the headquarters of the Central Committee there is both

18. *János Kádár: Selected Speeches and Interviews*, p. 450.

19. There have been several instances over the years when such "provocative" books already published were suddenly withdrawn from the bookstores. One such book was a 1971 biography of Béla Kun by György Borsányi, a well-known historian associated with the [Hungarian] Institute of Party History. Another was the memoirs of Endre Sik, Kádár's foreign minister from 1958 to 1961. Both described the Stalinist terror of the 1930s in the Soviet Union as seen and experienced by Hungarian Communist émigrés then living in Moscow. The Soviet embassy in Budapest was said to have complained about the books' unfavorable characterization of the Soviet Union. Censorship of a different type has been applied to other books, published only after major cuts had been made. The prime example is Zoltán Vas's memoirs, the published version of which bears almost no resemblance to the original. In this case, too, the main objection was Vas's description of his encounters with Soviet leaders.

a Lenin portrait and a clock on the wall, and they're very suggestive. When we look at both, Lenin and the clock together tell us what to do, when, in what spirit, and in what direction. The clock by itself also suggests that time is rapidly passing by, let's hurry as much as we can.[20]

Kádár's life-style complements the simplicity of his speeches. He is known to be a chess fan, is often seen at soccer games, and apparently enjoys playing cards—preferring neither a sophisticated game like bridge nor the gambler's favorite, poker, but the Hungarian equivalent of gin rummy called *ulti*.[21] He has also been observed taking leisurely walks in Budapest and doing so at times without a police escort. In contrast to other politicians—in Eastern Europe or for that matter elsewhere—who feel they must humble themselves to display human qualities, Kádár is not burdened with a complicated intellect and can therefore make people feel at ease in his company. As a result, while he has probably not converted anyone to the subtleties of Marxism-Leninism, his simplicity has made him, and through him the system he has built, palatable if not popular.

As to Kádár's style of decision-making, he has followed an apparently consistent pattern during much of his political life. At first he collects information, avoids commitments, delays action, and tests the political climate. Because of such circumspection, he arouses the expectation of compromise, of a necessary reconciliation of differing positions. Given his reputation as the pragmatic centrist he is, he is always thought to seek a middle course between the "extremes" of right and left. Yet, on closer examination, Kádár's most important decisions suggest another interpretation: that while he is cautious in the first phase of the decision-making process, he is quite prepared to act in a firm and authoritative manner subsequently, at the time when policy decisions are actually finalized, announced, and implemented.

20. János Kádár, *A szocialista Magyarországért: Beszédek és cikkek, 1968–1972* [For a Socialist Hungary: Speeches and Articles, 1968–1972] (Budapest, 1972), p. 390.

21. In September 1960 Kádár traveled to a meeting of the United Nations in New York on the small passenger liner *Baltika* in the company of other leaders of the Soviet bloc. The Soviet diplomat Arkady N. Shevchenko, who subsequently defected, recalls that while Kádár struck him as "intelligent, shrewd, and energetic," "On the *Baltika* he had evidently decided to relax and enjoy himself, devoting himself to playing cards. Card-playing, indeed, seemed to be an obsession with the Hungarians: give them five free minutes, and they would break out a deck. On this trip, even Khrushchev got a little angry at the day-and-night card games. After playing around the clock, Kádár was frequently too tired to appear for breakfast." Arkady N. Shevchenko, *Breaking with Moscow* (New York: Alfred A. Knopf, 1985), p. 98.

Kádár has adhered to this pattern during the more dramatic turning points of his political career. In the first instance, when he was released from prison and rehabilitated in 1954, he joined neither Nagy's revisionist nor Rákosi's dogmatic party faction. He played a waiting game for two years, until the early summer of 1956, when he finally turned against Rákosi openly and, after the latter's removal, rejoined the reconstituted party leadership. In the second instance, Kádár appears to have weighed his alternatives for several years in the 1960s before taking steps to quash his opponents and critics on the left so as to allow him to prepare for the institution of the New Economic Mechanism (NEM) and generally to develop the character of his more tolerant regime.

In both cases, international rather than internal factors—primarily sensitivity to Soviet developments—appear to have constituted the major consideration for the timing of Kádár's policy shifts. In early 1956 it was the anti-Stalinism of the 20th CPSU Congress—and Mikoyan's and Suslov's visits to Budapest—that made Kádár an active opponent of Rákosi and Rákosi's Stalinist practices. In the early 1960s he assumed a moderate, reformist stance only after Khrushchev's decisive victory over the hard-line dogmatists at the 22nd Congress of the Communist Party of the Soviet Union in October 1961.

Economic aspects. The best known feature of "Kádárization" is of course the New Economic Reform.[22] Formally introduced in 1968, NEM has since had a few ups and downs: it was pursued quite vigorously from 1968 to 1972, all but shelved for several years in the mid-1970s,[23] and then pursued again after 1979.

In a nutshell, NEM has signified a few major, structural changes in the Hungarian economy, all aimed at encouraging decentralization and competition. Above all, the role of central economic agencies has been

22. For an analysis of NEM in the context of economic developments in the Soviet bloc, see Morris Bornstein, "Economic Reform in Eastern Europe," in Joint Economic Committee, U.S. Congress, *East European Economies Post-Helsinki* (Washington, D.C.: GPO, 1977), pp. 102–34. For a more recent evaluation of NEM, see Paul Marer, "Economic Reform in Hungary: From Central Planning to Regulated Market," in Joint Economic Committee, U.S. Congress, *East European Economies: Slow Growth in the 1980's* vol. 3 (Washington, D.C.: GPO, 1986), pp. 223–92. The most comprehensive account of the early years is William F. Robinson, *The Pattern of Reform in Hungary: A Political, Economic and Cultural Analysis* (New York: Praeger, 1973).

23. For a candid discussion of the political reasons for the reform's slowdown between 1972 and 1979, see Rezső Nyers, "A szocialista politika és a reformok" [Socialist Politics and the Reforms], *Jelenkor* 28, no. 12 (December 1985): 1027–37. Nyers is widely regarded as the "father" of NEM. In 1974 he lost his positions in both the Politburo and in the party's secretariat.

significantly reduced. The various Five Year and annual plans these agencies still issue no longer determine enterprise policy. Instead, they are treated as "indicators" that can and do influence enterprise production plans through fiscal and monetary incentives; but they are not binding directives. Similarly, while the government still controls all large investments, the enterprises can decide what to do with most of the profit they make. To some extent, prices and wages have been liberated from central control too: with many exceptions and within governmental guidelines, they are determined at the enterprise level. Furthermore, the breakup of unduly large trusts in industry and mining has led to the rise of new, smaller, and presumably more efficient industrial units.

In addition to enhancing enterprise autonomy, NEM has entailed the modernization of Hungarian agriculture. As the cooperatives, encompassing about 75 percent of the country's arable land, are almost free to choose their own leaders, almost free to purchase advanced machinery, fertilizers, and pesticides from the West, including the United States, and almost free to price and sell their products at home or abroad, a prosperous peasantry in the Hungarian countryside has become NEM's major achievement. Stimulated by tax concessions, agricultural growth rates have quite consistently surpassed industrial growth rates. Indeed, agriculture has become a major factor in Hungarian exports to the West and to the East alike, helping to overcome Hungary's persistent balance of trade and balance of payments deficits.

Moreover, because existing repair outlets could not meet the increasing demand for services, agricultural cooperatives have been encouraged to set up their own service facilities and utilize their members' free time (especially in the winter months). In both the countryside and in the cities, individuals have also been allowed to open private repair shops as well as small restaurants, boutiques, and the like. In Budapest there have come to be several taxi companies, for example, that engage in a lively and vigorous competition for business.

To assess NEM in economic terms is beyond the scope of this chapter. It is clear, however, that the semi-autonomous existence of enterprises has introduced an element of competition into the Hungarian economy. With profit rather than the quantitative fulfillment of the central plan as a primary consideration, an element of economic rationality has returned to economic management and decision-making. Perhaps most important, the wider availability of goods and wage differentiation have had the combined effect of prompting the ambitious, the skilled, and the talented to work hard. Therefore, despite all the resistance to these changes, especially during the "lost years" of 1972 to 1979, and despite inflation and an apparent decline in the standard of living in the early 1980s, NEM may still be regarded as a success.

Alas, various comparative economic indicators that would validate this conclusion are either unavailable or unreliable. It is not clear how to determine or even how to estimate Hungary's GNP or its growth rate, especially in comparison with other bloc countries.[24] There is no conclusive proof that would confirm the impression that the standard of living in Hungary is higher than it is elsewhere in the Warsaw Pact, except for East Germany and perhaps Czechoslovakia. To reach the conclusion that NEM is nonetheless a success, it is therefore necessary to ask the question: In the absence of reform, would the Hungarian economy have performed better or worse? In the unanimous judgment of economists, Hungarian and Western, the certain answer to *this* question is that NEM has made things better.

Yet, there remains considerable opposition to some of the more radical ideas economists and others have put forth to carry the reform forward and thus modernize the Hungarian economy. For example, a 1985 bill providing for poorly performing factories to go bankrupt was withdrawn at the last minute. Notwithstanding occasional reports in the press about people looking for jobs and not finding any, unemployment is still "illegal" and hence managers do not have proper authority to dismiss incompetent or unnecessary workers. Hence the most persistent challenges to NEM are not economic but ideological constraints. They have to do with the trade-off between equity and incentives and with the growing gap between the income of the poor and the well-to-do. Indeed, the most pressing problem, perhaps an insoluble task, for the Kádár regime has been to find the appropriate formula for the distribution of wealth and other resources in this socialist society. For example, there are strong advocates of "affirmative action" in Hungary. Should the universities encourage social mobility for the children of workers by making class origin rather than talent a decisive consideration for admission? If the Kádár regime were to return to the previous practice of favoring children of the working class, and hence

24. For a major effort to recalculate several bloc countries' per capita GNPs, see Paul Marer, "Alternative Estimates of the Dollar GNP and Growth Rates of the CMEA Countries," in Joint Economic Committee, U.S. Congress, *East European Economies: Slow Growth in the 1980's* vol. 1 (Washington, D.C.: GPO, 1985), pp. 133–93. Marer's study has produced the following figures for per capita GNP (in dollars) in 1975 and 1980, respectively: *German Democratic Republic*: $3,200 and $5,910; *Czechoslovakia*: $2,780 and $4,740; *Hungary*: $2,340 and $4,390; *Poland*: $2,340 and $3,730; *Romania*: $1,230 and $2,680; *Bulgaria*: Not available. The corresponding figures for the Soviet Union were $2,280 and $4,190. The Hungarian data is not unimpressive.

uphold the value of social mobility, would not the country deprive itself of the kind of manpower the increasingly sophisticated Hungarian economy needs?

In addition, there is the problem of wage differentiation. The New Economic Mechanism has opened the way for enterprises to compete for manpower. Moving from one job to another, even for marginal advantage, has become common practice—one that often complicates and impedes planned development. Far more disturbing, however, given the regime's socialist orientation, is the increasing gap between the poor and the well-to-do. In a remarkably candid study, Zsuzsa Ferge pointed out that already in the early 1970s incomes frequently varied by a factor of eight or ten and thus the country's wage structure was not markedly different from that prevalent in the capitalist world. Hence, she added, "it contains the seeds of social tension."[25]

In short, "Kádárization" has created its own "contradictions." It has reduced the role of central authorities in general and the party bureaucracy in particular in the process of giving effect to political and economic reforms. By assigning significance to profit and economic rationality, it has departed from the tradition of allowing political considerations to be the decisive factor in the making of economic policy. Its antiegalitarianism has had a pernicious effect on the industrial working class, which has benefited little from the reforms; it is also the group least comfortable with the entrepreneurial spirit NEM has brought to life. With class distinctions in evidence and class antagonisms only barely under the surface, the more orthodox party leaders—forming as they did in 1972 the so-called "workers opposition"—have cause in the mid-1980s too to press for equity and thus for a slowdown in, if not a reversal of, Kádár's reformist course.

Judging by his past patterns of behavior, Kádár is not about to be swayed by internal pressures alone. He is likely to continue to take them into account and thus veto a radical proposal or two that would give added weight to market or profit considerations. He might even promote some of the advocates of orthodoxy or sacrifice some of the advocates of reform —but only in the case of *increased Soviet pressure* against NEM would he alter his strategic direction. Given Kádár's apparently deep conviction that Hungary has embarked on the road to a workable model of socialism, as well as his proven political skills and determination to defend his

25. Zsuzsa Ferge, *Társadalmunk rétegeződése: Elvek és tények* [The Stratification of Our Society: Theories and Facts] (Budapest, 1973), pp. 190–98.

reformist course, "Kádárization" is the legacy he is going to leave to his successors.

Sources of the "Kádár Mystique"

Tito of Yugoslavia once pioneered political and economic reforms within the confines of a one-party, but independent, Communist system, but Kádár has pioneered and sustained political and economic reforms both within the confines of a one-party Communist system and of the Soviet bloc. His achievement is certainly not a function of either Kádár's economic or theoretical brilliance. Indeed, the Western view identifying "Kádárization" primarily with economic reform is erroneous. "Kádárization" is primarily a political act. More than anything else, Kádár is a masterful practitioner of the art of politics, of gradualism and circumspection.

Alas, despite frequent references to his past, Kádár's official biography,[26] his speeches, and interviews provide few clues to the "Kádár mystique." When and how did he discover his life's mission as pursued since the early 1960s? What in his background prepared him to be the cautious and yet persistent reformer he has become? Did any of his associates—if so, who?—play a role in tutoring him about the expedient exercise of authority vis-à-vis his more orthodox critics in the HSWP? When and how did he acquire his extraordinary skills to handle the shrewd proprietors of power in the Kremlin? How did he get to the point of asking—of telling—Alexander Dubček of Czechoslovakia three days before the Soviet leaders crushed the "Prague Spring" of 1968: "Do you really not know the kind of people you're dealing with?" Indeed, what has happened to Kádár's early idealism: has he turned into a calculating man of realpolitik he is often seen to have become?

These questions cannot be answered well; but the following tentative and certainly incomplete list of experiences in and influences on Kádár's life might shed some light on the sources of his conduct.

(1) In his dealings with the Soviet Union, Kádár has followed a pattern reminiscent of the Horthy regime's dealings with Hitler's Germany. Under Horthy, Hungary was Hitler's reluctant ally. Even as Hungarians fought and died for the Third Reich during World War II, Horthy—and particularly his prime minister, Miklós Kállay—tried to keep the door open to the Western allies, Great Britain and the United States. Kállay's diplomatic

---

26. L. Gyurkó, "Introductory Biography," in *János Kádár: Selected Speeches and Interviews*, pp. 1–165.

stance became known as *hintapolitika*, literally "seesaw policy," meaning a small state's maneuvers to gain a measure of independence under the shadow of a dominant great power. It was in response to this *hintapolitika* that the Germans occupied Hungary in March 1944 and removed Kállay from office.

In his speeches, Kádár has frequently referred to Horthy as a Fascist, and he has never made a positive reference to *hintapolitika*. Indeed, having joined the illegal Communist party in 1932, Kádár fought the Horthy regime all his youth. Hence the evidence for the conclusion that he has learned something from Horthy's and especially Kállay's wily maneuvers is admittedly slim. It is a fact, however, that Kádár's formative political experiences were during World War II when he observed these complex and somewhat pathetic diplomatic maneuvers. It is also quite telling that Hungarian historical scholarship has recently discovered some positive elements in the politics of the Horthy era. For example, the country's leading historian, who is also director of the Historical Institute of the Hungarian Academy of Science, recently published a provocative essay about geopolitical continuity, suggesting that it is always the fate of small states to look for realistic ways to reduce rather than either accept or eliminate the influence of their larger, dominant neighbors.[27]

(2) As far as Kádár's personality is concerned, it may be significant—*he* thinks it is significant—that he grew up living a "double life," full of ambiguity, short of friends and deep roots. This is how he recalled those years in an interview:

> For about the first ten years of my stay in Budapest I led a kind of "double" life. During the school year I went to school and worked here, like any other "Budapest resident"; in the summer months I lived in the country on the farmsteads, for the first years in Somogy, later in Pest and Békés Counties. . . . The drawback of the "double life" which I led in my childhood was that I suffered a lot for it; in Budapest I was called a "country boy" while in the village I was a "city boy," so that in fact my contemporaries looked upon me as fundamentally alien both here and there.[28]

It seems that as an adult Kádár has also led a "double life." He has become something of a political commuter; he is not fully at home either in Budapest or in Moscow. Even though he is not regarded as "funda-

27. György Ránki, "Mozgástér és kényszerpálya" [approx. Elbowroom and Constraints], *Valóság*, November 1983: 1–15.

28. "Conversation with Lajos Mesterházi, Editor in Chief of 'Budapest' Magazine, February 1967," in *János Kádár: Selected Speeches and Interviews*, p. 290.

mentally alien both here and there," his childhood appears to have prepared him to adjust quickly to different customs and different demands on
him. The flexibility he had to have as a child to make himself accepted has
served him well ever since.[29]

(3) One of Kádár's most important traits is his political finesse. He
moves his colleagues up, down, sideways, and out. He also remembers
well who let him down or who supported him and under what
circumstances. He tends to wait for the appropriate political moment to
penalize a disingenuous or reward a helpful associate.

Kádár's ability to keep his cards close to his chest and to plan ahead may
well have developed in his youth. Playing *ulti*, still one of his favorite
pastimes, he learned early on how to finesse an opponent's high cards (as in
bridge) and why not to play his aces too early. Moreover, as a fine junior
chess player in the 1930s (who still reads chess books), Kádár acquired
some of the skills and characteristics he continues to display: patience,
deliberation, persistence, making your moves at the right time, taking
advantage of an opponent's occasional lack of attention, and above all
playing for long-term advantage.

(4) Another source of Kádár's tenacity is his past as an underdog. He
was an illegitimate child. He was a member and then a leader of an
illegal—the Communist—movement. He spent time in jail. He never
had a chance to get a formal education. As a young boy, he played soccer

29. There is a strangely recurring theme in Kádár's speeches that psychologists would
likely interpret as "compensation"—an attempt to keep stressing and repeating a particular disposition or attitude in order to assure the self and perhaps others as well that the
opposite disposition or attitude is invalid or nonexistent. In Kádár's case, he defends himself
frequently—too frequently—against feelings of equivocation, ambiguity, excessive
flexibility, and even double-dealing. On too many occasions he has found it necessary to
assert the following: "Our policy has always been characterized by frankness and a lack of
ambiguity. . . . We feel that a socialist country cannot pursue a double-dealing policy,
that a Marxist-Leninist, a Communist party cannot represent an equivocal policy vis-à-vis
its own class, its own people, and others. We feel that people listen to us and trust us if we
say the same thing on the same issue in Budapest, New York, and Moscow alike and do not
deviate from it according to where we say it." *Népszabadság*, March 30, 1974. Six years later
Kádár told a party Congress: "You may rest assured that, whether here at home or abroad,
whether at the seat of the United Nations or at the Helsinki Conference, whether in
Moscow, Warsaw, Prague, Berlin, Bucharest, Belgrade, Sofia, Vienna, Rome, Bonn, or
Paris, we advocate the same policy, we uphold the same position. By saying this, we should
like people whose thinking is close to ours and those whose thinking is far from ours to
know and understand that when Hungarians say yes, they mean yes, and when they say no,
they mean no. . . . We have never concealed our stand from anyone, anywhere." *János
Kádár: Selected Speeches and Interviews*, p. 449. Of course, Kádár has said different things and
has behaved differently in different places and under different circumstances, perhaps still
leading the "double life" as he once learned to do as a child.

but he was not good enough to make it in the first league. After the war, when he occupied high positions in the party and the government, he always found himself intellectually outclassed by Rákosi, Révai, and the other widely read, cultivated Muscovites. The group around Imre Nagy was also made up of people who spoke several languages and who in other ways too were intellectually superior to him.

There is a word in Hungarian that identifies a simple, uneducated worker. It is *proli*, a word derived from *proletár*; it is a rather derogatory term. All his life, Kádár was such a *proli*. However many books he has read (and he is said to be an avid reader of Hungarian literature) and however much he has come to be recognized around the world (and he is probably the most famous Hungarian that country has ever had), he continues to identify with the industrial working class and with the cause of socialism he has always regarded as the best cure for the ills of *proli* life.

As the underdog he used to be and as the advocate of socialism he has always been, Kádár has had to prove many other proponents of "socialism" wrong. More than anything else, in my view, this is what has motivated him: to prove Rákosi wrong, to prove Imre Nagy wrong, to prove the Kremlin wrong. Separately and collectively, they had spoiled his dream of rising above all the problems and difficulties and still building a viable socialist society. Kádár has had to revenge them by showing that he could do what they failed to do: making Hungary a showpiece for "Kádárization," for his expedient version of socialism.

Surely an idealist without illusions, Kádár has thus steered a course between what he feels is desirable and what he knows is possible under the circumstances. In the process, he has deprived his people of some of *their* aspirations, of their hope to be free. From their perspective, this is the tragedy of "Kádárization." Its virtue, from Kádár's perspective, is that only this way could he keep Moscow at an arm's length.

Kádár and the Kremlin

For almost twenty-five years, until about 1980 or so, Kádár had supported Soviet foreign policy without fail; on no significant international issue had Hungary departed from Soviet positions. In words, too, Kádár had seldom missed an opportunity to acknowledge Moscow's claim to foreign policy hegemony in the bloc. "It is our conviction," he said in 1967, for example, "that neither here nor in any other socialist country nor in a capitalist country can anyone call himself a Communist, an internationalist or even a progressive person if he turns against the Soviet Union or advocates anti-Soviet views."[30] "We know," Kádár explained in a less bombastic fashion in 1978, "that in our society there are people who applaud Hungarian-Soviet friendship, though in reality they think and act otherwise. . . . [But the] essential element of Hungarian-Soviet friendship is that our principles, goals and interests are the same and coincide."[31]

To gain sufficient elbow room for "Kádárization" at home, Kádár had regarded it essential not to take foreign policy positions different from those of the Kremlin. To the extent differences had existed at all, they had to do with issues related to economics.

In 1972, in the first and only case of strong and public disagreement between Hungary and the Soviet Union, Prime Minister Jenő Fock acknowledged "both minor and major difficulties" in economic relations between the two countries. The issue arose because of Moscow's unwillingness to agree to long-term deliveries of Soviet raw materials, particularly energy. Conceding that he was "unable to get a definite answer at present from the Soviet comrades," Fock added: "To tell the truth, I didn't even expect an answer, but I wished to sow this seed so that the Soviet comrades might ponder the fact that we, as a country poor in raw materials, cannot plan without knowing that our raw material requirements—including, in the first place, fuel oil and natural gas—are assured."[32]

An article in *Pravda* preceding Fock's visit had indicated why Moscow was not more forthcoming; it alluded to "petty-bourgeois tendencies" in Hungary and implied Soviet reservations about NEM.[33] No doubt encouraged by such Soviet signals, the "workers' opposition" elements in the party leadership then attempted and succeeded in reversing the country's reformist course in a few months. Kádár was compelled to defend himself,[34] while Fock, a reformist, resigned as prime minister in 1975.

Economic considerations had also played a role in an earlier and rather muted dispute in 1968 that had to do with the Soviet treatment of the "Prague Spring" in Czechoslovakia. This was the first time since 1956 that Hungary had pursued an active foreign policy aimed at protecting the Czechoslovak experiment in "socialism with a human face." Kádár's appar-

30. *Népszabadság*, September 8, 1967. Many similar statements can be found in *Yanosh Kadar: Izbrannye stati i rechi (oktyabr 1964-aprel 1970 g.)* (Moscow, 1970).

31. *János Kádár: Selected Speeches and Interviews*, p. 408.

32. Radio Budapest, March 29, 1972, as quoted in "Soviet-Hungarian Disagreements," *Radio Liberty Dispatch*, May 3, 1972.

33. *Pravda*, February 3, 1972.

34. Cf. Charles Gati, "The Kádár Mystique," *Problems of Communism* 22, no. 3 (May–June 1974): 23–35.

ent purpose was to limit the scope of the Czechoslovak reforms and to keep the Russians out—and thereby legitimize Hungary's own New Economic Mechanism.

At a meeting of bloc leaders in Warsaw, Kádár therefore advised patience. From the vivid account of the meeting supplied by Władysław Gomułka's interpreter,[35] who subsequently defected, it turns out that this was a most acrimonious gathering. Kádár's main antagonist was Walter Ulbricht of the German Democratic Republic, an early advocate of intervention against the Dubček regime: "If you think, Comrade Kádár, that you are helping the cause of socialism with your objections and reservations, you are making a big mistake. And you have no idea what will happen next. Once the American-West German imperialists have got Czechoslovakia in their control, then you will be next to go, Comrade Kádár. But that is something you can't or won't understand!" Although Ulbricht was not speaking for the Kremlin, the subsequent Warsaw Pact intervention cast a shadow on Kádár's relations with the Soviet leaders. In Hungary itself, Kádár's popularity was at its peak, perhaps, as Kádár had allowed only a token Hungarian contingent to take part in the invasion and he remained silent for several weeks before finally voicing his reluctant and very grudging approval of the action taken by the Kremlin.

During all these years, then, the only discordant note in the otherwise harmonious relationship between Budapest and Moscow had to do with Kádár's hope for a strong Soviet endorsement of NEM and the Soviet reluctance to give him such an endorsement. But, despite the initial green light both Khrushchev and Leonid Brezhnev had given it, the New Economic Mechanism was never fully supported by the Kremlin; its attitude was always ambiguous.

On the one hand, all Soviet leaders appeared to welcome Hungary's relative economic prosperity and especially its political stability. After all, where was another country in Eastern Europe with a genuinely popular leader? Khrushchev was particularly boastful of Kádár's "goulash Communism"; he seemed to appreciate the message this viable Communist system was sending to Western Europe. With all the trouble Poland was to give the Kremlin in 1970, 1976, and then in 1980–81, it must have been comforting to observe Kádár's successful effort to tame the Hungarian people. Even Brezhnev, who was probably quite skeptical about NEM, missed few opportunities to praise the successes of Hungarian agriculture.[36]

35. Erwin Weit, *At the Red Summit: Interpreter Behind the Iron Curtain* (New York: Macmillan, 1973), pp. 193–217.
36. For a detailed discussion, see Charles Gati, "The Soviet Stake in Eastern Europe," in

On the other hand, however, the more Hungary pursued its reformist course and the more it needed Western credit and technology to keep NEM on track, the more anxious the Kremlin appeared to be. After all these years of loyalty and indeed subservience, was Hungary adopting an activist foreign policy? In the early 1980s (for details, see chapter 9) tension between the two countries grew *over words* as the Kádár regime began to advocate a new formulation about the legitimacy of upholding the "national interest" in a socialist country's foreign policy. As late as 1978, as noted above, Kádár had still argued that Hungarian and Soviet "principles, goals and interests [were] the same"; now the emphasis turned to the special role of "small- and medium-size European countries" in maintaining cordial relations even at a time of "superpower" discord.

While Hungary was obviously advancing such views primarily in order to protect and to continue its beneficial commercial relations with Western Europe, *Pravda* editorialists in 1985 responded by calling attention to the danger of "revisionism" in an as yet unnamed fraternal country. However, referring to the two million Western tourists visiting Hungary every year, by 1986 another *Pravda* article warned the Kádár regime explicitly about some Westerners who "seek to exploit commercial contacts, scientific and cultural exchanges, and tourist trips in order to spread bourgeois ideology and anti-socialist propaganda."[37] Although Mikhail S. Gorbachev was reportedly impressed by NEM, particularly by the performance of Hungarian agriculture, some Soviet economists also became anxious. At a 1985 conference of Soviet and Hungarian economists in Moscow, one Soviet participant was said to have turned to his Hungarian colleagues: "Comrades, could you just answer me one question? In your country, is it still the plan which determines the market or is it now the market which determines the plan?"[38] The implication was clear: with its emphasis on market conditions, the Hungarian economy was moving away from the path of socialism—at least the Soviet-style path of socialism.

The pointed question underlines growing Soviet concern about the quiet and rather innocuous signals Hungary has been sending the West in the mid-1980s. *Just signals? Just words?* Or is it possible that the Kádár regime has embarked on a more flexible foreign policy in order to realize its domestic priorities? On this score, at least, the Kremlin appears to have little to worry about. The legacy of "Kádárization" is domestic reform, political and economic, and Kádár is not likely to endanger his

Seweryn Bialer and Thane Gustafson, eds., *Russia at the Crossroads: The 26th Congress of the CPSU* (London: Allen & Unwin, 1982), pp. 178–91.

37. I. Vorozheikin and V. Gerasimov, "Grani vzaimnosti," *Pravda*, January 22, 1986.

38. Information by two Hungarian economists who attended this closed conference.

achievements by testing Soviet tolerance in the foreign policy realm as well.

At the end of his long political career, Kádár remains a cautious reformer interested in achievable goals.

PART THREE

The Soviet Bloc at Century's End

8

Stalin's Foreign Policy Is Alive and Well

The three central arguments of this chapter are that Stalin's foreign policy was less consistently aggressive and revolutionary than is commonly assumed; that his successors' foreign policy has been more aggressive and revolutionary than is commonly assumed; and that there has therefore been more continuity in the conduct of Soviet foreign policy than is commonly assumed. All of these arguments run counter to widely held Western views.

Since Stalin's death in 1953, many Western students of Soviet foreign policy have emphasized "change" rather than "continuity" in the international orientation of the Soviet Union—change for the better, evolution toward moderation and restraint.[1] In the 1970s, in particular, it was frequently observed that Soviet foreign policy—responding both to a new external environment and to different internal circumstances—had successfully shed its Stalinist past. Having substantially reduced its revolutionary commitments, the Soviet Union was said to have become an essentially status quo power—steady and ambitious but not reckless, at times assertive but not adventurist, and invariably pragmatic.[2]

1. In American culture, "change" often denotes "improvement." Manufacturers tend to celebrate "change," for example, when they market a "new, improved toothpaste." I define change as the act or process of substitution. To give but one illustration, Moscow has long understood a "sphere of influence" to signify "exclusive control." If it were to understand that concept to signify only "extensive influence"—the classical meaning of the concept —then Soviet foreign policy could be said to have "changed" in that respect.

2. Similar observations were once made about Stalin's Russia as well. In 1933, for example, the historian Michael T. Florinsky wrote that, "The former crusaders of world revolution at any cost have exchanged their swords for machine tools. . . ." In 1943 Senator Tom Connally of Texas found that the "Russians for years have been changing their economy and approaching the abandonment of Communism. . . ." After quoting such nonsense, Henry A. Kissinger explained the context succinctly and well:

Is such a general appraisal of post-Stalin foreign policy, and the cautious optimism it has produced in the West, really warranted? Did de-Stalinization in foreign policy accompany Soviet domestic de-Stalinization?

I think not. With the important exception of Moscow's modified approach to Eastern Europe, the year 1953 was not a watershed in Soviet foreign policy. A comparison of post-Stalin Soviet foreign policy patterns with Stalinist behavior from 1928 to 1953 reveals far more continuity than change. As a basic approach to the outside world, Stalin's conduct of foreign policy was calculating and circumspect, and his historic mix of expansion and accommodation, revolutionary assertiveness and peaceful coexistence, the "exclusionary" and the "inclusionary" approaches—a clever blend of the hard line and the soft line that served the Soviet state so well for so long—has remained deeply ingrained in the Soviet political mind. On balance, Stalin cannot be said to have placed more emphasis on revolution making than his successors have on upholding or maintaining the status quo. Essentially cautious and opportunistic, the Soviet leaders since Lenin have displayed revolutionary assertiveness when and where it seemed safe to do so, while favoring the status quo and peaceful coexistence when and where it seemed necessary or useful to do so. All of them, and perhaps especially Stalin, consistently refused to risk the security of the Soviet Union for distant, revolutionary goals. After all, as early as the mid-1920s Stalin had already advocated for the emerging Soviet state the largely inward-looking posture of "socialism in one country" against Leon Trotsky's more radical, outward-looking alternative of "permanent revolution."

It is true, of course, that the *scope* of Soviet foreign policy has changed. Stalin did not develop a coherent policy toward the colonial areas of Asia and Africa, for example, while his successors have certainly done so toward what is now called the Third World. It is also true that some of the *issues*

There is a measure of pathos in our continued effort to discover "reasonable" motives for the Soviet leaders to cease being Bolsheviks: the opportunities to develop the resources of their own country, the unlimited possibilities of nuclear energy, or the advantages of expanding international trade. The Kremlin has been able to exploit this attitude by periodically launching policies of "peaceful coexistence," which have inevitably raised the debate whether a "fundamental" shift has occurred in Soviet purposes, thus lulling us before the next onslaught.
The Florinsky and Connally quotes are from Henry A. Kissinger, *The Troubled Partnership: A Reappraisal of the Atlantic Alliance* (Garden City, N.Y.: Doubleday Anchor Books, 1966), pp. 190–91. The Kissinger quote is from Henry A. Kissinger, *Nuclear Weapons and Foreign Policy* (Garden City, N.Y.: Doubleday Anchor Books, 1958), p. 7.

on the Soviet agenda are new, such as the current preoccupation with and the management of nuclear weapons systems. And it is also true that some of the foreign policy *problems* are different, especially those having to do with the less than obedient Communist parties and Communist states of the world. Yet, important as some of these changes in the scope, issues, and problems of Soviet foreign policy may seem, they are not so far-reaching as to conclude that Stalin himself would not have made them. Indeed, if Stalin could now survey the achievements, strategies, and methods of Soviet foreign policy since 1953, he would likely endorse its general thrust and congratulate his successors on their skillful adaptation of his approach to new international circumstances.

Furthermore, even if one were inclined to dismiss as political rhetoric Khrushchev's remark that so far as foreign policy toward the West was concerned he and his colleagues continued to regard themselves as Stalinists, the fact remains that Stalin's foreign policy has never been subjected to extensive criticism in the Soviet Union—not even during the height of the domestic de-Stalinization campaign in the mid-1950s. In fact, Stalin was criticized for only two foreign policy faults: the country's military unpreparedness on the eve of World War II and his unduly harsh and ultimately counterproductive treatment of Yugoslavia in 1948 and 1949 (and, by implication, the rest of Eastern Europe). It is not by accident, as *Pravda* might say, that precisely in the two areas of military preparedness and policy toward Eastern Europe have the new Soviet leaders tried —albeit not very successfully in the East European case—to avoid Stalin's mistakes. At any rate, Stalin's successors never accused the old master of excessive aggressiveness or adventurism, nor did they ever promise to de-Stalinize Soviet foreign policy and indeed place it on new foundations.

The reason for the apparent gap between the promise and early pursuit of domestic de-Stalinization, on the one hand, and the lack of de-Stalinization in foreign policy, on the other, is self-evident. While his successors believed that Stalin's domestic policies, particularly the intimidation and terror aimed against the Soviet elite, began to threaten the cause of socialism within the Soviet Union, his foreign policy record spoke well of his skills in promoting Soviet security and the cause of socialism abroad. After all, when Stalin became primus inter pares in 1928, the Soviet Union was weak and vulnerable, an essentially second-rate power; yet by 1953 it was recognized as one of the two superpowers. His successors, having inherited a tested and successful approach to the outside world, have had no reason either to criticize or to change the basic orientation of Stalin's foreign policy.

Continuity or Change?

The emphasis in Western studies on "change" rather than "continuity" in Soviet foreign policy since 1953 stems in part from an undue emphasis on Stalin's foreign policies after World War II. Admittedly, this was an era of expansion in Soviet foreign relations, beginning with the Soviet domination of Eastern Europe, the gradual takeovers in East Central Europe via the "salami tactics," the Berlin crisis of 1948–49, and the unnecessary and avoidable conflict with Yugoslavia—all coupled with intransigent statements and undiplomatic posturing. While some of these policies were indicated by the geopolitical opportunity that World War II had created, Stalin probably did push too hard during the early years of the cold war, especially from the time of the Szklarska Poreba meeting of the Cominform in 1947 to 1950–51. His aggressiveness provided the glue for Western unity against the Soviet Union—as manifested by the Truman Doctrine, the establishment of NATO in 1949, and even the consideration of such countermeasures as the use of atomic weapons against Moscow during the Berlin confrontation (recommended by Churchill, by then a private citizen, but quickly rejected by both Britain and the United States). To the extent that Stalin's policies led to the eventual mobilization of the West and the containment of further Soviet advances, these policies were not only unduly assertive but, from the perspective of long-term Soviet interests, probably counterproductive.

Aggressive Soviet behavior in the early years of the cold war, however, was only one aspect of the Stalinist pattern in Soviet foreign policy. In the early 1930s the Soviet Union concluded a number of treaties and cooperative agreements with such bourgeois states as France, Poland, and Czechoslovakia. In 1935 the 7th Congress of the Communist International, reversing the decisions of the Comintern's 1928 6th Congress, issued an analysis that justified the broad, flexible, coalition-seeking approach—the Popular Front strategy—adopted by Communist parties everywhere. Communists fought together with non-Communists in the Spanish Civil War. During Stalin's reign, a pragmatic Soviet Union first allied itself with Nazi Germany and then formed a grand coalition with such bastions of imperialism as Great Britain and the United States against Nazi Germany. And to accommodate the Soviet Union's immediate foreign policy needs, Stalin repeatedly modified certain features of Marxist-Leninist ideology pertaining to international relations.

Stalin's thinking in nonideological, power-political terms—meaning that he recognized both the uses and the limitations of Soviet power—was even demonstrated during the expansionary postwar era. A reluctant supporter of uncertain revolutionary causes abroad, Stalin denied extensive assistance not only to his comrades in the French and Italian Communist parties (as shown in chapter 1), but also to Mao's revolutionary forces in the Chinese civil war. He maintained relations with Mao's enemy, the Kuomintang's Chiang Kai-shek, as long as the outcome of the civil war was in doubt. Even in Eastern and in East Central Europe, when Stalin thought that he might need Western cooperation in the fall of 1945, he ordered new elections in Bulgaria and agreed to free elections in Hungary. Moreover, while purging Jews in the Soviet Union, he supported the Zionist cause for the establishment of a Jewish state in Palestine—no doubt calculating that such a state would weaken the British in the Middle East. And, finally, Stalin gave new emphasis to the old concept of "peaceful coexistence" and subsequently initiated the coalitionary "peace campaign" of the early 1950s.

Although this brief summary cannot do justice to the complexities of Stalin's foreign policy, it does suggest that Stalin was a rather cautious guardian of the Soviet Union's international interests. During his last years, as Adam Ulam noted, his policies "created an air of tension which, apart from being a source of danger to Russia, was largely unnecessary."[3] Moreover, the language he used to assess international developments and explain Soviet goals abroad contained more ideological referents than can be found in his successors' pronouncements. But Stalin's actual policies invariably reflected his sensitivity to the international balance of forces. As a result, he made all the necessary compromises in order to gain time and strength.

Has any really important change taken place since Stalin's time? Surely both the internal and external environments of Soviet foreign policy have changed: neither the Soviet domestic scene nor the world at large is the same as it was in the 1940s and early 1950s. Very much at issue, however, is the influence these internal and external environments have had on the actual conduct of Soviet foreign policy. In the discussion that follows below these "influences" will be first analyzed in general terms.

Three Internal Influences on Soviet Foreign Policy

The first and by far the most important change in the internal environment of Soviet foreign policy has been the substantially increased relative power of the Soviet Union since Stalin's reign. Although its economy

3. Adam B. Ulam, *Expansion and Coexistence* (New York: Praeger, 1968), p. 543.

remains uneven and technologically inferior to that of the West, the diverse and steadily growing military capability of the post-Stalin Soviet Union attests to its new status in world politics. This important change raises the following question: If Stalin's foreign policy had in part stemmed from a sense of weakness and insecurity, what foreign policy would follow enhanced Soviet domestic strength in the post-Stalin era?

To answer this question, one might assume that the Soviet leaders believe some or most of their self-congratulatory messages about the successes of the Soviet state. In that case, logic suggests that their new confidence about internal strength should help them overcome their often-noted historic sense of insecurity vis-à-vis the outside world, especially the West, and prompt them to pursue a more accommodating foreign policy.

Alternatively, one might suppose that, despite their remarkable achievements, the post-Stalin leaders still lack sufficient confidence in the viability of the Soviet domestic order. Perhaps they measure their accomplishments against more ambitious ultimate objectives or against the power of the United States, and therefore they find these accomplishments lacking. Their self-congratulatory messages may be no more than the official optimism and wishful thinking characteristic of political discourse everywhere. In that case, logic suggests that the Soviet leaders' apparent lack of self-confidence about the internal health of the Soviet Union would only reinforce their historic sense of inferiority vis-à-vis the outside world, especially the West, and prompt them to compensate for perceived weakness at home by pursuing an assertive or even aggressive foreign policy.

The underlying issue is thus one of causality, about which Western analysts cannot agree at all. Take two typical examples: In his perceptive analysis of the interwar period—an era of considerable Soviet weakness—Alexander Dallin concluded that "perceived weakness need not always produce a conciliatory mood in Moscow; nor does the willingness to seek a détente or a compromise need to stem from weakness alone."[4] Speaking of the post-Stalin years—an era of increasing Soviet strength—Morton Schwartz explicitly presented both interpretations as equally plausible. In one passage, he wrote: "Convinced of their superiority—a conviction strengthened by their vast military power—the Kremlin leaders may be anxious to flex their new muscles. Thus, in the years ahead they may probe for ways to expand Soviet influence around the world." In another passage,

4. Alexander Dallin, "Soviet Foreign Policy and Domestic Politics: A Framework for Analysis," in Erik P. Hoffmann and Frederic J. Fleron, eds., *The Conduct of Soviet Foreign Policy*, 2d ed. (Hawthorne, N.Y.: Aldine, 1980), pp. 41–42.

however, Schwartz concluded: "A secure Soviet leadership has already become a somewhat more relaxed Soviet leadership."[5]

Unable to reach a firm conclusion about causality, Western analysts are thus unable to confirm the validity of any of the following hypotheses:

1. Domestic weakness leads to foreign policy accommodation.
2. Domestic weakness leads to foreign policy assertiveness.
3. Domestic strength leads to foreign policy accommodation.
4. Domestic strength leads to foreign policy assertiveness.

The validation of any of these hypotheses would not only explain why Soviet conduct does or does not change; it would also have considerable implications for Western policy. It would indicate whether the West should try to encourage a strong and confident Soviet Union or whether it should try to keep Moscow weak and uncertain of its relative power position. But without such a validation, the Soviet Union's newly acquired domestic strength in the post-Stalin era has no explanatory value at all.

The second frequently discussed change in the post-Stalin domestic order has been the apparent decline of ideological rigidity. The reason given for a more pragmatic and flexible Soviet approach to the outside world is that the new leaders did not experience the early, prerevolutionary days and that their mindset was thus formed during the years of socialist construction. As party bureaucrats, managers, soldiers, lawyers, and engineers, they have devoted their lives to practical tasks, not to the making of revolution. While they have participated in political intrigues, most of them did not take part in prerevolutionary conspiracies.

Moreover, the new Soviet leaders, from Khrushchev to Gorbachev, have repeatedly modified Stalin's ideology of international affairs. Wars were once said to be inevitable; now they are not. Revolutions were once said to be inevitable; now there can be a peaceful transition to socialism. The international class struggle used to be the major dogma of foreign policy; now it receives less public emphasis than peaceful coexistence. Automation used to show capitalist inhumanity; now computers (often imported) are considered the new signposts of the scientific-technological revolution. At Lenin's grave, Stalin pledged to uphold the sacred and unshakable unity of the international Communist movement; now his successors have yet to find an ideologically adequate explanation for Soviet military contingency plans against China.

5. Morton Schwartz, *The Foreign Policy of the USSR: Domestic Factors* (Encino & Belmont, Calif.: Dickenson, 1975), pp. 89–91.

Without denying the steady erosion of faith since Lenin's days and the possibly far-reaching implications of this process for the future of Soviet political culture, what should not be forgotten is that the necessity of legitimizing every twist and turn in foreign policy by ideological incantation is hardly a novel phenomenon in Soviet history. Stalin offered an eloquent ideological rationale for the hard line adopted in 1928 as he did for the soft line in 1935. His successors presented an ideological explanation for their 1968 military intervention in Czechoslovakia (the "Brezhnev Doctrine") and for their détente policies toward the West ("peaceful coexistence").

Consider also Soviet views on war and peace. For his part, Stalin stated that there was no way to avoid confrontations between the forces of socialism and imperialism. In 1953 and 1954 Malenkov revised Stalin's assessment, stating that because of the destructive quality of atomic weapons and the increasing might of the Soviet Union, an all-out war with imperialism was no longer inevitable. That was good news, of course, but one must note that (1) Stalin's belief in the inevitability of war did not propel him to begin such wars (as he always sought to enhance Soviet power and influence gradually, indeed incrementally); and that (2) his successors have not denounced such "small" or "just" wars as the so-called wars of national liberation (e.g., Cuba, Vietnam, Cambodia, and Nicaragua) and military intervention in their self-proclaimed sphere (e.g., Hungary, Czechoslovakia, and Afghanistan). In the final analysis, Malenkov's revision of Stalin's dogma merely signifies the acceptance of, and the concurrent ideological rationalization for, what Stalin had practiced. The same can be said about other "changes" in the ideological environment of Soviet foreign policy since Stalin's time. After all, *Pravda* still holds that "there are essentially no neutrals in the struggle between the two world systems."[6] And according to the authoritative Soviet *Diplomatic Dictionary*, peaceful coexistence "is a specific form of class struggle between socialism and capitalism."

Hence Stalin's successors appear to have been no less influenced by ideological precepts than Stalin was supposed to have been. After all, ideological innovation and foreign policy flexibility, not doctrinal rigidity, were Stalin's traits, and his successors have only outperformed him in ideological gymnastics. But even if one were to assume otherwise, does the professed decline of ideological rigidity amount to flexibility? And does more flexibility necessarily translate into an accommodating or moderate

6. April 30, 1969.

foreign policy? It may well be, instead, that neither of these hypotheses is accurate:

1. Rigid ideological environment leads to foreign policy assertiveness.
2. Decline of ideological zeal leads to foreign policy accommodation.

The third change in the domestic environment of Soviet foreign policy since Stalin has been identified as the broadening of the decision-making process, including the rise of elite factions and competing interests. Foreign policy alternatives are debated more openly among a wider circle of advisers and decisionmakers. Resource allocation between military and nonmilitary uses, for example, is a particularly lively issue. Concurrently, the Soviet view of international life has become more sophisticated, with specialists now covering all conceivable aspects of foreign policy analysis and international relations theory from the classical balance of power to simulation and beyond.

The controversial issue here is not the existence of "competing domestic pressures" and factional political struggle (which had been particularly evident during the three succession crises of 1953–57, 1964–69, and the early 1980s), but their consequence for foreign policy. For no one can doubt that the three succession crises had *some* effect on foreign policy. One such effect was the paralysis of the decision-making process, a measure of immobilism leading to the postponement of difficult choices. Another effect was evident in Moscow's policy toward Eastern Europe (see chapter 9), which—during periods of leadership turbulence—has been characterized by confusing and even contradictory signals being sent to the region's leaders and attentive publics.

Such effects aside, the evidence certainly does not suggest that either the succession struggle or the broadening of the decision-making process necessarily result in a somewhat accommodating Soviet foreign policy. Around 1955 it did; around 1965 and 1980 it did not. Political deals and compromises in the Kremlin—and even the need for a breathing spell during times of trouble at the top—*can* produce a temporary thaw abroad and emphasis on discipline at home, but they may also produce a general compromise of the other variety—a thaw at home and a hard line abroad. In other words, the mere existence of divergent interests, needs, views, perceptions, and approaches cannot be said to ensure any consistent pattern in Soviet foreign policy—conciliatory, centrist, or belligerent. A compromise among competing groups and individuals does not require a foreign policy of restraint. Nor can one necessarily expect moderation from a divided post-Stalin foreign policy elite, even if it is better informed and more sophisticated. After all, more expertise does not necessarily mean more caution.

Especially because outsiders do not know the parameters of the foreign policy debates, the validity of any of the following hypotheses cannot be ascertained either:

1. Narrow (Stalinist) decision-making leads to foreign policy assertiveness.
2. Broadening of the decision-making process or factional struggle leads to foreign policy accommodation.
3. Limited knowledge of international life leads to foreign policy assertiveness.
4. Expanding knowledge of international life leads to foreign policy accommodation.

External Influences on Soviet Foreign Policy

The apparent lack of causality between the three major domestic "inputs" and foreign policy makes it particularly apposite to explore the external environment of Soviet conduct. Still keeping the discussion on a fairly general level, could that environment be the source of change in Soviet foreign policy?

To begin with, most members of the international community engage in activities that have a bearing on the Soviet Union. States engage in generally self-serving activities, though not necessarily or always pursuing goals that are contrary to Soviet interests. Under all circumstances, however, given the military might, economic power, political influence, and the global reach of the Soviet Union—in short, its preeminent position in the international system—most states have reason to seek to alter some aspect of Soviet foreign policy. In turn, since the Soviet Union does not operate in a political, military, or economic vacuum, it has to respond to at least some of these attempts to influence its behavior.

The primary external demands on the Soviet Union are (1) for foreign policy "moderation" (i.e., demands on Moscow to help maintain the status quo by refraining from war and intervention) and (2) for "assistance" (i.e., demands to help change the status quo by extending political support and economic as well as military aid). Since these two broad categories of demands are mutually exclusive, the Soviet Union must evaluate and respond to such contradictory external demands, trying to satisfy as many of its more important or more powerful foreign audiences and constituencies as possible. Simply stated, the Soviet Union is linked to many external causes, issues, and audiences whose demands on and expectations of the Soviet Union greatly differ. Moscow can satisfy some of these demands and expectations some of the time; it cannot satisfy all of them all of the time.

Since Stalin's reign, the international environment has dramatically changed. The world Communist movement has disintegrated. The Communist bloc that Stalin built after World War II has all but ceased to act as a united entity. Almost one hundred new and, in many cases, radical states have emerged. Interdependence is a new economic fact of international life. The "leading role" of the United States in the Atlantic alliance has eroded. The "liberation" of Eastern Europe is no longer on the Western agenda. The extraordinarily rapid modernization of weapons systems, spearheaded by the United States, has led to fundamental revisions in the concepts and strategies of warfare.

Some of the changes in the international system, such as the development of new weapons, require Moscow to exercise caution and accommodation; others, such as the rise of new states, may mean opportunities for the expansion of Soviet influence. How can the Soviet Union respond to external influences calling for accommodation? First, it can respond tactically by making a limited and short-term adjustment to external demands. This response is the well-known "one step backward," a temporary concession whose primary purpose is to gain time. This type of response originated with Lenin, and it has long been recognized as part of the repertoire of Soviet diplomacy. The other kind of reaction, as suggested by William Zimmerman, is far more complex and seldom recognized. While it may begin as a tactical adjustment to international reality, over time—if properly stimulated and reinforced—it would transform itself into a learned response. Learning from the benefits of experience and subjected to carefully orchestrated external stimuli, the Soviet Union would thus become capable of genuine and lasting attitude modification and "structural adaptation."[7]

If the Soviet Union indeed has the capability to produce such a response, as Zimmerman argued, the policy implications would be far-reaching indeed. It would signal a major opportunity—and responsibility—for the outside world to influence the Soviet foreign policy elite and to contribute to lasting change. The United States, for example, could act and speak in such a way as to reinforce the position of "moderates" in the Kremlin; it could attempt to show, by words and deeds, the benefits of détente and cooperation for both sides.

7. William Zimmerman, "Choices in the Postwar World: Containment and the Soviet Union," in Charles Gati, ed., *Caging the Bear: Containment and the Cold War* (Indianapolis: Bobbs-Merrill, 1974), pp. 85–108.

Unfortunately, there is reason to be skeptical about the possibility of achieving a lasting adaptation in Soviet foreign policy as a consequence of external influences. For one thing, there is the practical problem of policy coordination by the outside world. Neither now nor in the future can Western leaders know the parameters of internal debates on foreign policy in the Kremlin. But, assuming that they could make a good guess at the choices discussed, can the outside world then coordinate its policies in such a way as to bring about the desired result? Even though the United States is the most closely watched and surely the most important single external input, it is not the only one; and even if it could develop a set of finely tuned policies aimed at properly "educating" and influencing the Kremlin, the foreign policies of other states are likely to cancel out or at least mitigate the impact of the United States's efforts.

Even more fundamental is the problem of conceiving the appropriate mix of external inputs. It is not at all clear whether the outside world should be or should appear to be weak or strong, reassuring or threatening, in order to generate moderation in Soviet foreign policy. Soviet strategic superiority, for example, might help the Soviet leaders overcome their historic sense of inferiority vis-à-vis the West—a possibly valid but rather risky assumption—and thus help to produce a more accommodating Soviet foreign policy. Alternatively, the United States could seek strategic superiority, following the long-held belief that it can influence the Soviet Union only from a position of strength. But if that approach only reinforces a sense of inferiority in the Soviet leadership, the concessions if any will likely be only tactical or short-lived.

Accordingly, unless the West has some reasonably accurate assessment of the impact of external "strength" versus external "weakness" on the Soviet foreign policy debates—in other words, unless it knows what combination of external incentives and prohibitions may pave the way to a lasting tendency toward foreign policy moderation—it cannot be confident about the international environment producing such moderation in Moscow. This is not to deny the import of what the non-Soviet world does or is, or how it goes about conducting its relations with the Soviet Union; it is only to suggest that external environmental influences entering into the calculations of the Soviet leadership will generate no *enduring change* in Soviet conduct. For a set of often conflicting external demands, conditions, or policy inputs cannot make for change; only the balance of perceived needs can. The Soviet leaders themselves must recognize that external developments demand policy reassessment.

The Balance of Perceived Needs:
Key to "Change?"

So far, this chapter has focused in rather general terms on the *logic* of assigning change to Soviet foreign policy on the basis of analyzing the internal and external environments of Soviet conduct. Yet, fascinating as it is to engage in such a semiabstract, academic exercise, the ultimate criterion for a judgment about the sources of change has to be the *record*—the output—of Soviet foreign policy itself.

Reviewing the history of Soviet foreign policy, what changes, what new departures stand out? Under what circumstances did such changes for the better or for the worse come to be?

1. The Soviet Union discarded the early ideal of "revolutionary diplomacy" almost immediately after its establishment in 1917. Accepting the practice of what it had once regarded as "bourgeois" diplomatic intercourse with the outside world, the Soviet leaders promptly decided to enter into regular negotiations with other states and to observe diplomatic protocol. Mainly because Lenin wanted to make peace with Germany and thus to cement his shaky regime at home, he did not hesitate to tell Trotsky that the very survival of the Soviet state required a return to "old" diplomatic practices.

2. The Communist International's post-1928 "exclusionary" strategy —also known as the "United Front from below"—was replaced in the early 1930s by the "inclusionary," Popular Front strategy. Sanctioned at the Soviet-dominated 7th Comintern Congress in 1935, the new approach encouraged all Communist parties to cooperate with the non-Communist left in order to form a united front against the rise of Fascism. Inherent in this fundamental shift was the danger of reducing the once-sacred "leading role" and ideological purity of Communist parties. Yet Stalin presently accepted the potential danger of ideological erosion by socialists, social democrats, and others—those he used to call "social Fascists"—because he assumed that only a broader left coalition could ensure the security of the Soviet Union and defeat the greater danger—Nazi Germany and its allies.

3. Compared with his cautious, quasi-isolationist posture in the interwar period, Stalin initiated an expansionary phase in Soviet foreign policy after World War II, particularly after 1947. With the establishment of pro-Soviet regimes in Eastern Europe, "socialism in one country" gave way to "socialism in one region," because the prewar revolutionary rhetoric could now be translated into policy. As noted earlier, the change was due to the opportunity created by World War II and especially to the lack of counter-vailing power in the international system.

4. Around 1950—51 the confrontationist strategy of the post-1947 period was replaced by the peace campaign in Europe and the gradual opening to the Third World. Unable to break the European impasse and unwilling to risk a military showdown with the United States, Stalin, and subsequently his successors, shelved the rigid "two-camp" doctrine of 1947, resuscitated the "peaceful coexistence" line, and shifted to a rather low-tension policy toward the outside world. Clearly, the Berlin crisis and the Korean War demonstrated that the confrontationist strategy had failed to advance Soviet interests and should therefore be modified. For years to come, the Soviet Union was to look beyond the old world for new gains, relying less on the military than on the economic instrument of foreign policy.

5. Since the mid-1950s Stalin's successors have come to accept, however grudgingly, a degree of experimentation in Eastern Europe. Khrushchev's overture to Tito in 1955 marked the beginning of greater Soviet tolerance toward national traditions and characteristics in Eastern Europe. Despite subsequent interventions aimed at curtailing "excessive" liberalization in the region, Stalin's insistence on strict uniformity has been altered. In order to avoid the chronic and dangerous instability of the Stalin era, Moscow has added the goal of East European viability, however much it entails concessions, to the old goal of bloc cohesion.

6. The Soviet Union, having learned during the Cuban missile crisis that its inferior military posture vis-à-vis the United States had been a major political handicap, initiated a massive program of military investments in the 1960s to catch up with, and possibly surpass, the United States in the arms race. An estimated 12 to 15 percent of the Soviet GNP has since been devoted to military procurements, presumably in order to avoid the kind of humiliation that Moscow suffered in 1962.

These are among the more important new departures—some accommodating, some assertive in character—in the history of Soviet foreign policy. They suggest three conclusions.

First, the Soviet leaders embarked on a new course either when they reached the conclusion that the previous policy had failed or when a new opportunity for expansion had presented itself. Irrespective of whether the new course was initiated under Stalin or his successors, it was usually the Soviet leaders' perception of the failure of the previous policy that prompted the adoption of new approaches and solutions. True, in 1955 Khrushchev used the issue of Tito's rehabilitation as part of his political struggle against those who, like Molotov and Malenkov, had been implicated in the early anti-Tito campaign under Stalin. Yet, even in Eastern Europe, it was mainly the perceived needs of the Soviet state rather than political infighting that produced change in Soviet conduct.

Second, the record of Soviet foreign policy indicates tactical adjustments rather than lasting adaptations. While it may be premature to make a definitive judgment about the most recent period under Gorbachev, it is quite clear, as Zbigniew Brzezinski has noted, that Soviet policy toward the outside world has been characterized by a cyclical pattern—"by alternating offensive and defensive phases."[8] On the same point, Henry Kissinger said: "Peace offensives, of course, are not new in Soviet history. Peaceful coexistence has been avowed since the advent of Communism in Russia. It was stressed particularly between 1934–39; between 1941–46; at the time of the Geneva Summit Conference of 1955; again on the occasion of Khrushchev's visit to the United States in 1959; and following the Cuban Missile Crisis in 1962. . . . On each occasion the period of relaxation ended when an opportunity for expanding Communism presented itself."[9] Given the cyclical pattern of the past, it would require excessive optimism, if not naiveté, to emphasize aspects of lasting change in Soviet foreign policy since Stalin.

Third, the record of both Stalin and his successors suggest neither a rigid "master plan" for global conquest nor a conservative policy aimed at the maintenance of the status quo. If there has been a basic pattern in Soviet foreign policy since Lenin, it is characterized by the persistent, though cautious, pursuit of opportunities abroad—"persistent" because the overall objective of advancing Soviet influence has not changed and "cautious" because the Soviet leaders have usually sought to promote Soviet influence so gradually as to make strong and concerted Western countermeasures unjustifiable.

In the final analysis, then, post-Stalin Soviet foreign policy reflects a curious paradox. While the internal and external environments in which it operates *are* different, the new Soviet leaders—under conflicting pressures, impulses, and demands for both change and continuity—have nonetheless continued to rely on the old, historic mix of assertiveness-and-accommodation. Stalin's heirs must consider this mix to have been effective, and hence they see no need for the kind of change that de-Stalinization has signified in the domestic realm. Of course, as Edmund Burke once observed, one should "never plan for the future by the past." By the same token, however, it makes even less sense to project one's hopes about the Soviet future upon Moscow's past performance.

8. Zbigniew Brzezinski, "The Competitive Relationship," ibid., pp. 157–99.
9. Henry A. Kissinger, *The Troubled Partnership*, pp. 189–90.

9

The Soviet Bloc Is Alive but Not Well

Over four decades have passed since the Soviet bloc that Stalin conceived began to take shape. During these turbulent years, two types of challenges have confronted Soviet authority over Eastern Europe.

First, Moscow has had to cope with popular movements, riots, uprisings, and revolutions such as those that erupted in East Berlin (1953), Poznan (1956), Budapest (1956), Warsaw (1968), Prague (1968), several Polish cities (1970 and 1976), and—most dramatically—throughout Poland under the banner of the Solidarity movement (1980–81). When facing spontaneous challenges from below—popular movements seeking freedom, economic well-being, as well as independence—Moscow, acting directly or indirectly, invariably managed to reestablish its authority.

Second, the Soviet Union has had to cope with individual regime claims such as those that were advanced by Yugoslavia (1948), Albania (1961), and Romania (1964). When facing more or less controlled challenges from the top—demands by a single Communist party leadership for autonomy —Moscow invariably failed to reestablish its authority.

Conceptually, the Soviet Union of the post-Stalin era has responded to these challenges by accepting, however grudgingly, a modicum of diversity in the region. In what may well be the only foreign policy change of broad significance since 1953 (as argued in chapter 8), Moscow has expanded its goals in Eastern Europe by stressing not only Stalin's old notion of bloc cohesion, but also assigning responsibility to each regime for domestic order and stability. To be discussed below, this new definition of Soviet objectives has signified the practice of greater tolerance toward experimentation so as to allow the East European regimes to pursue their own, national "path" to socialism and thus obtain a measure of popular approbation.

Of course, both popular outbursts and individual regime claims for autonomy have still reoccurred time and again since 1953. Worse, a third and different challenge has emerged recently as well: the growing dissatisfaction and assertiveness of Moscow's essentially loyal allies in the Warsaw Pact. For the first time acting concurrently, though not conspiratorially, several like-minded regimes have begun to make an effort in the mid-1980s to trim excessive Soviet influence over their policies. Lacking the dramatic quality of past confrontations and rooted in a common desire for more "elbow room" rather than real independence, several East European regimes are engaged in a subtle attempt to reach out to Europe without offending or provoking the Soviet Union; indeed, they are making an attempt to move toward the West without appearing to move away from the East. By so trying to square the circle, a few East European regimes hope to reap Western economic benefits and gain a measure of respectability at home —and keep Moscow satisfied as well. At a deeper level, they are responding to a sense of European identity and consciousness that has been growing on the continent, East and West. But by proceeding cautiously and by affirming their commitment to the Soviet bloc, that is, to "socialist internationalism," the East European regimes are also responding to the most fundamental political fact of life in the region: their continued dependence on Soviet power for survival.

What are the causes and manifestations of this maneuver by the leaders of Eastern Europe? When it began to emerge, prior to Mikhail S. Gorbachev's appointment, was it related to Soviet leadership changes? Can Moscow stop the further erosion of its authority in the region? Are we witnessing the gradual decline of the Soviet empire or merely a new phase in its evolution?

Causes of Regime Discontent

The East European maneuver of the mid-1980s, which is spearheaded by Hungary, Romania, and the German Democratic Republic (GDR), reflects East European apprehensions about the direction of Soviet foreign policy generally and, in particular, about Soviet economic policy toward Eastern Europe.

As for the direction of Soviet conduct abroad, a large segment of the East European Communist elites appears to have grown critical of Moscow's lack of diplomatic skill and mistaken priorities. Without disagreeing with broad Soviet foreign policy objectives, they are particularly disturbed by the Soviet Union's heavy-handed treatment of Afghanistan; its inability to improve not only party-to-party but also state-to-state relations with China; and, above all, its clumsy and counterproductive handling of, and subsequent withdrawal from, the intermediate-range nuclear forces (INF) talks in Geneva in late 1983. Although only the Romanian government has addressed these issues directly in public, extensive contacts with Hungarian, East German, and Polish functionaries indicate that, from their perspective, too, Soviet conduct appears plagued by miscalculations and missteps.

While granting that the Soviet Union had to do "something" about Afghanistan in 1979, these functionaries wonder if the Kremlin accurately estimated the difficulties the Soviet armed forces would encounter. They wonder if the political and economic costs of the operation will not ultimately exceed the presumed benefits of military victory. Like many a Western observer, they wonder if Afghanistan will turn out to have been "Moscow's Vietnam." Without having specific measures in mind, they speculate whether the Soviet Union should not adopt an "alternative" to the policy it is presently pursuing there. In their view, then, Moscow has allowed itself to be bogged down in a war that it cannot easily win and from which it cannot extricate itself—but for which Eastern Europe has also had to pay in terms of Western diplomatic complaints and economic penalties.

The East European political elites seem to be equally puzzled by Soviet policy toward China. They applaud improvements in state-to-state relations between China and the Soviet Union (and Eastern Europe as well),[1] but they are dissatisfied with the slow pace of the normalization process. Although they share Moscow's suspicions over China's rapprochement with the United States and Western Europe, and believe that Chinese attacks on Soviet "hegemonism" have been unnecessarily harsh, they find the Soviet position altogether inconsistent. If the issue is ideology, they ask, then why does Moscow respond in the same way to present-day Chinese statements and policies as it once did to Mao's statements and policies? If, on the other hand, the primary issue is power rather than ideology, then why cannot Moscow find a diplomatic formula to ease tensions between the two countries? In the East Europeans' view, then, it is primarily though not exclusively the Kremlin's inflexibility that stands in the way of at least partial reconciliation. In the meantime, all of the East European regimes, with the exception of Romania, feel compelled to emulate publicly the Soviet posture toward China that they regard as deeply flawed and believe

    1. For the improvement in Sino-Soviet relations, see the *New York Times*, December 30, 1984. On January 20, 1985, Xinhua reported the departure of a high-level Chinese trade delegation to Czechoslovakia, Hungary, and Poland to sign economic agreements with those states. See Foreign Broadcast Information Service, *Daily Report: China*, January 23, 1985, p. H/2.

to be rooted in the Soviet leadership's grudge against a former—more tractable—ally.

Closer to home, the East European political elites appear especially critical of Soviet policies toward Western Europe in general and of Soviet handling of the INF talks in particular. Rightly or wrongly, it is a widely held view that the Soviet Union could have prevented the deployment of Pershing II ballistic and Tomahawk cruise missiles in Western Europe.[2] They maintain that a more subtle Soviet diplomatic effort—to encourage West European hopes about substantial Soviet concessions—would have so altered the political balance in the Netherlands, Belgium, and even the Federal Republic of Germany (FRG) that the installation of U.S. missiles would have had to be canceled or at least postponed. By first threatening to withdraw from the Geneva INF talks (if the missiles were deployed) and then actually withdrawing (when the missiles were deployed), the Kremlin made it easier for the United States to accomplish that which the Soviet leaders so vigorously and indeed vehemently sought to circumvent. In other words, Moscow should have temporized, not so much in order to conclude an agreement but in order to keep the Atlantic alliance guessing —and divided.

Especially before but even since the appointment of Gorbachev, the common element in the East European elites' critique of Soviet conduct toward Afghanistan, China, and the INF talks has been an increasing concern, mixed with condescension, about the lack of subtlety in the Kremlin's approach to the outside world. In a critique reminiscent of West European reservations about U.S. foreign policy, East European functionaries think of their Soviet ally as being unduly heavy-handed, inflexible, much too self-righteous and clumsy, and insufficiently appreciative of the merits of quiet diplomacy. They are concerned, clearly, because an intransigent Soviet policy creates an unfavorable atmosphere for the expansion of their own economic, cultural, and political relations with the West, particularly with Western Europe.

The expansion of economic relations with the West has become an especially urgent priority for Eastern Europe, and it is so perceived by all of the regimes in the Soviet bloc (with the possible exception of Czechoslovakia). The main reason for the urgency—and the second general cause of unease with Soviet conduct—is that since the early 1980s

2. Even that most loyal ally of the USSR, the Czechoslovak government appeared less than eager to receive Soviet missiles in retaliation for the INF deployments. See RFE-RL *Radio Free Europe Research* (Munich—hereafter RFE *Research*), December 23, 1983, Czechoslovak Situation Report 21/83.

Soviet subsidies to Eastern Europe have steadily declined and there has been a concurrent—and steep—deterioration in Eastern Europe's terms of trade with the Soviet Union. While acknowledging that the Soviet Union has its own economic problems, the East European regimes nevertheless resent getting less in the 1980s than they did in the middle and late 1970s. With a feeling of indignation, they wonder whether the Soviet Union could not afford to do more for them if it did not waste its resources fighting an elusive enemy in Afghanistan, keeping a vast army along its Chinese border, and installing modern and expensive intermediate-range missiles in the GDR and Czechoslovakia.

The essential facts are quite simple and well-known. To alleviate the impact on its East European allies of the sudden rise in the world-market price of energy in the early 1970s, Moscow agreed to provide oil and gas to the East European countries at a price that would only gradually catch up with the prices other countries were paying on the world market. Because of cheap energy as well as the overpricing of East European manufactures, Eastern Europe is estimated to have received an implicit Soviet subsidy amounting to $5.8 billion a year in the 1974–78 period, about $11.6 billion in 1979, about $17.8 billion in 1980, and about $18.7 billion in 1981. The average subsidy for 1982–84 is thought to have dropped to $12.1 billion per year, reaching about $10 to $11 billion in 1984.[3] Although some Western economists consider these staggering estimates excessive, there is no disagreement about either the existence of Soviet subsidies in the 1970s or their decline since 1981.[4] Due to the decline and the seeming disappearance of Soviet energy subsidies since 1984, the overall amount has sharply decreased. Concurrently, the steady deterioration in the terms of Soviet-East European trade—by approximately 20 percent since 1980—means that the East European regimes must sell more of their products in exchange for the same amount of goods received from the Soviet Union. A simple (although admittedly extreme) example illustrates the extraordinary change that has taken place. In 1974 Hungary sold

---

3. See Michael Marrese and Jan Vanous, *Implicit Subsidies and Non-Market Benefits in Soviet Trade with Eastern Europe* (Berkeley and Los Angeles: University of California Press, 1982). More recent information is derived from periodic reports by PlanEcon, Washington, D.C. See also Charles Wolf, Jr., et al. *The Costs of the Soviet Empire*, R3073-1-NA (Santa Monica, Calif.: Rand Corporation, 1983).

4. For an excellent analysis of Soviet-East European economic relations, see Paul Marer, "The Political Economy of Soviet Relations with Eastern Europe," in Sarah M. Terry, ed., *Soviet Policy in Eastern Europe* (New Haven and London: Yale University Press, 1984), pp. 155–88; Marer (p. 179) speaks of a "net cumulative subsidy of about $14 billion" in 1971–78.

eight hundred Ikarus buses to the Soviet Union in order to purchase one million tons of Soviet oil. In 1981 it had to sell twenty-three hundred Ikarus buses for one million tons of Soviet oil. By 1986 the "price" of the same amount of Soviet oil may have reached forty-five hundred Ikarus buses.[5]

From a purely economic point of view as well as from the Soviet perspective, such changes in Soviet-East European trade relations are fully warranted. The Soviet Union has to cope with its own serious economic stringencies. Keeping up in the military competition with the United States is expensive. The availability of cheap Soviet energy has substantially declined in recent years, while the cost of producing new oil has significantly risen.[6] Why should Moscow not receive the world-market price at long last for the energy its allies so desperately need? The answer from the East Europeans is that they made an implicit contract with the Soviet Union in the 1970s. That contract, or understanding, called for Moscow to protect the East European states from the worst effects of international economic turbulence in exchange for which the East European regimes would maintain domestic stability and support Soviet foreign policy objectives. To the extent that, with the notable exception of Poland, there has been relative peace and quiet in Eastern Europe, the Soviet Union is blamed for reneging on this tacit understanding.[7]

As they derive decreasing advantage from the Soviet economic connection and as they must pay a price for heavy-handed Soviet behavior abroad, the East European regimes have ample reason to reconsider their relations both with the Soviet Union and with the West. For, looking ahead to century's end, they wonder how they will be able to maintain domestic stability and support all the twists and turns in Soviet foreign policy as well.

Manifestations of Concern

Precisely because the current maneuver by several East European governments—the process of inching toward the West—is so incremental, its public manifestations are only occasional and are frequently subtle. In fact, one indicator of this trend—the relative share of East European trade with non-Communist countries (see table 9.1)—shows a decline since 1981,

5. *Magyarország*, July 31, 1983. The figure for 1986 is my rough estimate.

6. John P. Hardt, "Soviet Energy Policy in Eastern Europe," in Terry, *Soviet Policy*, pp. 210–12.

7. For a well-informed discussion of East European expectations vis-à-vis the Soviet Union, see F. Stephen Larrabee, *The Challenge to Soviet Interests in Eastern Europe: Romania, Hungary and East Germany*, R-3190-AF (Santa Monica, Calif.: Rand Corporation, 1984).

Table 9.1   East European Foreign Trade with Non-Communist
Countries, 1960−1984 (percentages of total foreign trade)

	Exports	Imports
1960	27.6	28.5
1970	30.9	32.5
1980	36.3	38.5
1981	36.0	34.5
1982	33.8	29.6
1983	31.5	27.2
1984*	30.9	27.0

*Preliminary.
Source: Adapted from Central Intelligence Agency, *Yearbook of Economic Statistics 1985*
(Washington, D.C., September 1985), pp. 100−101.

though this is hardly due to political intent in Eastern Europe or even
Western Europe. Indeed, it is a function of the region's still-growing hard
currency debt (see table 9.2), which has made Western credit available to
Eastern Europe only on a selective basis since the Polish crisis of 1980−81.
Every country in the area, but especially Romania and Hungary, has made
it a top priority to reduce Western imports in order to save hard currency,
and Poland has been all but unable to renew its once-extensive commercial
ties with the West.

Notwithstanding the temporary setback in East European trade with
the West, most other trends point to rising political dissonance in the
bloc, especially in the GDR, Hungary, and Romania.

Most surprising, and potentially significant, has been the apparent
breakdown of synchronization between Soviet and East German approaches
toward the Federal Republic.[8] Beginning in November 1983 and continuing after the INF talks had collapsed, the GDR turned out to be
only a reluctant supporter of a vehement and vociferous Soviet-led Warsaw
Pact campaign against NATO aggressiveness and, later, West German
"revanchism."[9] Although all East European leaders, except Nicolae Ceauşescu
of Romania, added their denunciations and innuendoes, the GDR's Erich

8. Charles Gati, "East Europe's Communists are Tugging at Russia's Leash," *Washington
Post*, Outlook Section, July 8, 1984. Ronald D. Asmus has written several perceptive
reports on the subject, including "Moscow's Campaign Against East-West German
Relations," RFE *Research*, August 29, 1984, RAD Background Report no. 160.

9. Moscow initiated the campaign in late spring 1984, accusing the Bonn government
of seeking to revise Europe's postwar borders and of trying to "erode the socialist system in
the GDR." For particularly salient examples, see *Pravda*, July 27 and August 2, 1984, and
Izvestia, August 11, 1984.

Table 9.2   Eastern Europe's Net Hard-Currency Debt to the West,
1970–1990 (in current U.S. dollars, billions)

	1970	1975	1980	1981	1984	1985	1990
Bulgaria	0.7	2.1	2.7	2.2	0.8	0.8	2.9
Czechoslovakia	0.6	1.2	3.6	3.4	2.4	1.8	2.0
GDR	1.4	4.8	11.6	12.3	7.2	6.9	9.3
Hungary	0.6	2.3	5.8	5.8	4.5	5.1	7.4
Poland	1.1	7.7	23.1	24.3	24.1	27.1	30.6
Romania	1.6	3.1	8.3	8.7	4.4	3.0	3.0
Totals	6.0	21.2	55.1	56.7	43.4	44.7	55.2

Source: For the years 1970 and 1975: Jan Vanous, Wharton Econometric Forecasting Associates, Washington, D.C. For the years 1980 to 1990, including the projections for 1985 and 1990: Jan Vanous, PlanEcon, Washington, D.C.

Honecker (as well as Hungary's János Kádár) made a point of pleading for restraint. Honecker asked for a "coalition of reason" in both German states, adding that such a coalition would serve the interests of "the German people"—a formulation contrary to the GDR claim positing the existence of two German nations since the formation of the GDR in 1949.[10] Echoing Kádár's favorite phrase, Honecker also appealed to the "small- and medium-sized states" of Europe to do what they can to "limit the damage" to intra-European cooperation caused by Soviet-American tensions.[11]

Some actions by the GDR were also out of phase with the Soviet campaign against the FRG. In the first half of 1984, the GDR allowed an estimated 25,000 people to leave for West Germany. In July 1984 at the height of a virulent Soviet campaign against the Federal Republic, the two German states reached an agreement that provided for new West German bank credits in exchange for East German concessions concerning emigration, family reunification cases, and the like.[12] Although the GDR's "concessions" were rather minor, the fact that a deal was struck at this time signaled Honecker's desire to distance himself from the latest Soviet position.

True, it is quite possible that *before* November 1983 the GDR might

10. *RFE Research*, April 30, 1984, RAD Background Report no. 68.

11. For a survey of the dispute between East Berlin and Moscow over relations with Bonn, see *RFE Research*, August 31, 1984, RAD Background Report no. 158.

12. On July 26, 1984, the GDR reached a $330 million (950,000,000 Deutsche Mark) credit agreement with the FRG. See Foreign Broadcast Information Service, *Daily Report: Eastern Europe* (Washington, D.C.—hereafter *FBIS-EEU*), July 26, 1984, p. E/1.

have been encouraged by Moscow to feign tolerance toward the unofficial East German peace movement and present itself to the West in other ways too as a state dedicated to peace and harmony in Europe. There might well have been collusion between Moscow and East Berlin in an effort to make the West German peace activists believe that both Washington and Moscow were under pressure from their respective allies.[13] Granted the utility of such "fraternal cooperation" prior to the collapse of the INF talks, it is still all but impossible to find similar reasons or, indeed, any rationale from the Soviet perspective for continued dissonance. Hence, the likely explanation for what has happened since then is that Honecker, having earlier received either mixed or confusing signals from Moscow and eager to take advantage of leadership change in the Kremlin, has decided to pursue the inter-German dialogue much more on his own than was the case before.

Soviet attacks on the continuing "limited détente" between East and West Germany, and East Germany's spirited defense of it, lend credence to this interpretation.[14] Although Soviet newspapers focused on Bonn's aggressive intentions, the real target was East Berlin. For example, even in mid-1984 and hence after the collapse of the INF talks, an article in *Pravda* stressed that the relationship between the two German states must be evaluated in the context of general East-West relations and cannot be isolated from them. It reminded East Berlin of NATO's present "crusade against socialism" and of Bonn's desire to "solicit concessions on matters of principle that affect the GDR's sovereignty." Another *Pravda* piece, which repeated some of the same accusations, was meant to underline Moscow's anxiety. It was an unsigned editorial (and hence fully authoritative and official), and it made mention of the nine hundred and fifty million Deutsche Mark credit deal that the two Germanies had just concluded. The editorial expressed specific reservations about travel concessions that, it claimed, would only serve to allow Bonn to have "new channels for political and ideological influence."

At first, the GDR rather vigorously defended its position. Responding to the July 27 *Pravda* article in its August 1 issue, *Neues Deutschland* maintained that Bonn was being pressured both by "revanchist" forces and by "realistic" elements and that it was not self-evident which side would turn out to be more influential. Of course, this was precisely the argument

---

13. Pedro Ramet, "Church and Peace in the GDR," *Problems of Communism*, July–August 1984, pp. 44–57; also Ronald D. Asmus, "Is There a Peace Movement in the GDR?" *Orbis*, Summer 1983, pp. 301–41.

14. Lev Bezymenski, "In the Shadow of American Missiles," *Pravda*, July 27, 1983, and "On the Wrong Track," ibid., August 2, 1984.

on which Moscow had based its own policies toward the FRG a year or so earlier—but now the situation was said to be different and the old policy was considered untimely and inoperative. In its article, *Neues Deutschland* also asserted that both German states were "independent in their internal and external affairs."

When, under growing Soviet pressure, Honecker ultimately postponed his visit scheduled for September 1984 to the Federal Republic, it was not clear for how long and to what extent the East Germans would place their "internationalist obligations" ahead of their self-interest. [15] Down but not out, Honecker showed up in maverick Romania on the fortieth anniversary of that country's liberation—the only top Communist leader from the Soviet bloc to do so. [16] This not-so-subtle expression of displeasure with Moscow notwithstanding, East Berlin shied away from engaging Moscow any further in public disagreements. The unstated compromise they appear to have reached allowed the GDR to improve ties with the Federal Republic and thus continue the dialogue in the spirit of the Helsinki process, but it could do so on condition that East Berlin proceed slowly, without publicity, and calibrate each step along the way so as not to embarrass the Soviet Union or counter its policies toward the West.

Ironically, but not surprisingly, Hungary—once the object of East Germany's ire for Kádár's reformist experiments—became the primary defender and promoter of Honecker's course. Indeed, it was an authoritative Hungarian statement issued at the beginning of 1984 that gave a much-needed ideological rationale for the GDR's (and Hungary's) approach to European cooperation. [17] Written by Mátyás Szűrős, the Central Committee secretary in charge of foreign policy, and published in the official party monthly *Társadalmi Szemle*, the article rejected the traditional (read Soviet) view according to which the "national interests [of the East European states] necessarily had to play a secondary role and generally had to be subordinated to interests and objectives that were seen as common ones." Szűrős added: "There is no question of this kind of subordination today." He also argued against "uniform solutions," calling instead for "methods that make optimum allowance for [national] characteristics." Turning directly to the realm of foreign policy, Szűrős maintained that, in

15. See Ronald D. Asmus, "A Postmortem on Honecker's Visit," RFE *Research*, October 17, 1984, RAD Background Report no. 191.

16. *FBIS-EEU*, August 24, 1984, pp. H/3-6. En route to Romania, Honecker sent a telegram of greetings to Gustáv Husák while flying over Czechoslovak territory. Ibid., August 22, 1984, p. D/6.

17. Mátyás Szűrős, "The Reciprocal Effect of the National and International in the Development of Socialism in Hungary," *Társadalmi Szemle*, January 1984, pp. 13-21.

the absence of a world Communist movement with a recognized center, each East European country had the right to take advantage of "specific possibilities." Alluding to one of the "specific possibilities," Szűrős wrote: "Historical traditions and contemporary characteristics do make it possible for relations between a particular socialist and capitalist country to flourish [even] when the general trend is one of deterioration of East-West relations and of a narrowing of contacts."

So much for a common front against imperialist machinations! Whether or not Szűrős—formerly the Hungarian ambassador to Moscow as well as to East Berlin—sent a copy of his article to Honecker will probably never be known, but the East Germans certainly found his arguments useful and convincing. Indeed, when—in the aftermath of a predictable rebuttal by two Prague diehards published in the Czechoslovak party daily *Rudé Právo* and the Soviet foreign affairs weekly *Novoye Vremya*[18]—Szűrős reiterated his views in the form of an interview,[19] *Neues Deutschland* promptly reprinted it in full.[20] In subsequent articles, too, the Hungarians sought to encourage the GDR's *Westpolitik*, praising Honecker's meetings with the leaders of Sweden, Greece, and Italy, and enthusiastically endorsing his proclaimed preference for diplomatic solutions.[21]

That the normally so very circumspect Kádár regime allowed itself to be embroiled in a debate over the relative merits of international and national obligations was the result of a conscious decision. The original Szűrős article was intended to serve four major objectives. First, it was to signal to the Hungarian party apparatus and to the country's attentive public the regime's recognition of the need to back up the economic reform movement at home with an activist foreign policy based to a greater extent than before on the country's national interest.[22] Second, it was to signal to the Soviet Union that while Hungary would remain a loyal ally and fulfill its bloc obligations, it must also look West both for economic reasons and for the purpose of satisfying the public's urge to belong to "Europe." Third, it was to signal to West European governments—to the Federal Republic

18. Michael Stefanak and Ivan Hlivka, "The National and the International in the Policy of the KSČ," *Rudé Právo*, March 30, 1984; "On the National and the International," *Novoye Vremya*, no. 16, April 1984.

19. *Magyar Hírlap*, April 4, 1984.

20. *Neues Deutschland*, April 4, 1984.

21. See Tibor Thurzó, "GDR Diplomacy: A Sense of Responsibility and Activity," *Népszava*, July 26, 1984 and Jenő Bocskor, "East German Foreign Relations: A Multilateral Dialogue," *Magyarország*, August 5, 1984.

22. On the relationship between Hungarian domestic policies and pressures for increased contacts with the West, see Rudolf L. Tőkés, "Hungarian Reform Imperatives," *Problems of Communism*, September–October 1984, pp. 1–23.

and Austria in particular—the Kádár regime's commitment to the Western connection even at a time of high tension between the Soviet Union and the United States. Fourth, it was to signal to some of the more orthodox Warsaw Pact states, especially neighboring Czechoslovakia, Hungary's pride in its achievements and its growing impatience with innuendoes questioning the validity of its socialist path.

As for Romania, it has continued to live up to its reputation as the Soviet bloc's leading maverick. It continues to irritate Moscow by maintaining fraternal ties with China regardless of the state of Sino-Soviet relations; by differing from Soviet positions on a multitude of issues, including Afghanistan, Kampuchea, and the Middle East; and by refusing to join the Soviet-ordained boycott of the 1984 Los Angeles Olympic Games. Also, unlike Honecker and Bulgarian leader Todor Zhivkov, Ceauşescu did visit the Federal Republic in October 1984.[23] In addition, Romania remains the only Warsaw Pact state to have officially and publicly opposed both NATO's INF deployments *and* Soviet counterdeployments. Thus, it is a fair guess that the Romanian regime is pleased with the emerging East Berlin-Budapest maneuver. One leading member of the Romanian Communist party's Political Executive Committee (Politburo) is known to have approached a Hungarian official and informally inquired about the possibility of coordinated political activity.

However intriguing such a constellation might be, Ceauşescu's leadership style as well as some of his policies preclude consistent cooperation with the other East European states in the Warsaw Pact. Romania suffers not only from a deep economic crisis but also from the consequences of Ceauşescu's apparent megalomania. It has come to be that the president's closest associates, including Politburo members, feel obliged to make recommendations or advance fresh initiatives as if they had been devised by Ceauşescu, for only then do these proposals have a chance of being seriously considered. The resulting alienation of the political elite has led to a paralysis of the decision-making process that no amount of posturing can hide or overcome.[24] The problem is further exacerbated by the president's unwillingness or inability to offer any rationale for his frequent tactical shifts in policy, which seem unrelated to his own professed strategic direction, and by his excessive preoccupation with prestige and protocol at the expense of substance. The upshot of these developments is that Romania's long-standing and potentially still significant position as a

23. For an analysis of the cancellation of the Honecker and Zhivkov visits, see RFE *Research*, October 19, 1984, RAD Background Report no. 189.

24. For an evaluation of Ceauşescu's recent leadership, see Trond Gilberg, "Romania's Growing Difficulties," *Current History*, November 1984, pp. 375–89.

semiindependent member of the Warsaw Pact has lost much of the attraction it might have once had for the other East European leaderships. Moreover, as long as the harsh Romanian treatment of the large Hungarian minority in Transylvania continues, Kádár will find it impossible to find a common cause with Ceauşescu.

Among other Warsaw Pact members, the Polish regime—overwhelmed by seemingly insoluble economic problems, facing popular hostility, and still mired in factional infighting—remains on the sidelines. Czechoslovakia and, to a lesser extent, Bulgaria continue to back Soviet orthodoxy.[25] Thus, the most that can be expected is East European mini-coalitions countering Moscow on some specific issues.

Judging by the admittedly sketchy evidence available about the proceedings of the Council for Mutual Economic Assistance (CMEA), such a mini-coalition appears to have come into being, with Romania, Hungary, and the GDR together pressing Moscow for concessions on the present CMEA price structure and on a variety of energy-related issues.[26] If they can further harmonize their views, act concurrently and yet unobtrusively, and place political topics on the agenda of the bloc's multilateral institutions, they could also press Moscow for sufficient "elbow room" in order to protect their Western connections from the vicissitudes of Soviet-American relations. Of course, the central question is the Soviet Union's response to such a maneuver by a coadjutant East European mini-coalition, however unobtrusive.

Soviet Dilemmas

There is every reason to assume that Moscow is deeply concerned about the "Europeanization" of East European Communism.[27] At the same time, it is not self-evident that this is a process that Moscow can readily arrest or contain. For as James F. Brown once astutely observed,[28] the Soviet Union pursues two competing, if not altogether contradictory, objectives in East-

25. Czechoslovak official statements echo the Soviet position; Bulgarian statements are occasionally somewhat more circumspect. For example, while during the Sofia celebrations marking the fortieth anniversary of "socialist" Bulgaria's founding, Mikhail Gorbachev, the leader of the Soviet delegation, spoke of West German "revanchism," Zhivkov avoided any such references and repeated his suggestion to turn the "Balkan Peninsula into a zone free from nuclear weapons." RFE Research, October 5, 1985, Bulgarian Situation Report 12/84.

26. See RFE Research, June 15, 1984, August 31, 1984, October 19, 1984, RAD Background Report nos. 94, 95, 155 and 189.

27. See Charles Gati, "The 'Europeanization' of Communism?" Foreign Affairs 55, no. 3 (April 1977): 539–53.

28. J. F. Brown, Relations Between the Soviet Union and its East European Allies: A Survey (Santa Monica, Calif.: Rand Corporation, 1975).

ern Europe. On the one hand, it seeks *bloc cohesion*—strict conformity with its own values, patterns, and policies. This goal, if realized, would help legitimize the Soviet experience at home and enhance the power of the Soviet Union abroad; its implementation, however, entails the use of coercive measures, including Soviet military intervention. To avoid that eventuality, and for other reasons as well, Moscow has as its other goal the *viability* of the East European regimes and indeed the *stability* of the region as a whole. A viable and stable Eastern Europe would, among other benefits, enhance the appeal of Soviet foreign policy to the West, the Third World, and the more independent-minded and presently anti-Soviet Communist parties throughout the world.

But the elusive goal of East European stability demands a high price from the Soviet Union. Short of granting the region independence, an option Moscow is not considering, there are only two noncoercive ways to obtain a measure of stability. One is to allow the East European regimes to attempt economic policies of a kind that produce consumer satisfaction by transforming "gulag Communism" into "goulash Communism." The other way is for the regimes to adopt political approaches of a kind that satisfy national or even nationalist aspirations by being informed less by Soviet values and interests than by each country's own customs and traditions. In short, the alternatives are bloc cohesion enforced by Soviet military power and economic subsidies, or a modicum of East European stability made possible by Soviet tolerance of "goulash Communism," "national Communism," or some combination of the two.

In the abstract, Moscow does not object to "goulash Communism." True, there are Soviet—and East European—diehards who regard excessive reliance on consumer satisfaction as a "petty-bourgeois" deviation. Such stale complaints aside, all Communist regimes would like nothing better than economic well-being, partly to demonstrate the superiority of centrally planned economic systems and mainly to take the edge off popular economic and political discontent. The problem is not only that Soviet-type economies have not done well in Eastern Europe. They are also not *seen* to have done well because the populations in Eastern Europe tend to assess their prevailing living standards less by comparing them with their own past than by comparing them to present living standards in such countries as the Federal Republic, Austria, or Finland. To achieve anything approaching that kind of consumer satisfaction, however, would require larger Soviet subsidies, a reformist course on the Hungarian (or Chinese) pattern, and a political opening to the West to encourage credit, investments, and the transfer of advanced technology—measures that entail considerable economic restructuring and political risk. Therefore, despite official endorsements of "goulash Communism," the policies that might lead to consumer satisfaction and hence to political stability are, in fact, abhorrent to most Soviet and many East European leaders.

The Soviet Union is also concerned about stability obtained by paying more than lip service to the East Europeans' national or nationalist aspirations. While Moscow does encourage nationalism in the Third World or Western Europe—wherever it might spark anti-American or anti-Western sentiments—it is certainly less favorably disposed toward East European expressions of nationalism. When the GDR celebrates the 500th anniversary of Martin Luther's birth, or Czechoslovakia takes pride in its national hockey team's victories, that's fine. When successive Polish regimes feel compelled to accommodate themselves to the traditional influence of the Catholic Church, that's fine, too, provided that the regime retains its capacity to inhibit and, if necessary, to control the Church's activities. But, in the Soviet view, respect for national values must not entail any policy aimed at fulfilling the region's traditional longing to be accepted by, and indeed to rejoin, the European community. For, as long as the Soviet Union itself is not perceived as belonging to the European community, the East European desire to belong is suggestive of anti-Soviet tendencies.

Herein lies the essential reason for the persistent tug of war between the proprietors of power in the Soviet Union and Eastern Europe. As several East European regimes now see it, they must, for the sake of domestic political stability, actively, if cautiously, inch toward the West. They certainly do not want Soviet interventions; they cannot, as Poland found out, count on sufficient Soviet economic help; and most of them worry about the unforeseeable consequences of market-oriented reforms. The only alternative they do see is a gradual opening to the West, which, despite obvious risks, offers the promise of public approval. From a Soviet perspective, however, the reasons for such an opening are less compelling. Genuinely afraid of Western influences, the Soviet leaders also appear to underestimate the region's persistent instability and the major sources of that instability—nationalist and economic pressures. Their attitude is shared by the typical Soviet tourist visiting Warsaw, let alone Budapest, when he asks: "Why are these people complaining when they live better than we do?" Thus, even after more than forty years of experience, Moscow cannot accept the fact that East Europeans judge the performance of their political and economic order by European and not by Soviet standards.

Of course, the Soviet Union has gone to considerable lengths to have peace and quiet, if not genuine stability, in Eastern Europe. It has long tried to steer a middle course between the objectives of cohesion and stability, bending now in one direction and then in another, and hoping all along that its problems of empire will some day, somehow, disappear.

"When the Cat's Away . . ."

Whether Moscow can continue to muddle through in this way in the years ahead depends as much or more on its capacity to shape a *properly calibrated* policy toward the region than on economic conditions. The evidence of the post-Stalin era (see table 9.3) indicates a significant correlation between the unity or lack of unity of the Soviet leadership, on the one hand, and East European popular movements and regime assertiveness, on the other. Specifically, it has been all but impossible for the Soviet Union to pursue its two competing goals of bloc cohesion and East European stability in a judicious and calibrated fashion at times of unsettled leadership in the Kremlin. Under such circumstances, the Soviet leaders, preoccupied with the struggle for power, have tended to send mixed signals to their East European clients. Sensing confusion in the Kremlin, East Europeans —leaders and people alike—have then tried to use the opportunity to

Table 9.3 Kremlin Politics and Eastern Europe, 1953–85

State of Soviet leadership		East European assertiveness	
Periods of relative turbulence	Periods of relative tranquility	Popular movements	Regime demands for autonomy
1953–57		East Berlin, 1953 Poznan, 1956 Warsaw, 1956 Budapest, 1956	Poland, 1956 Hungary, 1956
	1957–64		Albania, 1961 to present
1964–69		Warsaw, 1968	Romania, 1964 to present
		Prague, 1968	Hungary, 1968 to present Czechoslovakia, 1968
	1969–79	Polish cities, 1970 and 1976	
1979–85		Poland Solidarity, 1980–81	Mini-coalitions, 1983 to present

shift the balance of decision-making authority to their side. "When the cat's away, the mice will play."

Of the three periods of Soviet leadership turbulence so far, the volatile and highly personalized struggle for power in 1953–57 resulted in several popular upheavals and considerable elite disorientation in Eastern Europe.[29] To recall briefly, this was the time when Beria was reportedly rethinking the "German question"; when at first Malenkov and then Khrushchev advocated a "new course" for Eastern Europe; when Khrushchev and Mikoyan urged, while Molotov and others opposed, reconciliation with "national Communist" Yugoslavia; when a divided Soviet leadership felt it needed Tito's blessing to invade Hungary; and when a visibly shaken Kremlin first tried to obstruct and then grudgingly accepted Gomułka's appointment as Poland's new leader.

Apparent confusion in Moscow led to unparalleled factional infighting in the East European Communist parties, too, especially in Poland and Hungary. Sensing divisions at the top in Eastern Europe, no wonder that large segments of the attentive public, led by intellectuals and followed by the people as well, gained courage and expressed their long-suppressed convictions.[30] Of course, in the end they did not get their way, for the Soviet leaders, facing the prospective disintegration of their empire, managed to pull themselves together and reestablish their authority. For about seven years after the defeat of the "anti-party" group in 1957, they appear to have united behind Khrushchev and followed a rather calibrated policy toward Eastern Europe, one that stressed the goal of cohesion without necessarily stifling every national experiment.[31]

The second—certainly far less volatile—period of Kremlin turbulence began in 1964 as a palace conspiracy against Khrushchev and continued until 1969 or so with intense jockeying for position after his ouster (primarily between Leonid Brezhnev and Aleksei Kosygin).[32] While Brezhnev was only primus inter pares, Soviet policy in Eastern Europe once again lacked a sure hand.

29. Of the vast literature on Soviet politics in the mid-1950s, the East European connection is explored most usefully in Veljko Mičunović, *Moscow Diary* (Garden City, N.Y.: Doubleday, 1980) and in *Khrushchev Remembers,* translated and edited by Strobe Talbot (Boston: Little, Brown, 1970).

30. For two excellent books on Poland and Hungary in 1956, see Flora Lewis, *A Case History of Hope* (Garden City, N.Y.: Doubleday, 1958) and Ferenc A. Váli, *Rift and Revolt in Hungary* (Cambridge: Harvard University Press, 1961).

31. Zbigniew Brzezinski, *The Soviet Bloc: Unity and Conflict* (Cambridge: Harvard University Press, 1967).

32. See, e.g., Michael Tatu, *Power in the Kremlin: From Khrushchev to Kosygin* (New York: Viking, 1969).

While Khrushchev's confusing on-again, off-again campaign for CMEA integration was an important factor in creating the proper conditions for Romania's 1964 declaration of semiindependence, it was the Kremlin's subsequent preoccupation with Khrushchev's ouster that allowed Romania to make stick its claim for a measure of autonomy in the Warsaw Pact. The Hungarian and Czechoslovak reform movements, which started in the mid-1960s, also received considerable stimulation from the Kremlin's ongoing debate about economic reform.[33] It is highly instructive that most Czechoslovak leaders were under the strong impression that what they were doing met with Soviet approval. Even after their economic reform movement became the political "Prague Spring" in 1968, many of them continued to believe that the "Soviet comrades" at least understood and probably supported their efforts for "socialism with a human face." In point of fact, according to Zdeněk Mlynář's vivid testimony and other evidence,[34] *some* of the Soviet leaders did. Even if one accepts the premise that the Czechoslovak reformists around Alexander Dubček were somewhat naive about Soviet intentions, they operated on the basis of frequent consultations with Kremlin leaders at the highest level—and received contradictory signals.

The third period of Kremlin leadership turbulence can be traced to about 1979, when Brezhnev's illnesses and absences became chronic. Eventually an intense struggle to succeed him developed between Yuri Andropov and Konstantin Chernenko. Andropov's rule was short-lived, and Chernenko's rule as primus inter pares in the Politburo (as his mentor Brezhnev's once was) turned out to be of even shorter duration. Yet this power struggle had important repercussions, too, all the more so because it was taking place at a time of economic stagnation affecting the entire bloc. For the first time, concerned about a recurrence of a "time of troubles" in the Kremlin, several East European leaders allowed their preference for or against a specific contender to succeed Brezhnev to come out, with Ceauşescu reportedly opting for Chernenko and Andropov

33. On Soviet economic reform debates in the mid-1960s, see Fyodor I. Kushnirsky, "The Limits of Soviet Economic Reform," *Problems of Communism*, July–August 1984, pp. 33–43.

34. See Zdeněk Mlynář's, *Nightfrost in Prague* (New York: Katz, 1980). For a systematic treatment of differing Soviet positions concerning Czechoslovakia, see Jiri Valenta, *Soviet Intervention in Czechoslovakia, 1968: Anatomy of a Decision* (Baltimore: Johns Hopkins University Press, 1979). For two studies that find the evidence of differing Soviet positions somewhat less convincing, see Karen Dawisha, *The Kremlin and the Prague Spring* (Berkeley and Los Angeles: University of California Press, 1984) and especially H. Gordon Skilling, *Czechoslovakia's Interrupted Revolution* (Princeton, N.J.: Princeton University Press, 1976).

receiving the endorsements of Kádár and Czechoslovakia's Gustáv Husák.[35]
As Moscow may see it, the East European regimes, once compelled to
accept taxation without representation, began to seek representation without taxation.

In addition to fostering the incipient mini-coalition described earlier,
the absence of a firm leadership in the Kremlin had adversely affected the
Polish regime's management of the 1980–81 crisis in that country. The
paralysis of power in the Kremlin had a profoundly unsettling influence on
the Polish leadership, which for almost eighteen long months could not
decide what it should or should not do.[36] True, the rise of Solidarity was
primarily a function of internal developments, both economic and political.
It is also true that the Polish party had always tended to be deeply divided,
probably more so than any other ruling Communist party in the world.
One can further assume that Moscow, anxious to avoid fighting two wars at
the same time (in Afghanistan and Poland) and perhaps concerned about
Western sanctions, preferred not to intervene militarily if at all possible.
Finally, it is quite likely that the Kremlin kept postponing the decision to
act in the hope of further exacerbating the Polish crisis—that it waited for
the political order to become chaotic and economic conditions to become
unbearable—so that the likes of General Wojciech Jaruzelski—surely a
"moderate" by Soviet standards—would at last see no alternative to a
comprehensive and brutal crackdown.

Yet, the question still remains: Why did the Kremlin tolerate such an
extraordinary display of pluralism for a year and a half? What kind of

35. See, e.g., "Hungary's Hope for Continuity," *Neue Zürcher Zeitung*, February 29,
1984; and RFE *Research*, December 8, 1982, Romanian Situation Report 21/82.

36. Both before and after the December 1981 "crackdown," Soviet treatment of Poland
was marked by a good deal of vacillation and apparently confusing signals. For an early
analysis of Soviet options and immobilism, see Charles Gati, "Polish Futures, Western
Options," *Foreign Affairs* 61, no. 2 (Winter 1982/83): 292–308. The release of Lech
Wałesa from house arrest in November 1982, less than twenty-four hours after Brezhnev's
death, prompted Warsaw wits to make up the following story: Andropov, the new Kremlin
chief, calls Jaruzelski: "On whose authority did you release Wałesa?" Jaruzelski: "I
discussed the matter with Comrade Brezhnev." Andropov: "And what did our beloved
Leonid Il'ich tell you?" Jaruzelski: "He said and I quote: 'You may release that no good Pole
only over my dead body.'" The public trial of four security police officers charged with the
Rev. Jerzy Popiełuszko's murder was also seen in Poland as a function of General Jaruzelski's
ability "to take advantage of what many believe to be disarray in the Kremlin as a result of a
struggle to succeed Konstantin U. Chernenko as the Soviet leader." *New York Times*, February 9, 1985. That at least *some* Soviet leaders disapproved of such a public trial was implied
by a TASS report, which identified the four security police officers only as "four citizens"
who "attributed their act" to their desire to prevent Father Popiełuszko from pursuing
"activities harmful to the state." Ibid.

Leninist leadership would hesitate for so long to protect the Soviet empire from such a fundamental challenge to its existence? Indeed, did Moscow seek only to intimidate Poland by completing all preparations for intervention in December 1980 and again in March 1981, or did the preparations for, and subsequent cancellations of, military action indicate vacillation and drift, an inability to take a decisive step?

In my opinion, there is no question but that all Soviet leaders knew what they wanted. In one way or another, they were determined that Poland must remain in the fold. But for well over a year they could not decide how to achieve that goal, primarily because no Soviet leader wanted to be held responsible for the failure of either policy option: accepting the process of "socialist renewal" or ordering an end to it. Responsibility for a failed option would have spelled political defeat for its proponent, and hence no Soviet leader—and certainly none of the contenders for the top position—was willing to press for the adoption of either of the two high-risk alternatives. Put another way, an in-between policy of muddling through was a political imperative dictated by political ambitions permeating the intrigue-filled atmosphere of the Kremlin at that time.

Therefore, it is as misleading to assign "prudence" to the Soviet leaders for having waited as long as they did as it is to shout "deception" every time they appear to have emitted confusing signals. Given Brezhnev's incapacitating illnesses, the irregular participation of East European troubleshooter Mikhail A. Suslov in the decision-making process, and the intense struggle for succession under way, only the most cautious or circumspect policy response was politically palatable. Indeed, the ultimate decision to instigate an internal coup that would reestablish Communist authority was adopted precisely because it entailed fewer risks than the alternative of direct Soviet military intervention. More important, the fact that such an internal coup was not attempted earlier must be understood as a symptom of Soviet immobility, which, in turn, exacerbated divisions within the Polish party and generated false hopes among the Polish people as well.

Under Gorbachev and Beyond

Can Gorbachev stop the pervasive drift that characterized the Kremlin's East European policy during Brezhnev's last years and under Andropov and Chernenko?

To answer that question, two observations are in order. First, Soviet leadership immobility, by itself, has never caused either regime assertiveness or popular defiance in Eastern Europe. Rather, such assertiveness and defiance occur in the Soviet bloc because of the absence of autonomy, because of repression, because of the gap between economic promise and performance. It is only that these deep-rooted, substantive, and systemic causes of pervasive discontent *generate crises mainly when East Europeans sense division and drift in Moscow*; when they believe that they can get away with "more"—usually more independence—than they might be able to do when the Soviet leadership appears less preoccupied with the struggle for power. In short, Kremlin turbulence does not create crises in Eastern Europe; it turns inherent instability into explicit regime demands or popular explosions.

Second, the continuing, post-1985 tug of war in Soviet-East European relations points to Moscow's—indeed Gorbachev's—inability to put Humpty Dumpty back together again. In time he may succeed, but early indications suggest that some East European leaders, having grown used to receiving mixed Soviet signals and hence making decisions largely on their own, are not inclined to reassume the excessively subservient role of earlier times. With Gorbachev already at the helm, Romania's Ceauşescu has visited China and agreed to the opening of a Chinese consulate in Constanta, a Black Sea town well situated to observe the Soviet Navy's activities. With Gorbachev at the helm, Hungary's Kádár has continued to stress the role of "small- and medium-sized countries" in the maintenance and strengthening of inter-European détente, pleading for "agreements with respect to every disputed or resolvable international problem."[37] With Gorbachev at the helm, the GDR's Honecker has removed from his Politburo Konrad Naumann, the leading hard-line critic of his policies toward the Federal Republic, and *Neues Deutschland* kept reprinting Hungarian statements regarding the importance of the "national interest" in the foreign policies of the East European countries.[38] With Gorbachev at the helm, Poland's Jaruzelski has dismissed from the Politburo the most blatantly pro-Soviet member of that body, Stefan Olszowski.

In the meantime, Gorbachev has given no clear indication of his approach to Eastern Europe. What is clear is that, concerned as he must be about both the "Polish syndrome" and the lack of sufficient cohesion in the bloc, he has made the region one of his top priorities. "The first precept of the Party and the state," he told a 1985 plenary session of his Central

37. János Kádár, "European Peace," *Magyarország* 22, no. 44 (November 3, 1985): 3–4.

38. An article along these lines by Mátyás Szűrős appeared in *Népszabadság* on November 2, 1985; *Neues Deutschland* reprinted it on November 6, 1985. For an expanded version of the Szűrős article in English, see Mátyás Szűrős, "Hungarian Foreign Policy in the Mid-1980s," *Külpolitika* [special English edition], no. 4, (1985): 11–26.

Committee, "is to preserve and strengthen in every way fraternal friendship with our closest friends and allies—the countries of the great socialist community."[39]

Putting the matter in blunt language, several Soviet commentaries followed up by treating all nationalist departures from Soviet norms and policies as expressions of "pragmatism" and even "revisionism" (an accusatory term seldom used since the "Prague Spring" of 1968). Alluding to Hungary, Romania, and the GDR, a particularly vehement article in *Pravda* asked: "What question can there be of any mediation by particular socialist countries in resolving disagreements between the USSR and the United States if on key international questions the foreign policy of the USSR and of the Marxist-Leninist nucleus of world socialism is identical?"[40] Symptomatic of continuing debates in the Soviet political elite, *New Times* responded with an article by Nikolai Shishlin, a prominent Central Committee staffer, who conceded that the national interests of socialist countries "have not disappeared with the rise of the world socialist system and the formation of the socialist community," and hence "the ruling Communist parties must be masters of the art of combining the national and international interests of the socialist countries."[41]

On another occasion, a Soviet theoretician went out of his way to confirm that the pursuit of national interests by each member of the socialist community was both natural and legitimate. Writing in *Rabochi klass i sovremenni mir*, Yuri S. Novopashin of the Soviet Academy of Science's Institute of the Economics of the World Socialist System argued that "the national and state interests" of the East European countries had not declined, with the result that "contradictions" and indeed a lack of harmony rather than "international relations of a new type" characterized the Soviet bloc for the time being. Echoing the view advanced by the much-criticized Mátyás Szűrős, the Hungarian party's specialist on foreign affairs, Novopashin appeared to be placing national interests ahead of bloc cohesion when he specifically denied that "the principle of respect for national sovereignty can be subordinated to some higher principle . . .—namely, that of unity."[42] As if to rebut these conciliatory words, *Pravda* used a

39. As quoted in *New Times*, no. 35 (August 1985): 9.

40. O. Vladimirov, "The Main Factor in the World Revolutionary Process," *Pravda*, June 21, 1985.

41. Nikolai Shishlin, "Top-Priority Task," *New Times*, no. 35 (August 1985): 9–11.

42. Yuri S. Novopashin, "Political Relations of the Socialist Countries," *Rabochi klass i sovremenni mir*, no. 5 (1985): 55–65 as quoted in Elizabeth Teague, "Soviet Author Repudiates 'Brezhnev Doctrine,'" *Radio Liberty Research*, RL 4/86 (December 20, 1985), p. 3.

rather obscure anniversary to state the opposite view: "The unity and cohesion of the ruling Marxist-Leninist parties is a reliable guarantee that the intrigues of imperialist, anti-socialist, and revisionist forces will never be able to undermine the revolutionary gains in any fraternal country or weaken the might of world socialism as a whole."[43] What made the message conveyed by this article ominous was not only that it was published in *Pravda* but that its author, Igor Biryukov, served as deputy chief of that paper's department dealing with Eastern Europe.

Even under Gorbachev, then, the tug of war both within the Soviet hierarchy and in Soviet-East European relations continues. Gorbachev has not been able to calibrate the Kremlin's East European policy the same way Khrushchev did between 1957 and 1964 and Brezhnev did from about 1969 to 1979. Demanding cohesion but tolerating diversity, he has failed to discourage some of the East Europeans from pursuing their national interests. At the same time, some of the leaders of Eastern Europe have gained sufficient experience and finesse to calibrate the processes of change in the policies of *their* countries. Above all, these leaders have learned since the Polish crisis of 1980–81 to make timely, if meager, concessions to their people so as to avert popular pressures that might push them beyond the limits of Soviet tolerance.

Having proved unable so far to put Humpty Dumpty together again, one of Gorbachev's "first precepts" in the years ahead is to cope with the serious challenge that the East European mini-coalitions pose to Moscow's concept of cohesion. Like his predecessors, his task is to stop the continuing if slow decline of Soviet authority in the region. Given the growing incompatibility of interests between the Soviet Union and its dependencies, he is not likely to succeed. For under Gorbachev, too, the Soviet bloc, though still alive, remains chronically ill.

43. Igor Biryukov, "An Important Political Covenant," *Pravda*, December 14, 1985.

10

The United States and Eastern Europe: In Defense of "Differentiation"

The political condition of the Soviet bloc, and particularly the growing incompatibility of interests among its members in the 1980s, should prompt the United States to take notice. Is another rift in the making? If so, will it resemble the open split between the Soviet Union and Yugoslavia, or between the Soviet Union and Albania, or perhaps between the Soviet Union and China? Alternatively, is the apparent decline of Soviet authority over Eastern Europe going to continue to be gradual and hence the changes in relationships less dramatic—if still significant? If either development occurs, should it be or indeed could it be exploited to serve U.S. interests?

Known as "differentiation" since the 1970s, American foreign policy toward Eastern Europe is in place. Its goals are limited. In contrast to postwar successes in Greece and Yugoslavia, its more recent accomplishments have been limited, too. The United States might well have enhanced Romania's ability to remain the maverick of the Soviet bloc it has been since the mid-1960s. The United States might well have made a contribution to Hungary's ability to pursue domestic liberalization and even display a modicum of independence in foreign relations. Yet, at first glance at least, the failures of American policy are more obvious, more easily identifiable. After all, the Soviet sphere is intact; the people of Eastern Europe are not free; the region's states are not independent. Given their membership in the Warsaw Pact and CMEA, Bulgaria, Czechoslovakia, the GDR, Hungary, Poland, and even Romania are still on "the other side." Should the United States be doing something it is not doing now?

Why Limited Goals? Why Restraint?

Judging by its deeds—as, occasionally, confirmed by its words, too—the United States has long recognized the division of Europe and hence the

Soviet sphere in Eastern Europe. The main reason for U.S. acquiescence in the status quo is self-evident. Lacking appropriate power, military, political, or economic, to challenge Soviet power, the United States has had no option but to accept prevailing reality.

The absence of adequate *means* to change the European status quo has served to define the limits of American *objectives* toward Eastern Europe. Given the circumstances, these objectives have been modest. By offering minor rewards and occasional penalties, the United States has sought to encourage evolution toward *semi*-independence and *semi*-authoritarianism by the region's Communist regimes; hence the goals of "diversity" and "liberalization."

Time and again, the United States has declined to provide active support to East Europeans who pressed for more substantial, fundamental changes. In 1956, when Hungary withdrew from the Warsaw Pact and fashioned a multiparty political order, the United States watched helplessly as Soviet armed forces put an end to that brave effort. In 1968, when Czechoslovakia tried to introduce a more lenient, humanitarian form of socialism, Soviet military intervention took place in the face of American passivity. In 1981 the Reagan administration condemned Moscow for instigating the Polish military coup and the Jaruzelski regime for implementing it, and then added a series of economic sanctions as well, but it was clear from the beginning that no American policy would, or could, return Poland to the path of "renewal" inspired by the "Solidarity" movement and supported by the Polish people.

Such restraint by the United States—a marked unwillingness to confront Soviet preponderance in Moscow's front yard—has been based on the following considerations and circumstances:

First, U.S. restraint has had much to do with the hopelessness of any direct East European confrontation with the Soviet Union. Courageous and determined as the Poles and the Hungarians may be, they can no more defeat the Soviet Army than they can extract meaningful concessions from Moscow through militant confrontation. As demonstrated repeatedly, moreover, the Soviet leaders are prepared to do whatever it takes to assure the survival of their imperium. Under the circumstances, the United States has been reluctant to encourage East European actions that would invite a Soviet backlash.

Second, the United States has long assumed that the Soviet Union considers the political orientation of the East European states as nonnegotiable; indeed, it regards any Western attempt to support systemic changes in the region as a challenge not only to its East European dependencies but to its own security. In the Soviet view, therefore, Washington should refrain from assisting indigenous opposition forces lest it is willing to renounce all hope for East-West accommodation. Arrogantly, Moscow has even linked U.S. acquiescence in the East European status quo to progress in arms control and perhaps other bilateral and "negotiable" issues.

Third, the United States, given its global role, has always faced more urgent priorities than the old, if persistent, problems of Eastern Europe. In point of fact, the region finds its way to the American agenda only in times of major crises. At best, Eastern Europe is subsidiary to other, more pressing and more immediate, U.S. concerns; at worst, it is a forgotten region.[1]

Finally, American restraint has been due to the increasingly divergent interests of members of the Western alliance toward Eastern Europe. The most pronounced difference, apparent since the late 1960s, has been between the Federal Republic of Germany and the United States. In brief, the Federal Republic seeks less the general encouragement of East European semi-independence and liberalization than the creation of such political conditions that would make it conceivable for the two Germanys to find a modus vivendi, perhaps a confederal status of sorts, at some admittedly distant future date. As part of its long-term, grand design, the Federal Republic has therefore bestowed considerable economic favors on the East German regime, and its policies have been somewhat more accommodating toward the Soviet bloc as a whole. Recognizing the centrality of the issue for its important ally and seeking a Western consensus, the United States has made but a small effort to divert the Federal Republic from its course.

Restrained by such considerations and circumstances, the United States has thus long set out to achieve considerably less, of course, than the "liberation" of the people and the full "independence" of the states of Eastern Europe.

As early as 1949, the National Security Council's first comprehensive statement on U.S. policy (NSC 58) — then "top secret" — explicitly addressed the issue of expediency: "[S]hould it be our aim to replace, as a first step, Kremlin authority with (a) governments immediately friendly to us or (b) any governments free of Moscow's domination, even though they be Communist regimes?" Significantly, the answer was (b), meaning that Washington should and will "foster a heretical drifting-away process on the part of the satellite states." As "a first step," the United States was

---

1. Cf. Charles Gati, "The Forgotten Region," *Foreign Policy* 19 (Summer 1975): 135–45. For a comprehensive treatment of the evolution of American policy toward Eastern Europe, see Bennett Kovrig, *The Myth of Liberation: East-Central Europe in U.S. Diplomacy and Politics Since 1941* (Baltimore: Johns Hopkins University Press, 1973).

prepared to confine itself to the goal of replacing "Kremlin authority with *any governments free of Moscow's domination, even though they be Communist regimes.*"[2]

On the record, the Eisenhower administration's strongly anti-Communist secretary of state, John Foster Dulles, endorsed his predecessors' approach when he remarked in 1956 that, "Communism on a national basis . . . offers a great prospect for the Poles, the Czechs, and so forth, who would much rather have their own national brand of Communism than be run by Moscow." In 1964 Secretary of State Dean Rusk also spoke of the United States seeking only "evolution within the Communist world." In 1983 Vice President George Bush reaffirmed that view: "Our policy is one of differentiation—that is, we look *to what degree* countries [in Eastern Europe] pursue autonomous foreign policies, independent of Moscow's direction, and *to what degree* they foster domestic liberalization."[3]

Thus, since 1949, policy directives as well as several public statements acknowledged that the United States sought diversity rather than democracy, liberalization rather than liberation. Today, too, the policy of differentiation consists of two propositions reflecting these goals:

\# Regarding diversity: Relying on peaceful means, the United States will encourage and reward those of the region's Communist regimes that attempt to take distance from at least some aspects of Soviet foreign policy and thus demonstrate a modicum of autonomy.

\# Regarding liberalization: Relying on peaceful means, the United States will also encourage and reward those of the region's Communist regimes that treat their own people in a more decent way [than the Soviet Union], and thus demonstrate a modicum of respect for human rights.

By so paving the way for a *measure* of foreign policy autonomy and a *measure* of liberalization, the United States aims at driving wedges between the Soviet Union and its junior allies. Given the content of NSC 58 and its early support for Tito's Yugoslavia, this was as much the Truman administration's definition of the U.S. national interest as it became the Reagan administration's objective as well.[4]

2. "NSC 58: United States Policy toward the Soviet Satellite States in Eastern Europe (September 14, 1949)," in T. H. Etzold and J. L. Gaddis, eds., *Containment: Documents on American Policy and Strategy* (New York: Columbia University Press, 1978), pp. 211–23. Emphasis added.

3. "Address by Vice-President George Bush to the Austrian Foreign Policy Association, Vienna, September 21, 1983," press release by the office of the press secretary to the vice president (Washington, D.C.). Emphasis added.

4. The Reagan administration's policy guidelines on Eastern Europe are contained in its secret National Security Decision Directive (NSDD-54), completed and signed by the president in August 1982. As reported by Raymond L. Garthoff, former U.S. ambassador

The Idealist Imperative

Still, the apparent realism of American policy toward Eastern Europe has always been accompanied by high-sounding, maximalist statements by officials whose grand proclamations had little or indeed nothing to do with achievable objectives. They have felt obliged, primarily though not exclusively on the level of political rhetoric, to give voice to American idealism—to the United States's "commitment" to the twin goals of freedom and independence for Eastern Europe.

In 1949, NSC 58—the same "top secret" National Security Council statement on U.S. policy that prudently distinguished between the Soviet Union and its dependencies—also stated: "Our ultimate aim must, of course, be the appearance in Eastern Europe of non-totalitarian administrations willing to accommodate themselves to, and participate in, the free world community." In 1953 Secretary of State Dulles, enunciating the replacement of the "negative, futile, and immoral" doctrine of containment with that of liberation, asserted: "To all those suffering under Communist slavery, the intimidated and weak peoples of the world, let us say this, you can count on us." In 1962 President John F. Kennedy declared: "[W]e must never—in any statement, declaration, treaty, or other manner —recognize Soviet domination of Eastern Europe as permanent."

Such maximalist rhetoric has changed but slightly since the early 1970s. Instead of merely demanding, unrealistically, that Moscow give up its imperium—and declaring that some day, somehow, it will—Washington, more unrealistically, has added insult to injury by telling Moscow to *concur* in the dissolution of its pride and joy in Eastern Europe.

For example: While continuing to deny Moscow's right to hegemony, President Richard Nixon put forth the U.S. position this way in 1970: "Ultimately, a workable system of security embracing all of Europe will require a willingness on the part of the Soviet Union to normalize its own relations with Eastern Europe. . . ." Secretary of State George Shultz

to Bulgaria, one of the issues debated prior to its adoption had to do with the precise definition of conditions under which the United States would reward East European regimes. One position held that rewards should be granted to regimes that show both a measure of independence in foreign policy *and* domestic liberalization. See Raymond L. Garthoff, "Eastern Europe in the Context of U.S.-Soviet Relations," in Sarah Meiklejohn Terry, ed., *Soviet Policy in Eastern Europe* (New Haven: Yale University Press, 1984), pp. 315–48. As adopted in the end, however, NSDD-54 favors differentiation when an East European regime demonstrates *either* foreign policy independence *or* internal liberalization. This crucial distinction means, for example, that Romania—a semiindependent but internally repressive regime—qualifies for whatever small favors the United States can grant to an East European country.

echoed that view in 1985: "We hope to see the day when the Soviet Union learns to think anew of its own security in terms compatible with the freedom, security, and independence of its neighbors." True, later that year Shultz also reaffirmed the classic formula when, during a visit to Berlin, he stated that the division of Europe was "unnatural and inhumane" and that the United States did not recognize the incorporation of Eastern Europe into the Soviet sphere.

What the record of the last four decades shows, then, is (1) continuity in the actual pursuit of evolutionary goals, (2) continuity in frequently avowed maximalist objectives, and hence (3) a discrepancy between (most) deeds and (many) words, between what the United States could in fact do and was doing on the one hand and what it claimed to do and promised to accomplish on the other.

Why the discrepancy? One answer is that while the propensity for stating maximalist objectives is derived from universal and idealistic values inherent in American political culture, the concurrent inclination to pursue an expedient course has stemmed from opportunities offered by a Soviet bloc riddled with tension and conflict. Hence on some occasions officials have found it politically rewarding, and perhaps emotionally satisfying, to voice support for the "legitimate aspirations" of the East Europeans; on other occasions they have let it be known how little Washington can realistically expect to achieve under prevailing geopolitical circumstances. Put another way, at times the United States asserted its hope—an independent and democratic Eastern Europe—and at most other times confined itself to that which seemed achievable—a semi-independent and semi-authoritarian Eastern Europe.

Another answer is that official statements advancing maximalist goals signify no more than political posturing. Indeed, when the United States failed to assist Hungary in 1956, the doctrine of liberation proved to be a hollow promise. John Spanier may well have been right that, "the [Republican] policy of liberation seems to have been devised primarily to roll back the Democrats in the United States, not the Red Army in Eastern Europe. And for this domestic purpose, liberation was a highly effective strategy."[5] True, too, the politician who, campaigning in the ethnic wards of Chicago or Buffalo, even today exaggerates his hope about what the United States can do in Eastern Europe is likely to be engaged in a cynical ploy for the Polish vote.

Yet the idealistic content of American discourse on Eastern Europe

5. John Spanier, *American Foreign Policy Since World War II*, 10th ed. (New York: Holt, Rinehart and Winston, 1985), p. 73.

should not be dismissed lightly; it has meaning as well as consequences, intended and unintended. To begin with, the fact that maximalist goals have appeared in *secret* official documents, and hence not only in campaign oratory and political platforms, suggests a widespread, pervasive need to believe in something more than marginal adjustments in the status quo. After all, even some of the best informed members of Congress and seasoned professionals in the Department of State, too, appear to be almost as incurably sanguine as their constituents. Products of the same political culture, they also believe, or want to believe, or sometimes believe what the public wants to hear: that if the United States had only tried hard enough, Eastern Europe could yet be free of Soviet domination "in the long run." In the aftermath of the 1981 Polish "crackdown," for example, whoever occupied the White House would have not only condemned the Soviet Union and the Polish military regime, and pressed the West Europeans to adopt economic sanctions, but he would have also declared that the United States will "never accept" a Soviet sphere in Eastern Europe.

To interpret such admittedly sentimental declarations as mere hypocrisy is to ignore the place of national interest *and* idealistic principle in American political culture. As Alfred T. Mahan, the early advocate of realpolitik and of the primacy of national interests, recognized: given human nature, ideals must invariably supplement reason in foreign policy. "The sentiment of a people is the most energetic element in national action," he wrote in 1910. "Whatever individual rulers may do, masses of men are aroused to effective action—other than spasmodic—only by the sense of wrong done, or right to be vindicated."[6]

Still, in the absence of an appropriate survey of public opinion, it is hard to tell what it is that the American public actually *expects* its leaders to deliver. It appears, however, that the goal of advancing human rights in Eastern Europe tops the agenda. Like motherhood and apple pie, everyone is for it. Let divided families unite, let political prisoners go, let the faithful observe their religion. The Helsinki "Final Act," a nonbinding agreement guaranteeing human rights and signed by all of the leaders of the Soviet bloc, must not become another empty promise. Witnesses line up before congressional committees to describe violations of the Helsinki accords. Without offering specific recommendations, they urge "prompt

6. Alfred T. Mahan, *The Interest of America in International Conditions* (Boston: Little, Brown, 1910), p. 168. In the 1980s (anti-Communist) idealism in foreign policy has found a home on the pages of *New Republic*. For a brilliant if somewhat unconvincing example, see Charles Krauthammer, "The Poverty of Realism," *New Republic* 194, no. 7 (February 17, 1986): 14–22.

and effective action" by the United States to assure the act's implementation. Since the mid-1970s, Romanian violations of human rights in particular have been frequently exposed.

There seems to be considerably less public concern about such strictly political issues as, for example, Romania's maverick role in the Warsaw Pact. The Ceauşescu regime's maneuverings are not a matter of particular public interest, except when Romanian athletes, unlike those of the rest of the bloc, show up at the Olympic Games in Los Angeles. Indeed, the vicissitudes of the Polish "Solidarity" movement in the early 1980s might have been the only important recent exception. But "Solidarity" made a deep impression on the American public not because it set out to alter the status quo, but because it set out to change some of the essential features of Polish political life. For many Americans, and apparently not only for ethnic East Europeans, the Polish future was pregnant with hope for a political order in which the Catholic Church and the labor movement could at least share power with the Communists. With political pluralism if not a genuine multiparty system on the horizon, something more than that country's liberalization became a possibility. What captured the public's imagination was almost certainly the prospect of Poland's *liberation*, for, if "Solidarity" had survived, the people would have been free to practice their religion, speak their mind, join an independent labor union.

Paradoxically, while professionals would have celebrated such an outcome as a momentous loss for the Soviet Union's strategic and political posture in Europe, and a corresponding gain for the West, the American public's response would have been inspired by the *apparent triumph of American values*. Accordingly, widespread interest in human rights and in Poland's political fate converged, suggesting that what arouses public sentiment are humanitarian concerns having to do with the transformation of the domestic political order in Eastern Europe.

In the final analysis, then, the discrepancy between (most) deeds and (many) words in the American approach to Eastern Europe is a function of the very real difference (1) between the public's idea of what should be achieved and the U.S. government's notion of what can be achieved, and (2) between the public's preoccupation with people-oriented, humanitarian issues and the government's preoccupation with state-oriented, political and foreign policy issues. The result is that differentiation—an approach seeking only limited goals and placing a premium on Eastern Europe's international conduct—cannot but lack sufficient domestic support.

If Not Differentiation, What?

The obvious alternative to differentiation is its absence, meaning a policy whereby the United States would treat all East European Communist regimes alike, with the possible exception of nonaligned Yugoslavia. The reasons for the "treat-them-alike" alternative, offered primarily by conservative and neoconservative critics, include the following:[7]

1. As the Polish "crackdown" demonstrated, peaceful evolution in the Soviet sphere is either altogether impossible or reversible. Therefore, American hopes for such evolution are unwarranted.

2. U.S. economic presence, however small, helps improve the East European economies—through, for example, granting most-favored-nation (MFN) tariff status to Hungary, Romania, and to pre-1982 Poland—and thereby alleviates the Soviet burden of empire in Eastern Europe. Hence American interests would be better served by the reduction or elimination of U.S. economic presence, which would force the Soviet Union to divert additional resources from its military programs in order to pay full price for its empire.

3. As some U.S. technology sold to Eastern Europe is reported to have been transferred to the Soviet Union and as some U.S. technology is known to have been stolen by East European intelligence agents for, if not on behalf of, the Soviet Union, the East European regimes have shown to serve the same master. Therefore, they should be treated the same way as the Soviet Union; indeed, all members of the Warsaw Pact should be treated alike.

4. Preferential treatment of some Communist regimes gives credence to

7. In this summary of the "treat-them-alike" approach, I draw on numerous interviews with government officials in Washington; the columns of George F. Will in *Newsweek* and in the *Washington Post*; articles in *Commentary* and the *Wall Street Journal*; and the lengthy interview given by former U.S. ambassador to Romania David Funderburk to the *Washington Post* on May 15, 1985. For a critique of Washington's inclination to pursue limited goals in Eastern Europe (and of my views on U.S. policy toward Poland), see also Jerzy Milewski, Krzysztof Pomian, and Jan Zielonka, "Poland: Four Years After," *Foreign Affairs* 64, no. 2 (Winter 1985/86): 337–59. The issue of human rights in Eastern Europe has been the subject of numerous hearings before various committees of Congress at least since the mid-1970s. Most witnesses questioned, but did not explicitly oppose, the extension of most-favored-nation (MFN) tariff status to Romania; they generally favored renewal to Hungary (and China). See, for example, *Most Favored Nation Status for Romania, Hungary and China*, Hearing before the Subcommittee on International Trade of the Committee on Finance, U.S. Senate, July 27, 1981 (Washington, D.C.: GPO, 1981) and *Human Rights in Romania*, Hearing before the Subcommittees on Europe and the Middle East and on Human Rights and International Organizations of the Committee on Foreign Affairs, House of Representatives, May 14, 1985 (Washington, D.C.: GPO, 1985).

the false impression, already widespread in Western Europe, that the primary issue between the United States and the Soviet Union is one of conflicting national interests rather than conflicting national interests *and* conflicting ideals. To counter that impression, and hence to avoid the danger of "ideological disarmament" in the West, it is imperative to clarify that all Communist regimes, of whom the Soviet Union is only the most powerful, represent a collective challenge to free people and their institutions. Therefore, as all members of the Warsaw Pact subscribe to the same Communist ideology, they should be treated alike.

5. As the case of Romania shows, differentiation does not necessarily encourage the one American goal that matters most: respect for human rights. That being the case the United States should cease rewarding repressive regimes, however much their foreign policies annoy the Soviet Union and foment division in the Warsaw Pact. In other words, the United States should make no distinctions on the basis of foreign conduct alone.

In Defense of Differentiation

The case against differentiation has the advantage of being easily understandable. It seems to rest on a simple premise: "When you've seen one Commie, you've seen them all." It is as if those who advocate a "treat-them-alike" approach have never compared the qualities of two Communist countries in Eastern Europe, say Hungary and Czechoslovakia. Could it be that they slept through the Soviet-Yugoslav dispute and the Sino-Soviet rift? Worse, could it be that they deny that such differences might serve American interests? In any case, the certain result of their approach would be to push some of the more independent-minded East European regimes into Moscow's (open) arms.

Looking at their specific points, as summarized above, consider the following:

1. Whether gradual and peaceful evolution—domestic liberalization—is or is not possible in the Soviet sphere depends on one's definition of "evolution"—and its limits. The record shows that systemic change of the type that would lead to the substitution of the Communist system by a pluralistic political order is, indeed, impossible. But the record also suggests that "Kádárization" is possible, which is to say that a Communist regime in Eastern Europe may increasingly rely on persuasion rather than coercion to obtain popular compliance. Without dismantling the apparatus of coercion, such a regime governs by seldom having to resort to the use of "administrative measures."

As "Kádárization" so defined is possible and as the people of Eastern Europe clearly prefer it to what they presently have, the question that remains is this: Does it serve the interests of the United States to see Eastern Europe evolve in such a way as to make the region's Communist regimes become more tolerable, and hence more acceptable, to their people? Would not the old (Stalinist) formulation apply—"the worse the better"—meaning that the worse the Soviet position in Eastern Europe, the better it is for the United States?

The answer depends on one's estimate of how desperate the Soviet position in Eastern Europe must become for Moscow not to defend its interests. In my view, under all circumstances, with the possible exception of a region-wide popular uprising, the Soviet Union can, and is going to, continue to have a presence in Eastern Europe. Serious as its domestic and foreign problems may be, the United States can expect to do no more than to *weaken* the Soviet empire. After all, if a once united West, led by a militarily superior and politically resolute United States, could not roll back Soviet power from the heart of Europe for four decades, how could it be done now from a position of military equivalence and apparent political purposelessness in the Western alliance?

If the United States is to weaken the Soviet bloc rather than vainly anticipate its collapse, and hence Soviet surrender, the most effective way to proceed is to offer incentives for the kind of East European behavior that can be realistically envisaged, that is, not an outright break with Moscow but distance, not democracy but reform. The resulting diversity of Communist systems would absorb the resources, energy, and time of the Soviet leaders, and it would also further deprive Soviet ideology of its universalist pretensions. Both American interests *and* ideals would thus be served.

Of course, like most everything else in political life, the evolution of Communist systems is reversible. However, if two Soviet criteria are met —party control and Warsaw Pact membership—Moscow is likely to continue to tolerate deviations from its own patterns and policies. After all, Poland—the main beneficiary of U.S. aid from 1957 to 1981—is once again rated ahead of all Warsaw Pact states except Hungary in Freedom House's comparative survey of political rights and civil liberties around the world.[8] And some freedom, however circumscribed and tenuous, is better than no freedom at all.

2. Does U.S. trade alleviate the Soviet burden of empire? The United States has but a limited economic presence in Eastern Europe. Although approximately 25 percent of the region's foreign trade is conducted with

8. *Freedom at Issue*, no. 88 (January–February 1986), pp. 8–11.

the West, much of it is with the Federal Republic of Germany, which is the leading trading partner of every member of the Warsaw Pact including the Soviet Union. For reasons of its own, as mentioned earlier, the Federal Republic has significantly aided East Germany's economy and contributed to its relative prosperity. With the GDR all but a silent member of the Common Market, intra-German trade is so tilted as to accord considerable benefits to the East German side. Elsewhere, Poland, Romania, and Hungary can be said to have benefited from economic interaction with Western Europe, the United States, Japan, and Canada.

Unilateral U.S. sanctions or an embargo, complete or partial, would barely harm Eastern Europe, though it might cause temporary hardships and dislocations. This is so not only because of the limited American economic presence in the region, but because other Western countries would not follow U.S. policy. Washington may then deplore, criticize, or condemn its allies; it cannot change their orientation on this issue. Therefore, the result of, say, denying MFN to its current recipients —Romania and Hungary—would be to compel them to find a West European replacement for the United States and to ask Moscow for assistance. Friction in the West and greater East European dependence on Moscow would inevitably ensue.

Does it follow, though, that the United States would have successfully shifted at least some of the burden of empire to the Soviet Union? Not at all. The cessation of U.S. commercial transactions with Eastern Europe is not an effective way to weaken either the Soviet Union or its dependencies. First, as mentioned above, such a policy would cause *certain* divisions in the Western alliance for the sake of causing *potential*, and in any case minor and short-lived, damage to the Soviet bloc. Second, under far worse economic conditions in the past, Moscow has never hesitated to tighten the belt at home and in Eastern Europe in order to continue to give its military programs the highest priority, and there is no reason to believe it would respond differently in the future. Third, whatever small damage might be done would harm the people of Eastern Europe more than their rulers. In short, much of the burden of empire would be born by Western Europe and the East European people. It may well be, then, that the best way to harm the empire is for the United States to provide extensive aid to anti-Soviet forces in Afghanistan and Nicaragua.

3. Critics of differentiation make a valid point when they find the surreptitious transfer of U.S. technology from Eastern Europe to the Soviet Union unacceptable. Not incidentally, it is also illegal. Thus, if and when an East European country is known to have engaged in such an activity, it should be immediately and permanently denied further access to Ameri-

can technology. U.S. denial of technology would be effective because, unlike regular commercial transactions, Eastern Europe's needs—in the area of communications, for example—cannot be readily satisfied by turning to West European and Japanese sources.

Yet the broader conclusion—that such transfers show all Communist regimes to serve "the same master"—is misleading. It ignores the prevalence of tension and conflict in the Soviet bloc. Of course they are "allies"; of course they cooperate with Moscow. But their persistent need for new and advanced technology can and in most cases does make them cautious guardians of technologies they know they can obtain only from the United States. Just in case, though, it is not unwarranted to insist on strict enforcement of appropriate American laws.

4. By treating some Communist regimes better than others, does differentiation reduce public awareness of the Communist, rather than the Soviet, threat to the West?

Granted that no Communist regime, however moderate at home and however moderate its foreign conduct, can approximate American values. Granted that there has always been a yearning in the United States (probably more so than in Western Europe) for a clarity of purpose. Granted, too, that it is legitimate for the United States to pursue a foreign policy that the American people find satisfying; it is certainly desirable for all to feel proud of what this country does abroad. Opposition to all Communist dictatorships could meet some of these considerations and needs.

Yet in the real world of limited American power and influence, with neither sufficient resources for nor sufficient public interest in conducting a global crusade, the *primary* obligation of the United States is to build as wide and as numerous a coalition against Soviet expansionism as possible. If China, Yugoslavia, Romania, or the Italian Communist party share American concerns about Soviet "hegemonism," then it is for the cause of freedom that the United States cooperates with them or co-opts them. Such cooperation need not be more than temporary, for this is a coalition shaped by a common cause, not by common values.

In its dealings with the Soviet bloc, then, the choice for the United States is between anti-Communism and antiexpansionism. Given existing constraints in the United States and generally in the West, this may be one of the easier choices to make.

5. Should respect for human rights supersede all other U.S. interests in American policy toward Eastern Europe?

In the mid-1980s the practical issue here is Romania. Should the United States discontinue MFN to the repressive regime of Nicolae Ceauşescu —the man a *Wall Street Journal* column identifies as "America's most favored tyrant"?[9] Admittedly, there is something to be said for reaching that conclusion and indeed for the growing indignation, in Congress and even within the executive branch, about human rights conditions in one of Eastern Europe's harshest dictatorships. Romania is a Communist police state. Its dictator shares power only with members of his family. Religious freedom is nonexistent. No one enjoys political rights, least of all the country's large Hungarian minority. Often denied, emigration is at best an expensive proposition.

Yet, when the United States extended MFN status to Romania in 1975, it did not do so because Romania was or was about to become a democracy. The United States was guided by considerations of self-interest, seeking to encourage nationalist tendencies in countries of the Warsaw Pact—much as the Soviet Union has always sought to do in NATO. Romania *has* pursued such a nationalist path for over two decades now. It refused to participate in the Soviet-led military intervention in Czechoslovakia in 1968, and it has been critical of the Soviet invasion of Afghanistan. It allows no Warsaw Pact military maneuvers on Romanian soil. Ceauşescu has aided American diplomatic efforts in the Middle East, Southeast Asia, and elsewhere. Alone among its allies, Romania has maintained cordial relations with both Israel and China.

Thus, while the novelty has worn off, essentially the same conditions that prompted the United States to grant MFN in 1975 still obtain today. Romania has not changed since then; in Congress, however, a curious coalition of conservatives and liberals has come to oppose Bucharest's MFN status. Conservatives deny serious differences among Communist states,[10] and thereby miss an opportunity to translate their anti-Communism into policy. Liberal human rights activists have turned into such effective lobbyists against Ceauşescu's Romania that they may still convince Congress to remove the only leverage the United States has to help realize their goals,[11] and thereby miss an opportunity to translate their human rights concerns into policy.

9. Ion Mihai Pacepa, "Ceauşescu: America's Most Favored Tyrant," *Wall Street Journal*, January 13, 1986. For a contrary view, see Charles Gati, "Realism on Romania," *Baltimore Sun*, December 13, 1985.

10. In his postresignation interview with *Washington Post*, former U.S. ambassador to Romania David Funderburk asserted that there was a large Soviet presence in Bucharest and hence Romania was just like all the other Soviet dependencies in Eastern Europe. His evidence? While in Bucharest, Funderburk and his staff counted the number of cars belonging to Soviet personnel and they found more than they had apparently expected to find. *Washington Post*, May 15, 1985.

11. See *Human Rights in Romania*.

If the issue is insufficient anti-Sovietism, then should Romania attempt to remove itself from the Warsaw Pact to satisfy some American conservatives—and invite the loss of its semiindependence? If the issue is insufficient respect for human rights, then why is there little or no lobbying against MFN for Yugoslavia and China—countries whose record on human rights is not markedly better than Romania's?[12] The questions suggest that human rights can no more serve as the sole guideline of an American approach toward the Soviet bloc than considerations of power alone—the policy of "driving wedges"—can be sustained by a country so engrossed in the promotion of its values. That is why current policy toward Eastern Europe (NSDD-54) correctly favors American rewards for regimes that demonstrate *either* a measure of domestic liberalization *or* a measure of foreign policy independence.

The Choices Ahead

The debate over differentiation reflects long-existing pressures and considerations that bear on American policy toward Eastern Europe. They include

1. the status of American-Soviet relations,
2. the public's apparent desire for a better life for the people of Eastern Europe,
3. the shortage of means by which an effective American policy can be implemented,
4. the interests of the West European allies, and
5. the receptivity of individual regimes in the region to U.S. policies and preferences.

Precisely because none of these pressures and considerations can be dismissed or even slighted, the United States cannot afford to "forget" Eastern Europe and to do little or nothing—even if possible conditions of détente with Moscow, the allies' frequent indifference, or frustration over the shortage of appropriate implements might make a casual approach to the region rather tempting. Nor can the United States afford to try to undermine the East European regimes and aim at "liberation"—even if possible conditions of high tension with Moscow and domestic pressures for transplanting humane values might make a resolute and indeed unwavering approach to the region rather tempting.

While, thus, there is no escape from complexity, and while there is no magical formula that would help establish a hierarchical order among conflicting pressures and considerations, the choices ahead might be made

12. For comparative data on human rights, see *Freedom at Issue*.

somewhat easier and U.S. policies might become somewhat more efficacious against the following reflections and conclusions:

First, the Soviet position in Eastern Europe is more vulnerable than commonly assumed. It can be subjected to peaceful challenge by the United States, and by the West in general, but it should be done without attempting to destabilize the region.

Second, the kind of change that is likely to take root is gradual and evolutionary in character; the prospects for open splits à la Yugoslavia or Albania are all but nonexistent. The United States should therefore encourage evolutionary, "within-system" change. There is absolutely nothing wrong, un-American, or immoral about aiming at that which is achievable: the "Kádárization" rather than the "Finlandization" or neutralization of Eastern Europe.

Third, to be effective, this objective can be and should be pursued in cooperation with Japan and with the West European allies. Their occasional reservations might be allowed to temper, but not to cancel, American policy. For however important it is to exploit Soviet vulnerability in Eastern Europe, it should not be done at the expense of America's *vital* interests in the viability of Westen Europe and NATO.

Fourth, to meet the public's interest in results, and to sustain a modicum of hope about the future, U.S. officials at the highest level must *always* combine talk about long-term aspirations with candid acknowledgment of the reality of Moscow's positional advantage in Eastern Europe. To speak of aspirations only, as is done on some public occasions, is to reinforce the American illusion of omnipotence. To speak of limits only, as is privately done at times, is defeatism.

To do more and better that which is already being done, and to explain complexities and limitations candidly, may not seem a particularly encouraging and creative conclusion. But, in this case, it is not daring and imagination that are called for but the persistent implementation of existing policy. The people of Eastern Europe, already profoundly pro-American, need not be prompted to press ahead, only they can set the pace of change. The proprietors of power in Eastern Europe need not be constantly reminded of what they must do to achieve genuine progress and stability; they know it only too well. But the Soviet Union, though it can be neither pushed out nor wished away from this region, can be put on the political defensive in Eastern Europe by the prudent and calibrated technique of differentiation. To do that job well, however, American policymakers and the public alike should come to believe that, in dealing with Eastern Europe, achieving something is infinitely more than seeking everything and getting nothing.

Selected Bibliography

The following bibliography of secondary sources lists books, chapters, and articles in major Western languages—almost exclusively in English—that readers may find useful to consult. Readers familiar with Hungarian should review sources incorporated into the footnotes.

Aczél, Tamás, and Tibor Méray, *The Revolt of the Mind: A Case History of Intellectual Resistance Behind the Iron Curtain* (New York: Praeger, 1959).

Bader, William B., *Austria Between East and West, 1944–1955* (Stanford, Calif.: Stanford University Press, 1966).

Barker, Elisabeth, *British Policy in South-East Europe in the Second World War* (London: Macmillan, 1976).

Bethell, Nicholas, *Gomułka: His Poland, His Communism* (New York: Holt, Rinehart & Winston, 1969).

Bialer, Seweryn, "The Three Schools of Kremlin Policy," *New Leader*, July 29, 1957.

Billington, James H., "Finland," in Cyril E. Black and Thomas P. Thornton, eds., *Communism and Revolution: The Strategic Uses of Political Violence* (Princeton, N.J.: Princeton University Press, 1964).

Black, Cyril E., *The Dynamics of Modernization: A Study in Comparative History* (New York: Harper & Row, 1966).

Blumstock, Robert, "Public Opinion in Hungary," in Walter Connor, Zvi Gitelman, et al., *Public Opinion in European Socialist Systems* (New York: Praeger, 1977).

Bognár, József, "Initiative and Equilibrium: Major Political and Economic Issues in Hungary," *New Hungarian Quarterly*, Vol. 11, No. 37 (Spring 1970).

Bornstein, Morris, "Economic Reform in Eastern Europe," in Joint Economic Committee, U.S. Congress, *East European Economies Post-Helsinki* (Washington, D.C.: GPO, 1977).

Brown, J. F., *Relations Between the Soviet Union and its East European Allies: A Survey* (Santa Monica: Rand Corporation, 1975).

Browne, Eric C., *Coalition Theories: A Logical and Empirical Critique* (Beverly Hills: Sage Publications, 1973).

Brzezinski, Zbigniew, "The Competitive Relationship," in Charles Gati, ed., *Caging the Bear: Containment and the Cold War* (Indianapolis: Bobbs-Merrill, 1974).

———, *The Soviet Bloc: Unity and Conflict* (Cambridge, Mass.: Harvard University Press, 1967).

Burks, R. V., *The Dynamics of Communism in Eastern Europe* (Princeton, N.J.: Princeton

University Press, 1961).

Churchill, Winston S., *Triumph and Tragedy* (Boston: Houghton Mifflin, 1953).

Clemens, Diane Shaver, *Yalta* (London: Oxford University Press, 1970).

Claudin, Fernando, *The Communist Movement: From Comintern to Cominform* (New York: Monthly Review Press, 1975).

Dallin, Alexander, "Soviet Foreign Policy and Domestic Politics: A Framework for Analysis," in Erik P. Hoffmann and Frederic J. Fleron, eds., *The Conduct of Soviet Foreign Policy*, 2d ed. (Hawthorne, N.Y.: Aldine, 1980).

———, "The Use of International Movements," in Ivo J. Lederer, ed., *Russian Foreign Policy: Essays in Historical Perspective* (New Haven: Yale University Press, 1962).

Davis, Lynn Etheridge, *The Cold War Begins: Soviet-American Conflict Over Eastern Europe* (Princeton, N.J.: Princeton University Press, 1974).

Dawisha, Karen, *The Kremlin and the Prague Spring* (Berkeley: University of California Press, 1984).

Deák, István, "Hungary," in Hans Rogger and Eugen Weber, eds., *The European Right: A Historical Profile* (Berkeley and Los Angeles: University of California Press, 1965).

Dedijer, Vladimir, *Tito* (New York: Simon & Schuster, 1953).

Djilas, Milovan, *Conversations with Stalin* (New York: Harcourt, Brace & World, 1962).

Dodd, Lawrence C., *Coalitions in Parliamentary Government* (Princeton, N.J.: Princeton University Press, 1976).

Eckstein, Alexander, "National Income and Capital Formation in Hungary, 1900–1950," in Simon Kuznets, ed., *Income and Wealth*, Ser. 5 (London, 1955).

Eden, Anthony, *The Reckoning* (Boston: Houghton Mifflin, 1965).

Etzold, T. H., and J. L. Gaddis, eds., *Containment: Documents on American Policy and Strategy* (New York: Columbia University Press, 1978).

Felix, Christopher (pseud.), *A Short Course in the Secret War* (New York: E. P. Dutton, 1963).

Galbraith, John Kenneth, *Economic Development in Perspective* (Cambridge, Mass.: Harvard University Press, 1962).

Garai, George, "The Policy toward the Jews, Zionism, and Israel of the Hungarian Communist Party, 1945–1953" (Ph.D. dissertation, London School of Economics and Political Science, 1979).

Garson, Robert, "Churchill's 'Spheres of Influence': Rumania and Bulgaria," *Survey*, Vol. 24, No. 3 (Summer 1979).

Garthoff, Raymond L., "Eastern Europe in the Context of U.S.-Soviet Relations," in Sarah M. Terry, ed., *Soviet Policy in Eastern Europe* (New Haven and London: Yale University Press, 1984).

Gati, Charles, "The 'Europeanization' of Communism?" *Foreign Affairs*, Vol. 55, No. 3 (April 1977).

———, "The Forgotten Region," *Foreign Policy*, No. 19 (Summer 1975).

———, "Polish Futures, Western Options," *Foreign Affairs*, Vol. 61, No. 2 (Winter 1982/83).

———, "The Populist Current in Hungarian Politics 1935–1944" (Ph.D. dissertation, Indiana University, 1965).

Gilberg, Trond, "Romania's Growing Difficulties," *Current History*, November 1984.

Groennings, Sven, E. W. Kelley, and Michael Leiserson, eds., *The Study of Coalition Behavior: Theoretical Perspectives and Cases from Four Continents* (New York: Holt, Rinehart & Winston, 1970).

Gyurkó, L., "Introductory Biography," in *János Kádár: Selected Speeches and Interviews*

(Budapest, 1985).

Hardt, John P., "Soviet Energy Policy in Eastern Europe," in Sarah M. Terry, ed., *Soviet Policy in Eastern Europe* (New Haven and London: Yale University Press, 1984).

Hay, Julius, *Born 1900: Memoirs* (La Salle, Ill.: Library Press, 1975).

Hiscocks, Richard, *Poland: Bridge to the Abyss?* (London: Oxford University Press, 1963).

Johnson, Chalmers, *Revolution and the Social System* (Stanford, Calif.: Hoover Institution Press, 1964).

———, *Revolutionary Change* (Boston and Toronto: Little, Brown, 1966).

Kertesz, Stephen D., *Diplomacy in a Whirlpool: Hungary Between Nazi Germany and Soviet Russia* (Notre Dame, Ind.: University of Notre Dame Press, 1953).

Khrushchev Remembers, translated and edited by Strobe Talbott (Boston: Little, Brown, 1970).

Kissinger, Henry A., *Nuclear Weapons and Foreign Policy* (Garden City, N.Y.: Doubleday Anchor Books, 1958).

———, *The Troubled Partnership: A Reappraisal of the Atlantic Alliance* (Garden City, N.Y.: Doubleday Anchor Books, 1966).

Korbel, Joseph, *The Communist Subversion of Czechoslovakia, 1928–1948: The Failure of Coexistence* (Princeton, N.J.: Princeton University Press, 1959).

Kővágó, József, *You Are All Alone* (New York: Praeger, 1959).

Kovrig, Bennett, *Communism in Hungary: From Kun to Kádár* (Stanford, Calif.: Hoover Institution Press, 1979).

———, *The Myth of Liberation: East-Central Europe in U.S. Diplomacy and Politics Since 1941* (Baltimore: Johns Hopkins University Press, 1973).

Kraus, Michael, "Communist Behavior in Coalition Governments: Czechoslovakia 1945–1948," paper delivered at the 1978 national convention of the American Association for the Advancement of Slavic Studies.

Krauthammer, Charles, "The Poverty of Realism," *New Republic*, Vol. 194, No. 7, Issue 3,709 (February 17, 1986).

Kushnirsky, Fyodor I., "The Limits of Soviet Economic Reform," *Problems of Communism*, July–August 1984.

Larrabee, F. Stephen, *The Challenge to Soviet Interests in Eastern Europe: Romania, Hungary, and East Germany* (Santa Monica: Rand Corporation, 1984).

Lasky, Melvin J., ed., *The Hungarian Revolution* (New York: Praeger, 1957).

Lendvai, Paul, *Anti-Semitism Without Jews* (New York: Doubleday, 1971).

Leonhard, Wolfgang, *Child of the Revolution* (Chicago: Regnery, 1958).

Lewis, Flora, *A Case History of Hope* (Garden City, N.Y.: Doubleday, 1958).

Lomax, Bill, translator, "Imre Nagy's Secret Speech," *Labour Focus on Eastern Europe*, Vol. 8, No. 1 (Summer 1985).

Lukacs, John, "The Night Stalin and Churchill Divided Europe," *New York Times Magazine*, October 5, 1969.

Lundestad, Geir, *The American Non-Policy toward Eastern Europe, 1943–1947* (New York: Humanities Press, 1975).

Luža, Radomir V., "February 1948 and the Czechoslovak Road to Socialism," *East Central Europe*, Vol. 4, No. 1 (1977).

McCagg, William O., Jr., "Domestic Politics and Soviet Foreign Policy at the Cominform Conference in 1947," *Slavic and Soviet Series* (Tel Aviv), Vol. 2, No. 1 (Spring 1977).

———, *Stalin Embattled 1943–1948* (Detroit: Wayne State University Press, 1978).

Macartney, C. A., *October Fifteenth: A History of Modern Hungary, 1929–1945* (Edinburgh: The University Press, 1961).

Mackintosh, Malcolm, "Stalin's Policies towards Eastern Europe: The General Picture," in
    Thomas T. Hammond, ed., *The Anatomy of Communist Takeovers* (New Haven: Yale
    University Press, 1975).
Mahan, Alfred T., *The Interest of America in International Conditions* (Boston: Little, Brown,
    1910).
Marcou, Lilly, *Le Kominform* (Paris: Presses de la Fondation Nationales des Sciences Politiques,
    1977).
Marer, Paul, "Alternative Estimates of the Dollar GNP and Growth Rates of the CMEA
    Countries," in Joint Economic Committee, U.S. Congress, *East European Economies:
    Slow Growth in the 1980's* (Washington, D.C.: GPO, 1985), Vol. 1.
————, "Economic Reform in Hungary: From Central Planning to Regulated Market," in
    Joint Economic Committee, U.S. Congress, *East European Economies: Slow Growth in the
    1980's* (Washington, D.C.: GPO, 1986), Vol. 3.
————, "The Political Economy of Soviet Relations with Eastern Europe," in Sarah M.
    Terry, ed., *Soviet Policy in Eastern Europe* (New Haven and London: Yale University
    Press, 1984).
Marrese, Michael, and Jan Vanous, *Implicit Subsidies and Non-Market Benefits in Soviet Trade
    with Eastern Europe* (Berkeley: University of California Press, 1982).
Mastny, Vojtech, *Russia's Road to the Cold War* (New York: Columbia University Press,
    1979).
Matossian, Mary, "Ideologies of Delayed Industrialization: Some Tensions and Ambiguities,"
    Economic Development and Cultural Change, Vol. 6, No. 3 (April 1958).
Merkl, Peter H., "Coalition Politics in West Germany," in Sven Groennings et al., eds., *The
    Study of Coalition Behavior: Theoretical Perspectives and Cases from Four Continents* (New
    York: Holt, Rinehart & Winston, 1970).
Méray, Tibor, *Thirteen Days that Shook the Kremlin: Imre Nagy and the Hungarian Revolution*
    (New York: Praeger, 1959).
Mičunovič, Veljko, *Moscow Diary* (Garden City, N.Y.: Doubleday, 1980).
Mikes, George, *The Hungarian Revolution* (London: Deutsch, 1957).
Molnár, Miklós, and László Nagy, *Imre Nagy: Réformateur ou révolutionnaire?* (Geneva: Droz,
    1959).
Mlynář, Zdeněk, *Nightfrost in Prague: The End of Humane Socialism* (New York: Karz,
    1980).
Nagy, Ferenc, *The Struggle Behind the Iron Curtain* (New York: Macmillan, 1948).
Nagy, Imre, *On Communism: In Defense of the New Course* (New York: Praeger, 1957).
Niemeyer, Gerhart, "Communists in Coalition Governments," in Frank R. Barnett et al.,
    eds., *Peace and War in the Modern Age: Premises, Myths, and Realities* (Garden City, N.Y.:
    Doubleday, 1965).
Organski, A. F. K., *The Stages of Political Development* (New York: Alfred A. Knopf, 1965).
Polonsky, Antony, and Bolesław Drukier, eds., *The Beginning of Communist Rule in Poland
    — December 1943 – June 1945* (London: Routledge & Kegan Paul, 1980).
Ramet, Pedro, "Church and Peace in the GDR," *Problems of Communism*, July–August
    1984.
Ránki, György, "The Fascist Vote in Budapest in 1939," in S. U. Larsen et al., eds., *Who
    Were the Fascists?* (Oslo: Universitetforlaget, 1980).
Reale, Eugenio, *Avec Jacques Duclos au banc des accusés* (Paris: Plon, 1958).
————, "The Founding of the Cominform," in Milorad M. Drachkovitch and Branko
    Lazitch, eds., *The Comintern: Historical Highlights* (New York: Praeger, 1966).
Reis, Albert, "The Churchill-Stalin Percentages Agreement," *American Historical Review*,
    Vol. 83, No. 2 (April 1978).

Révai, J., "The Character of a 'People's Democracy,'" *Foreign Affairs*, October 1949.

Robinson, William F., *The Pattern of Reform in Hungary: A Political, Economic and Cultural Analysis* (New York: Praeger, 1973).

Schwartz, Morton, *The Foreign Policy of the USSR: Domestic Factors* (Encino and Belmont, Calif.: Dickenson, 1975).

Seton-Watson, Hugh, *The East European Revolution* (New York: Praeger, 1965).

Shawcross, William, *Crime and Compromise: János Kádár and the Politics of Compromise Since 1956* (New York: E. P. Dutton, 1974).

Shevchenko, Arkady, *Breaking with Moscow* (New York: Alfred A. Knopf, 1985).

Skilling, H. Gordon, *Czechoslovakia's Interrupted Revolution* (Princeton, N.J.: Princeton University Press, 1976).

Spanier, John, *American Foreign Policy Since World War II*, 10th edition (New York: Holt, Rinehart & Winston, 1985).

Starobin, Joseph R., "Origins of the Cold War," *Foreign Affairs*, Vol. 47, No. 4 (July 1969).

Sterling, Claire, *The Masaryk Case: The Murder of Democracy in Czechoslovakia* (Boston: David R. Godine, 1982).

Szűrős, Mátyás, "Hungarian Foreign Policy in the Mid-1980s," *Külpolitika* (special English edition), No. 4, 1985.

Tatu, Michel, *Power in the Kremlin: From Khrushchev to Kosygin* (New York: Viking, 1969).

Taubman, William, *Stalin's American Policy: From Entente to Détente to Cold War* (New York: W. W. Norton, 1982).

Tigrid, Pavel, "The Prague Coup of 1948: The Elegant Takeover," in Thomas T. Hammond, ed., *The Anatomy of Communist Takeovers* (New Haven: Yale University Press, 1975).

Tőkés, Rudolf L., "Hungarian Reform Imperatives," *Problems of Communism*, September–October 1984.

——, "The Hungarian Populist 'Third Road' Ideology—Three Case Studies: 1932–1943" (M.A. thesis, Columbia University, 1961).

Ulam, Adam, *Expansion and Coexistence* (New York: Praeger, 1968).

——, *Titoism and the Cominform* (Cambridge, Mass.: Harvard University Press, 1952).

Valenta, Jiri, *Soviet Intervention in Czechoslovakia, 1968: Anatomy of a Decision* (Baltimore: Johns Hopkins University Press, 1979).

Váli, Ferenc A., *Rift and Revolt in Hungary: Nationalism versus Communism* (Cambridge, Mass.: Harvard University Press, 1961).

Völgyes, Iván, "Politics, Ideology and Culture: The STP's of Life in Communist Eastern Europe," *Social Science Journal*, October 1976.

Vulpuis, Alex, *Die Allparteinregierung* (Berlin: Metzner, 1957).

Weit, Erwin, *At the Red Summit: Interpreter Behind the Iron Curtain* (New York: Macmillan, 1973).

Wolf, Charles, Jr., et al., *The Costs of the Soviet Empire* (Santa Monica: Rand Corporation, 1983).

Wolff, Robert Lee, *The Balkans in Our Time* (Cambridge, Mass.: Harvard University Press, 1956).

Zimmerman, William, "Choices in the Postwar World: Containment and the Soviet Union," in Charles Gati, ed., *Caging the Bear: Containment and the Cold War* (Indianapolis: Bobbs-Merrill, 1974).

Zinner, Paul E., ed., *National Communism and Popular Revolt in Eastern Europe* (New York: Columbia University Press, 1957).

——, *Revolution in Hungary* (New York: Columbia University Press, 1962).

Index

Charles Gati is Professor of Political Science at Union
College, Schenectady, New York, and Senior Research
Scholar, Research Institute on International Change
at Columbia University

Library of Congress Cataloging-in-Publication Data
Gati, Charles.
Hungary and the Soviet bloc.
Bibliography: p.
Includes index.
1. Soviet Union—Foreign relations—Hungary.
2. Hungary—Foreign relations—Soviet Union.
3. Soviet Union—Foreign relations—Europe, Eastern.
4. Europe, Eastern—Foreign relations—Soviet Union.
5. Soviet Union—Foreign relations—1945–
I. Title.
DK67.5.H8G37   1986   327.470439   86-19739
ISBN 0-8223-0684-0
ISBN 0-8223-0747-2 (pbk.)